EXAM CRAM™ 2

Network+
Lab Manual

David L. Prowse

que®
CERTIFICATION

Network+ Exam Cram 2 Lab Manual

Copyright © 2006 by Que Publishing

International Standard Book Number: 0-7897-3293-9

Library of Congress Catalog Card Number: 2004108934

Printed in the United States of America

First Printing: August 2005

08   07   06   05   4   3   2   1

Trademarks

Warning and Disclaimer

Bulk Sales

Que Publishing offers excellent discounts on this book when ordered in quantity for bulk purchases or special sales. For more information, please contact

U.S. Corporate and Government Sales

1-800-382-3419

corpsales@pearsontechgroup.com

For sales outside the U.S., please contact

International Sales

international@pearsoned.com

Publisher
Paul Boger

Executive Editor
Jeff Riley

Development Editor
Steve Rowe

Managing Editor
Charlotte Clapp

Project Editor
Dan Knott

Copy Editor
Kate Shoup Welsh

Proofreader
Susan Eldridge

Interior Designer
Gary Adair

Cover Designer
Ann Jones

Page Layout
Michelle Mitchell

CERTIFICATION

Que Certification • 800 East 96th Street • Indianapolis, Indiana 46240

A Note from Series Editor Ed Tittel

You know better than to trust your certification preparation to just anybody. That's why you, and more than 2 million others, have purchased an Exam Cram book. As Series Editor for the new and improved Exam Cram 2 Series, I have worked with the staff at Que Certification to ensure you won't be disappointed. That's why we've taken the world's best-selling certification product—a two-time finalist for "Best Study Guide" in CertCities' reader polls—and made it even better.

As a two-time finalist for the "Favorite Study Guide Author" award as selected by CertCities readers, I know the value of good books. You'll be impressed with Que Certification's stringent review process, which ensures the books are high quality, relevant, and technically accurate.

As a 20-year-plus veteran of the computing industry and the original creator and editor of the Exam Cram Series, I've brought my IT experience to bear on these books. During my tenure at Novell from 1989 to 1994, I worked with and around its excellent education and certification department. At Novell, I witnessed the growth and development of the first really big, successful IT certification program—one that was to shape the industry forever afterward. This experience helped push my writing and teaching activities heavily in the certification direction. Since then, I've worked on nearly 100 certification related books, and I write about certification topics for numerous Web sites and for *Certification* magazine.

In 1996, while studying for various MCP exams, I became frustrated with the huge, unwieldy study guides that were the only preparation tools available. As an experienced IT professional and former instructor, I wanted "nothing but the facts" necessary to prepare for the exams. From this impetus, Exam Cram emerged: short, focused books that explain exam topics, detail exam skills and activities, and get IT professionals ready to take and pass their exams.

In 1997 when Exam Cram debuted, it quickly became the best-selling computer book series since "...*For Dummies*," and the best-selling certification book series ever. By maintaining an intense focus on subject matter, tracking errata and updates quickly, and following the certification market closely, Exam Cram established the dominant position in cert prep books.

You will not be disappointed in your decision to purchase this book. If you are, please contact me at etittel@jump.net. All suggestions, ideas, input, or constructive criticism are welcome!

Ed Tittel

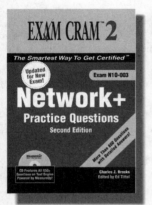

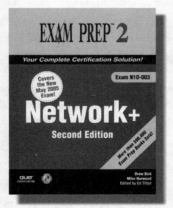

I'd like to dedicate this book to my wife Georgia. Without a complaint, she was there through yet another mind-numbing deadline! You're the best!

About the Author

David L. Prowse is owner of TSR Data, a technology-solutions company focusing on IT security, Web development, and training. He is a licensed Telecomm/Datacomm installer and is also the creator of www. TechnicalBlog.Com, an IT support site. Before going independent in the year 2002, his resume included eight years of IT experience, and six concurrent years of experience as a technical trainer in the live and virtual classroom environments.

At age 33, David now has 15 various IT certifications including the CompTIA Network+, which he has beta-tested twice since its inception. He has taught the Net+ course more than 30 times to such organizations as the FAA and Sungard. In addition, he is the technical editor for some of the top rated A+ and Network+ manuals by Que. His vision is of a world where he can sleep more than a few hours a day.

Acknowledgments

Let me give my sincere appreciation to the entities that made this book happen. Thanks, Jeff Riley, for believing in me and for giving me this opportunity. I'd like to also thank Steve Rowe, Pamalee Nelson, and the rest of the staff at Que for making everything go smoothly. My gratitude also goes to David Holder and Eugene Miranda from ArthurMcNeil.net for all the equipment and assistance in this project. Thanks to my best friend Kamran Chaudhri, who invokes the true writing skills. Let me also acknowledge who and what got me past the big hurdles: The Beatles, Stephen R. Donaldson, Gary Gygax, J.R.R. Tolkien, and Dunkin' Donuts. Finally, my wife Georgia, who can't be thanked enough! Thanks to all of you for helping to make this project a success.

Contents at a Glance

Table of Contents

We Want to Hear from You!

As the reader of this book, *you* are our most important critic and commentator. We value your opinion and want to know what we're doing right, what we could do better, what areas you'd like to see us publish in, and any other words of wisdom you're willing to pass our way.

As an executive editor for Que Publishing, I welcome your comments. You can email or write me directly to let me know what you did or didn't like about this book—as well as what we can do to make our books better.

Please note that I cannot help you with technical problems related to the topic of this book. We do have a User Services group, however, where I will forward specific technical questions related to the book.

When you write, please be sure to include this book's title and author as well as your name, email address, and phone number. I will carefully review your comments and share them with the author and editors who worked on the book.

Email: feedback@quepublishing.com

Mail: Jeff Riley
            Executive Editor
            Que Publishing
            800 East 96th Street
            Indianapolis, IN 46240 USA

For more information about this book or another Que Certification title, visit our Web site at www.examcram2.com. Type the ISBN (excluding hyphens) or the title of a book in the Search field to find the page you're looking for.

Introduction

Introduction to Your Lab Manual

Welcome to the *Network+ Exam Cram 2 Lab Manual*! This book is designed to be a perfect complement to the *Network+ Exam Prep 2, Network+ Exam Cram 2, Second Edition,* and the *Network+ Practice Questions Exam Cram 2* books. The *Network+ Exam Cram 2 Lab Manual* includes more than 25 labs with nearly 50 exercises that mimic tasks and present real-world scenarios that a network administrator might face on the job. The exercises were developed based on the Network+ exam objectives.

Written by a Network+ instructor, the *Network+ Exam Cram 2 Lab Manual* provides clear, step-by-step directions to help the reader through complex exercises and offers ample guidance to help the reader avoid potential pitfalls. For topics that don't lend themselves to hands-on exercises, this book includes research-based exercises, such as researching a topic on the Internet and/or in print media and answering a set of questions based on that research, or creating a report or other such document based on that research.

The author includes references to specific chapters and topics in the corresponding *Network+ Exam Cram 2, Second Edition* and *Network+ Exam Prep 2* books; however, this lab manual is a standalone product that can be used effectively both individually and in a class setting. If you feel that you could benefit both from buying this book *and* taking a class, check out the many third-party vendors who offer Network+ training in addition to training offered by CompTIA.

Undoubtedly, experience with the technologies on which you are going to be tested is critical. To truly be prepared for your certification exam it is recommended that you read and study, complete lots of practice questions, and gain solid experience with the technologies on which you will be tested. The last point is our intent with this book. We want to offer you plenty of opportunity to jump into the technologies the Network+ exam tests on, complete with plenty of guidance and feedback to assist you throughout your exercises. So, after you complete this lab manual, it is our hope that you will feel more confident and competent with networking fundamentals as well as the objectives you must master for the Network+ exam!

Who Is This Book For?

This is always a critical question that readers want to answer before purchasing any book. It can be frustrating to buy a book that doesn't fit your needs, to say the least—we know from experience! With that said, this book is for anyone studying for the Network+ exam who feels they are at a point in their study where they need to put the concepts and principles of Network+ into action for greater understanding. If you are qualified to be taking the Network+ exam, you are the person for this book. However, you should use the exercises in this book at the point you feel you are ready to get hands-on experience. This, of course, will vary for every reader, but knowing how you learn and what study techniques best breed success for you is the path to passing the Network+ exam.

A word of warning is necessary here! Don't use this book as your sole study vehicle. We know that saying our book is not the sole study guide needed for exam success may sound weird! Make no mistake, we want this book to succeed greatly, but we also know that successful certification students almost always have more than one study source. This is not a sales pitch for Que's other products, either! It is tried-and-true advice. Not every book covers items completely or to the degree you may need, so having several study aides gives you a greater chance of finding the information you need along with different viewpoints and experiences from various authors. That is truly a rich learning environment!

What Makes Up a Que Network+ Lab Manual?

By now, you are probably curious as to what makes up a Que Network+ lab manual. The following list will detail for you what a typical chapter contains.

- ➤ **Introduction.** Each chapter contains an introduction that gives insight as to what the chapter covers, why this content is important for the exam, and any other information you may need as you begin to do the exercises.

- ➤ **Objectives list.** This is simply a listing of the Network+ objectives, quoted from CompTIA, that your particular chapter will be covering.

- ➤ **Step-by-step lab procedures.** This is the meat of your lab manual's chapters. Here is where you will exercise your skills and develop that all-important set of experiences that will help you on the job *and* on the Network+ exam.

➤ **What Did I Just Learn?** This critical section follows your step-by-step exercises and sums up and reviews the concepts and skills you should have mastered after completing the exercises. If you don't feel confident that you picked up those skills or understood the concepts provided, try the steps again and consult some of your other study books for review.

➤ **Practice questions.** At the end of each chapter, we provide you with a small number of practice questions. There won't be a lot of these, but we include them to help you make sure that you have an understanding of the concepts and skills central to the chapter you are completing. If you become uncomfortable or unsure while answering these practice questions, be sure to visit other study guides to get more information or review.

Other Elements You Will Encounter

While the preceding list gives you the major elements each chapter in your Network+ lab manual contains, you will see some other elements floating around. The following list details these for you:

➤ **Figures.** Periodically, you will be offered a picture or diagram that will help you visualize something while you are doing your exercises.

➤ **Exam alerts.** Once in a while, you will encounter these elements, which are offered to you as a sort of early warning. If you see something in an exam alert, you should take great care to learn about it because you can be fairly certain that the topic(s) will be on the Network+ exam.

➤ **Hints.** These elements periodically appear to give a hint on how to do something differently or some extra advice on how to complete an exercise step. These will be placed in locations where we have students before you have had difficulty. This is our way of trying to head off potential trouble—as much as possible, at least!

➤ **Warnings.** Warnings are alarms to you that something could go really wrong if you aren't careful. Pay close attention to these!

About Network+

The CompTIA Network+ certification tests an individual's basic skills and knowledge of general networking concepts, data-communications methods, basic security, and communication protocols. Candidates are recommended to possess at least nine months of network-support work experience and the A+ certification or equivalent knowledge.

System Requirements

The following is a list of the recommended components and their minimum recommended requirements for this lab manual.

➤ A PII 266MHz PC with 64MB RAM, 2GB HDD, CD-ROM, and network interface card (installed with Windows 2000 Professional) This will be known as PC1.

➤ A PII 266MHz PC with 128MB RAM, 2GB HDD, CD-ROM, and network interface card (installed with Windows 2000 Professional or Server) This will be known as PC2.

➤ A four-port wireless/wired router with built-in firewall

➤ A wireless NIC

➤ Two straight-through patch cables

➤ Access to Windows 2000 Professional software

➤ Access to Windows 2000 Server software

➤ 25 feet or more of Category 5 or CAT5e cable

➤ A wire stripper

➤ An RJ-45 crimper

➤ A package of RJ-45 plugs

➤ A patch tester

➤ Access to the Internet

➤ (Optional) a two- or four-port KVM switch

For the labs we will be referring to the following:

➤ Compaq Deskpro PIII 533MHz computers with 256MB RAM and 3Com 3C905 XL 10/100 PCI TX network interface cards (these cards will automatically be recognized by Windows 2000 during the OS install)

➤ Linksys wireless router model WRT54G

➤ Linksys PCI wireless NIC model WMP54G

➤ WiedMuller wire stripper model AM 12

➤ Paladin Tools RJ-45 crimper

➤ Ideal RJ-45 plugs #85-346 or like-model plugs

➤ Paladin Tools Patch

➤ Check 1529 patch tester

➤ Belkin four-port KVM switch bundled with cables, PS/2, part #F1DJ104P

➤ Cable Internet access

Although it is highly recommended that you use two separate PCs, users who do not have access to multiple computers will find that virtual computer software such as VMWare Workstation or Microsoft Virtual PC is useful for emulating networks. Time-limited evaluation copies of both of these products are available. For more information, visit www.vmware.com/products/desktop/ws_features.html and http://www.microsoft.com/windowsxp/virtualpc/.

In Conclusion

This manual is created as a means for you to gain hands-on experience with the concepts and technologies on which you are likely to be tested. Although we can't guarantee you a passing score from using this book, we can offer you plenty of hands-on experience that will be sure to help you on the job and on the exam.

Remember, it is best to have several sources of study materials. Que offers, along with this lab manual, several products that you can use:

➤ *Network+ Exam Cram 2, Second Edition.* ISBN: 0-7897-3254-8. By Drew Bird and Mike Harwood.

➤ *Network+ Practice Questions Exam Cram 2.* ISBN: 0-7897-3352-8. By Charles J. Brooks.

➤ *Network+ Exam Prep 2.* ISBN: 0-7897-3255-6. By Drew Bird and Mike Harwood.

In conclusion, study hard, apply your knowledge, practice, practice, practice, and best of luck to you!

Media and Topologies

Welcome! The Network+ exam has become an industry standard networking certification. You are tested on a broad range of connectivity concepts. In this chapter, you will perform lab exercises that familiarize you with the installation of wired and wireless Ethernet LANs, NIC drivers, network cables, and firewalls. You will also learn about various Layer 1 and Layer 2 protocols. These topics will serve as a foundation to help build your networking skills. As mentioned in the introduction, this manual can be used at home or in the classroom setting. If you choose the latter, see Appendix A, "Classroom Setup," for the documentation on how to set up the classroom.

There is a lot of confusion in the networking arena, and because of this, I have been assigned to guide you through safely to the other side! In this chapter, you will learn the correct terminology, tools, methodologies, and strategies to help you excel in the IT field *and* pass the exam.

I'd also like you to know that I support every manual I write. To this end, I created a support Web site: http://www.technicalblog.com. It's free for you to use. So lay down your concerns, and let's rock!

Domain 1: Media and Topologies

The following is a list of the exam objectives, also known as subdomains, covered in this chapter:

1.1 Recognize the following logical or physical network topologies given a diagram, schematic or description: Star, Bus, Mesh, & Ring.

1.2 Specify the main features of 802.2 (Logical Link Control), 802.3 (Ethernet), 802.5 (token ring), 802.11 (wireless), and FDDI (Fiber Distributed Data Interface) networking technologies, including: Speed, Access Method (CSMA/CD), Topology, and Media.

1.3 Specify the characteristics (For example: speed, length, topology, and cable type) of the following cable standards: 10BASE-T and 10BASE-FL, 100BASE-TX and 100BASE-FX, 1000BASE-T, 1000BASE-CX, 1000BASE-SX and 1000BASE-LX, 10 GBASE-SR, 10 GBASE-LR and 10 GBASE-ER.

1.4 Recognize the following media connectors and describe their uses: RJ-11 (Registered Jack), RJ-45 (Registered Jack), F-Type, ST (Straight Tip), SC (Subscriber Connector or Standard Connector), IEEE 1394 (FireWire), Fiber LC (Local Connector), MT-RJ (Mechanical Transfer Registered Jack), USB (Universal Serial Bus).

1.5 Recognize the following media types and describe their uses: Category 3, 5, 5e, and 6, UTP (Unshielded Twisted Pair), STP (Shielded Twisted Pair), Coaxial cable, SMF (Single Mode Fiber) optic cable, MMF (Multimode Fiber) optic cable.

1.6 Identify the purposes, features and functions of the following network components: Hubs, Switches, Bridges, Routers, Gateways, CSU / DSU (Channel Service Unit / Data Service Unit), NICs (Network Interface Card), ISDN (Integrated Services Digital Network) adapters, WAPs (Wireless Access Point), Modems, Transceivers (media converters), & Firewalls.

1.7 Specify the general characteristics (For example: carrier speed, frequency, transmission type and topology) of the following wireless technologies: 802.11 (Frequency hopping spread spectrum), 802.11x (Direct sequence spread spectrum), Infrared, & Bluetooth.

1.8 Identify factors which affect the range and speed of wireless service (For example: interference, antenna type and environmental factors).

What You Will Need

The following is a list of the components and their minimum recommended requirements that you will need for the Chapter 1 labs:

➤ A PII 266MHz PC with 64MB RAM, 2GB HDD, CD-ROM, and network interface card (installed with Windows 2000 Professional) This will be known as PC1.

➤ PII 266MHz PC with 128MB RAM, 2GB HDD, CD-ROM, and network interface card (installed with Windows 2000 Professional or Server). This will be known as PC2.

➤ A four-port wireless/wired router with built-in firewall

➤ A wireless NIC

➤ Two straight-through patch cables

➤ Access to Windows 2000 Professional software

➤ Access to Windows 2000 Server software

➤ At least 25 feet of Category 5 or Category 5e cable

➤ A wire stripper

➤ An RJ-45 crimper

➤ A package of RJ-45 plugs

➤ A patch tester

➤ Access to the Internet

➤ (Optional) A two- or four-port KVM switch

For these labs we will be referring to the following:

➤ Compaq Deskpro PIII 533 MHz computers with 256MB RAM and 3Com 3C905 XL 10/100 PCI TX network interface cards. (These cards will automatically be recognized by Windows 2000 during the OS install.)

➤ Linksys wireless router: Model WRT54G

➤ Linksys PCI wireless NIC: Model WMP54G

➤ Wiedmuller wire stripper: Model AM 12

➤ Paladin Tools RJ-45 crimper

➤ Ideal RJ-45 plugs: Model #85-346 or like model plugs

➤ Paladin Tools Patch

➤ Check 1529 patch tester

➤ Belkin four-port KVM switch bundled with cables, PS/2, part #F1DJ104P

➤ Cable Internet access

A Word About the Minimum Requirements

Although Microsoft will tell you that you can run these OSes at lower processor speeds, we highly recommend that you follow our minimum recommended requirements; otherwise, you risk extremely slow response times from the software. In addition, you can use faster computers. That, of course, is up to you.

You may have noticed that Windows 2000 Professional and Windows XP are very much the same from an architectural standpoint, and most of the labs will work the same way on both platforms with slight navigational differences. The same holds true for Windows 2000 Server versus Windows 2003 Server.

 We do not cover the installation of Windows 2000 Professional or Server, as these topics are outside the scope of the Network+ exam. However, you can access step-by-step installation labs and other ancillary Network+ labs online at http://www.technicalblog.com/labs.

Lab 1: Installation of the Physical LAN

Orientation

In this procedure, you will accomplish the following:

➤ Establish network connectivity between two PCs using the physical star topology.

➤ Verify link lights on the NICs and router.

➤ Boot the computers and view them with My Network Places.

➤ Research other types of topologies on the Internet.

➤ Prepare for the Network+ subdomain 1.1.

When planning and installing the physical LAN, you need to take into account what type of topology to use. A *topology* is simply the way that computers are wired together. It is usually displayed in diagram format. There are four main types of topologies—bus, ring, star, and mesh—but hands down the most common of these is the star topology. When a star topology is used, all computers are wired to a central connecting device with twisted pair cabling. This device could be a hub, MSAU, switch, or SOHO (small office/home office) router. The star topology, which is illustrated in Figure 1.1, is what you will use in this lab (and in almost all other labs in this book).

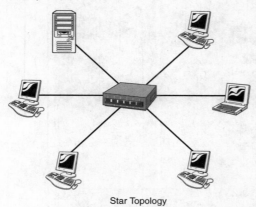

Star Topology

Figure 1.1 Example of a star topology.

Procedure

In this next section you will connect the PCs' network interface cards to the router, and will configure and view network connectivity. Although you can also use a hub or switch in this lab, we will be referring to the Linksys router mentioned in the beginning of the chapter. This is a good lab to start with as it is fairly simple. So here we go!

1. Verify that your two computers have network interface cards. This can be done by looking at the back of the PCs and locating a card with a port that looks like a large telephone jack. It may also be integrated into the motherboard. This port is known as an *RJ-45 port* and is shown in Figure 1.2. A photograph of a NIC inside a computer is shown in Figure 1.3. If either computer does not have a NIC, you will need to install one before continuing with this lab.

Figure 1.2 Network interface card with RJ-45 port.

Figure 1.3 Back view of a computer with a NIC.

Steps 2 and 3 deal with the router. If you have not yet installed the CD that came with the router, you will need to do that before continuing. Don't worry, it is very easy. You will notice that the router has a sticker warning not to connect computers to the router until you have run the CD. Always follow the manufacturer's directions. The CD will tell you exactly what to do step by step. It will ask you for a login to the router, which by default is set as a blank username and a password of **admin**. It will tell you what to connect in what order. Then it will copy files to the ROM chip on the router. It will also ask you for a new username and password, so pick a good one and jot it down—or better yet, memorize it! Then you should be ready to go. If you install the CD right now, you will probably be able to skip steps 2 and 3, as they will already be done.

2. Make sure that the computers are turned off and that the router is not plugged in. Then, take your two patch cables and attach one to each computer's NIC. Connect the other end of each cable to the router. An example of this is shown in Figure 1.4.

Figure 1.4   Example of network connectivity.

3. Use the supplied AC adapter to plug in the router. I recommend that you use a UPS for your equipment. At the very least, if a UPS is not available, you should use a surge protector. When you power up the router, you should see some lights come to life.

4. Connect the keyboards, monitors, and mice to your computers if you have not already done so. Alternatively, you can use a KVM switch as illustrated in Figure 1.5. Connect the power cables to the computers as well.

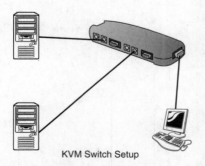

KVM Switch Setup

Figure 1.5   Example of a KVM switch setup.

5. Boot the two computers. While they are booting, take a look at the router. You should see the link lights turn on for each port to which you connected a computer. An example of this is shown in Figure 1.6.

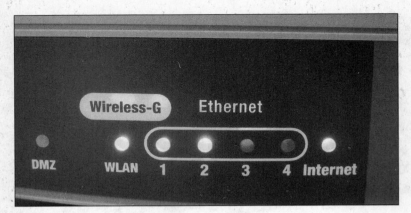

Figure 1.6 Example of link lights.

6. Great job so far! The physical connectivity is done. You have created a network utilizing the star topology! Now it's time to view your network and see if there is logical connectivity between the two computers:

   a. On your desktop, double-click the My Network Places icon. This will open the My Network Places window.

   b. Double-click the Computers Near Me icon. You should be able to see both PC1 and PC2, as displayed in Figure 1.7. If you can't, that's okay for now. In the upcoming labs, you will go through all the possible reasons behind this, and learn how to eliminate any of these problems.

Figure 1.7 The Computers Near Me window.

The last item in this lab is to research the other physical topologies beyond the star topology: bus, ring, mesh, and the combo topologies. Let's break each one down in a little more depth:

It is extremely important for the exam that you are able to identify the various topologies by definition and by illustration.

➤ **Bus**. You will rarely see this setup, and when you take a look at Figure 1.8, it's easy to understand why. Notice that all the computers are connected to a backbone, not a central connecting device like a hub. This means that if you want to add or remove computers from a bus network, you have to take the whole network down first. Also, notice the coaxial cable that is used. This type of cable is limited in speed and really can't handle today's network's data throughput.

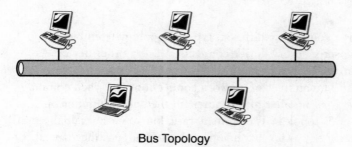

Bus Topology

Figure 1.8   Example of a bus topology.

➤ **Ring**. This is another uncommon type of topology, which also uses coaxial cable with no central connecting device, as shown in Figure 1.9. (Notice the ancient looking computers in the illustration; that's how old the ring topology is!) A ring topology is created by connecting both ends of the bus topology together, forming, as the name implies, a ring of computers. The physical ring, like the bus, is limited in speed and by the fact that if you want to add or remove computers, you will have to bring the whole network down first.

In addition to the ring topology shown in Figure 1.9, there are other types of ring topologies, including logical ring setups like token ring and configurations like FDDI. We will touch on these later in this book. As far as LANs go, however, ring topologies are uncommon.

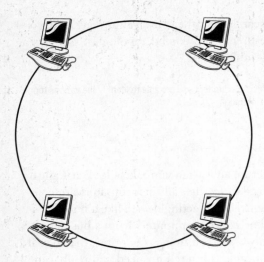

Ring Topology

Figure 1.9   Example of a ring topology.

> **Mesh**. Mesh is a completely different type of topology from bus and ring. In a mesh setup, every device connects to every other device. As shown in Figure 1.10, which shows a "full mesh," this can involve a lot of connections! The number of network connections that each computer will need is the total number of computers in the network minus one. As you can guess, this topology is extremely rare, but some special labs and think tanks may use it. A lesser version of this topology is the "partial mesh," where only a few of the computers on the network have secondary network connections to other systems. You may see this with database replication. These computers would then be known as "multi-homed systems."

> **Star-bus and hierarchical star**. In some cases, you may need to connect two star networks to each other. If this is the case, then the easiest way to do it is to connect the two central connecting devices to each other. Let's say that each star network has a hub at the center. By connecting the two hubs, you are effectively creating a bus between the two. Therefore, it is known as a *star-bus topology*. Now take it to the next level. Use one central hub or *switch* as a "backbone" and connect several hubs to it, each with its own star topology. Now you have the hierarchical star topology. This is extremely common in large corporate networks. An example of this is illustrated in Figure 1.11.

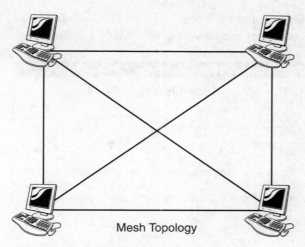

Mesh Topology

Figure 1.10   Example of a mesh topology.

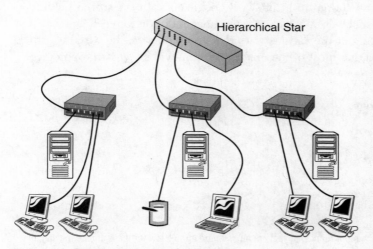

Figure 1.11   Example of a hierarchical star topology.

You should know the difference between a *physical topology* and a *logical topology*. The most common example of this is the standard Ethernet network. Using twisted pair cable, you connect all devices to a hub, which is considered a *physical star topology*. Unfortunately, it gets more involved. If you were to look inside a hub at the electronics, you would find that all the ports are actually connected to one copper circuit known as a bus! So logically, the topology would be referred to as bus, and physically it would be considered a star. The second example of this would be a token ring network. Physically, these are also connected as a star, with a central connecting device known as an MSAU instead of a hub. Internally, however, the MSAU sends frames of data from port to port in order, creating a logical ring. Table 1.1 sums it up.

Table 1.1 Physical versus logical topologies.		
Type of Network	**Physical Topology**	**Logical Topology**
Ethernet	Star	Bus
Token ring	Star	Ring

I know this confuses the issue somewhat, and we haven't gotten into the logical side of things yet, but I promise to make things more clear as we go through the rest of this chapter and through Chapter 2, "Protocols and Standards."

To learn more about topologies, go ahead and access the Internet (this is the fun part right?) and go to http://www.google.com. In the search field, type the queries listed below, and choose the Images option for each. Spend a few minutes looking at the various ways that computers can be wired together. Keep in mind that most of the images you find will be *physical* topologies.

➤ Star topology

➤ Bus topology

➤ Ring topology

➤ Mesh topology

➤ Star-bus topology

➤ Hierarchical-star topology

The four topologies that are most important to know for the exam are the star, bus, ring, and mesh topologies.

That's it! We are finished with Lab 1. Great work!

After completing this lab, you may think "Wow! That was easy!" If so, great! You are on your way. This was an easier initial lab, with limited steps, but rest assured that the labs will become more intense as we move on. Don't worry though; we will take it step by step, and I have every confidence that you will do just fine. Now let's go ahead and wrap this lab up!

What Did I Just Learn?

In the previous lab, you learned how to connect computers together to create a local area network (LAN). Moreover, you learned that when we connect computers, we normally use the star topology. You were also educated about viewing other computers on the network. You practiced the skills you need to:

➤ Recognize the logical and physical network topologies

➤ Network computers together to make a physical LAN

➤ Connect PCs by way of patch cables to a central connecting device, making a star topology

➤ Research diagrams of topologies on the Internet

➤ Use My Network Places to view other systems on the network

Lab 2: Configuration of the NIC and TCP/IP

Orientation

In this procedure, you will accomplish the following:

➤ Configure a network interface card's properties and services.

➤ Set the TCP/IP parameters in static and dynamic modes.

➤ View the differences between various 802 networking technologies.

➤ Identify several cabling standards.

➤ Prepare for the Network+ sub domains 1.2 and 1.3.

Now that we have set up our physical LAN we need to take a look at the type of networking technology we are using. We must also talk about other networking architectures and cabling standards. To help illustrate these topics, we will configure your NICs and work with several Internet Protocol parameters. Then, we will investigate further with references to the Internet and illustrations of the various cabling and networking technologies.

In order for your NIC to function, several components need to be in place. First, you need a working *driver*, which is the software that allows the card itself to "talk" to the operating system. Second, you need to be compliant with a networking technology. Third, the card has to be configured as a client of a specific type of network operating system. Next, you need to install and configure a communications protocol—for example, TCP/IP. This stands for Transmission Control Protocol/Internet Protocol and it is the most widely used protocol on the planet! Most of the Network+ exam refers to and asks questions about TCP/IP. Finally, you need to test the configuration and verify that everything is working properly. If you follow these steps, you will do well.

Most operating systems are capable of configuring settings for your network connection automatically. However, you cannot rely on the OS to do everything for you in all situations. You need to be able to prove your hands-on knowledge on the exam when it comes to NIC services and IP properties. In addition, when working in the field, you will be configuring many custom settings, so this could very well be the most important part of this chapter. Let's get started!

Procedure

In this lab you will verify the NIC driver, modify your NIC's speed, change the type of connection, and view services and their bindings. In addition, you will configure your TCP/IP properties. Next, you will verify your settings in the command prompt. After that, you will test your networking connections. Finally, you will research some additional networking technologies. You will use the same hardware and software setup as in Lab 1. In fact, you will use the same exact setup for all of the Chapter 1 labs. Okay? Let's go!

1. Verify the NIC drivers.

    a. Boot both of your Windows 2000 machines.

    b. On the Windows 2000 Professional client (PC1), go to your desktop and right-click My Computer.

    c. Select Manage from the drop-down menu to open the Computer Management Console, as shown in Figure 1.12.

    d. Click Device Manager to view all your hardware categories on the right-hand side of the window.

> **NOTE**
>
> You will notice that there is an unknown Ethernet Controller listed. This is your wireless NIC. Windows 2000 knows that a card is there and it understands that it is a networking card, but because the driver was written after Windows 2000 was released, it cannot plug-and-play the card. We will cover this installation in Lab 5.

Figure 1.12 The Computer Management Console window.

e. Locate the Network Adapters category and click the + sign next to it to open it. You'll see the network adapters installed in your machine, as shown in Figure 1.13.

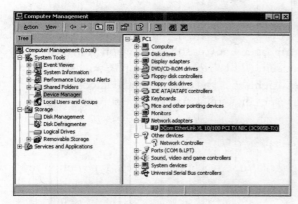

Figure 1.13 A 3Com network adapter.

f. Make sure that there are no icons or markings on the card itself. This means no exclamation points, question marks, or red Xs. If you see any of these, you need to troubleshoot the configuration. This should not be the case, though, because Windows 2000 Professional found our 3Com NIC and installed the driver without any problems. Leave this window open for step 2.

g. If for some reason you do need to install or re-install a driver, it is a pretty easy task. Here's how it's done:

    i. Right-click the card itself and choose Properties.

    ii. In the window that opens, click the Driver tab.

    iii. Click Update Driver. You will need to use the CD that was provided with the NIC or download the latest driver on the manufacturer's Web site from a known good computer.

A great place to obtain hard-to-find drivers is http://www.network-drivers.com.

    h. You are now finished with step 1. To sum up, you want to verify that the NIC driver is installed. The rule of thumb is to make sure that your Device Manager is clean. This means that all categories should be collapsed and you should see nothing but + signs. (Except, of course for our wireless NIC, which we will install later.)

2. Modify your NIC's speed.

    a. In the Computer Management Console window on your Windows 2000 Professional client (PC1), right-click your 3Com card under Network Adapters. Right-click the card itself and choose Properties. A Properties dialog box like the one shown in Figure 1.14 opens.

    b. Click the Advanced tab.

    c. On the left side, under Property, click the Media Type option to select it.

    d. On the right side, you should see a Value drop-down list with the Hardware Default option shown. Click the arrow to the right of the drop-down list to open it, as shown in Figure 1.15.

    e. Select 10BaseTx in the Value drop-down list and click the OK button. Your card will now run at 10Mbps. This is okay, because your router can handle what's known as auto-sensing. That is, it can run at 10Mbps or 100Mbps.

Figure 1.14   The 3Com network adapter Properties dialog box.

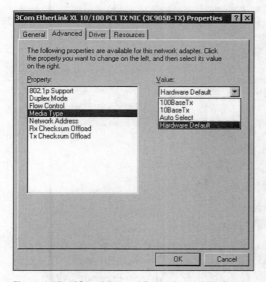

Figure 1.15   3Com Advanced Properties and Media type.

In some scenarios, you may have to change your NIC speed to 10Mbps. For example, if you are connecting to a switch that only accepts 10Mbps connections, your card will not function is set to 100Mbps. Because of this, it is important to know how to change the speed setting.

f. Let's go ahead and change the setting in the Value drop-down list back to Hardware Default. This will ensure that the card runs at its highest speed, 100Mbps. Leave this dialog box open when you are done.

3. Modify the type of NIC connection.

   a. In the Properties dialog box, click the Duplex Mode option in the Property list. Take a look at the new options in the Values drop-down list, noting that again, Hardware Default is the normal setting.

   b. In the Value drop-down list, choose Half Duplex, as shown in Figure 1.16.

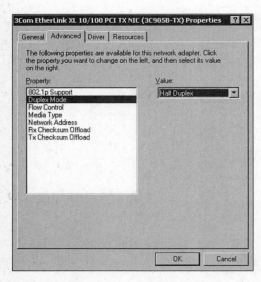

Figure 1.16 Network adapter duplex mode.

   c. Click the OK button to close the Properties dialog box. Your network operations should still function because the 3Com NIC can run at either half duplex or full duplex. Moreover, your SOHO router should be able to handle both, or will at least allow full-duplex cards to send data at half-duplex rates. Remember that *full duplex* means two-way transmission at the same time. *Half duplex* means two-way transmission, but not simultaneously.

   d. Go back to the 3Com NIC Properties dialog box and return to the Advanced tab. Change the Duplex Mode setting back to Hardware Default. Now, close the Properties dialog box and the Computer Management Console window.

4. View bindings and services.

   a. Minimize all windows.

You can quickly minimize all windows by clicking the Show Desktop icon in your Quick Launch area or by using the Windows+D shortcut key combination.

   b. Right-click My Network Places and select Properties. The Network and Dial-up Connections window opens, as shown in Figure 1.17.

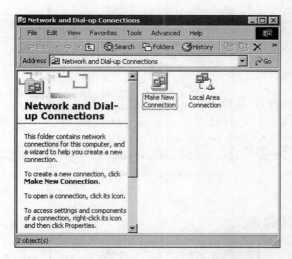

Figure 1.17   The Network and Dial-up Connections window.

   c. Click the Advanced menu and choose Advanced. This opens the Advanced Settings dialog box, as shown in Figure 1.18.

   d. Services such as File and Print Sharing are bound to your protocol, in this case TCP/IP. In addition to this, TCP/IP is bound to the NIC driver. The Bindings for Local Area Connection area is where your bindings can be configured and re-ordered if necessary. You want to make sure that if you have multiple services and/or protocols, the most commonly used ones are at the top of the list.

   e. Click the OK button to close the Advanced Settings dialog box.

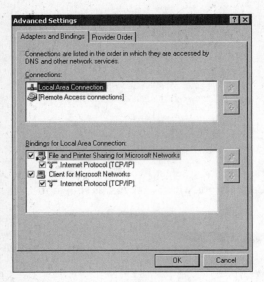

Figure 1.18 The Advanced Settings dialog box.

f. In the Network and Dial-up Connections window, which should
still be open, right-click Local Area Connection and choose
Properties. The Local Area Connection Properties dialog box
opens, as shown in Figure 1.19. This is where you can go to install,
uninstall, and disable common networking services like File and
Print Sharing.

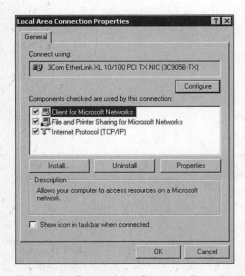

Figure 1.19 The Local Area Connection Properties dialog box.

5. Configure a static TCP/IP address.

   a. In the Local Area Connections Properties dialog box, select
Internet Protocol (TCP/IP) and click the Properties button. This
opens the Internet Protocol (TCP/IP) Properties dialog box, as
shown in Figure 1.20.

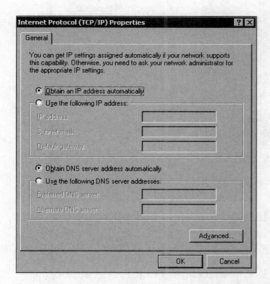

Figure 1.20   The Internet Protocol (TCP/IP) Properties dialog box.

   b. You have two options when it comes to IP addressing. You can get
one automatically (which is how it should be set right now), or you
can assign one manually. That is what we will do next. To begin,
click the Use the following IP address option button to select it.
Notice that the fields below the radio button become activated so
that you can enter information.

   c. Enter the following information:

      i. IP address: `10.10.1.1`

     ii. Subnet mask: `255.0.0.0`

    iii. You can leave the Default gateway field and the DNS server
information blank. Your dialog box should look like the one
shown in Figure 1.21.

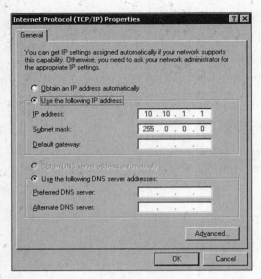

Figure 1.21   The modified Internet Protocol (TCP/IP) Properties dialog box.

d. Click OK to close the Internet Protocol (TCP/IP) Properties dialog box and return to the Local Area Connection Properties dialog box.

e. Click OK to close the Local Area Connection Properties dialog box. (Note that if you were to click Cancel instead of clicking OK, your IP configuration would be erased.)

f. Go to PC2, your Windows 2000 Server computer.

g. Navigate to the Internet Protocol (TCP/IP) Properties dialog box. (This is done the same way on both Windows 2000 Professional and Windows 2000 Server.) To do this, right-click My Network Places and select Properties. Then right-click Local Area Connection and choose Properties again. Finally, click the Internet Protocol option and click the Properties button.

h. Click the Use the following IP address radio button to activate it. Notice that the fields below the radio button become activated so that you can enter information.

i. Enter the following information:

   i. IP address: `10.10.1.2`

   ii. Subnet mask: `255.0.0.0`

   iii. You can leave the Default gateway field and DNS server information blank. We will cover these topics later.

j. Click OK to close both the Internet Protocol (TCP/IP) Properties dialog box and the Local Area Connection Properties dialog box for your changes to take effect. What you have done is to change the systems from obtaining a dynamic IP to using a manually assigned IP address. We put both computers on the 10.0.0.0 network. Because they are both on the same network, they should be able to communicate; in the next section, we will verify this.

It is imperative that you know how to configure and test TCP/IP addresses for the Network+ exam.

6. Verify the IP configuration and test.

a. Go back to PC1, the Windows 2000 Professional computer.

b. Click the Start button, choose the Run option, and type cmd in the window that appears to open the command prompt. A command prompt window opens, as shown in Figure 1.22.

Figure 1.22   The command prompt window.

c. Type ipconfig to view the system's IP address and subnet mask, which you just entered, as shown in Figure 1.23. This verifies what you entered earlier in the Internet Protocol (TCP/IP) Properties dialog box.

```
C:\WINNT\System32\cmd.exe                                    _ □ X
Microsoft Windows 2000 [Version 5.00.2195]
(C) Copyright 1985-1999 Microsoft Corp.

C:\>ipconfig

Windows 2000 IP Configuration

Ethernet adapter Local Area Connection:

        Connection-specific DNS Suffix  . :
        IP Address. . . . . . . . . . . . : 10.10.1.1
        Subnet Mask . . . . . . . . . . . : 255.0.0.0
        Default Gateway . . . . . . . . . :

C:\>_
```

Figure 1.23   The results of running the **ipconfig** command.

If the numbers you see in your command-line window don't match the numbers you entered for your system's IP address and subnet mask, then go back and re-enter that information (refer to exercise 5 in this chapter for that information.) It could be that you inadvertently clicked the Cancel button instead of clicking OK. Always watch to make sure you are clicking the correct button.

d. Switch to PC2, the Windows 2000 Server computer, and again run ipconfig from the command line to verify that the IP address and subnet mask are correct.

You can also type **ipconfig/all** for more detailed information about your NIC.

e. Return to PC1 to test your connection with the *ping* command. To do so, type ping 10.10.1.2. You should get replies, as illustrated in Figure 1.24.

f. Great job! This means that both computers can communicate. If you did not get replies, you want to make sure of the following:

i. The network adapter drivers are installed.

ii. The network cables are connected.

iii. The router is powered on.

iv. You have correctly configured the IP addresses on both machines.

```
C:\WINNT\System32\cmd.exe                                    _ □ ×
Windows 2000 IP Configuration

Ethernet adapter Local Area Connection:

        Connection-specific DNS Suffix  . :
        IP Address. . . . . . . . . . . . : 10.10.1.1
        Subnet Mask . . . . . . . . . . . : 255.0.0.0
        Default Gateway . . . . . . . . . :

C:\>ping 10.10.1.2

Pinging 10.10.1.2 with 32 bytes of data:

Reply from 10.10.1.2: bytes=32 time=10ms TTL=128
Reply from 10.10.1.2: bytes=32 time<10ms TTL=128
Reply from 10.10.1.2: bytes=32 time<10ms TTL=128
Reply from 10.10.1.2: bytes=32 time<10ms TTL=128

Ping statistics for 10.10.1.2:
    Packets: Sent = 4, Received = 4, Lost = 0 (0% loss),
Approximate round trip times in milli-seconds:
    Minimum = 0ms, Maximum =   10ms, Average =   2ms
C:\>
```

Figure 1.24   The ping command with replies.

The simplest of errors when working with TCP/IP will render your computer use-less on the network. Make sure the syntax is correct!

7. Return the computer to normal.

a. Return the systems to their original state—that is, such that they obtain an IP address automatically. The address they will obtain will be the one that was originally given to them by the Linksys router. To begin, on PC1, right-click My Network Places and select Properties.

b. Right-click Local Area Connection and select Properties.

c. Select the IP Protocol option and click the Properties button.

d. Click the Obtain an IP address automatically radio button.

e. If it is not already selected, click the Obtain DNS Server address automatically radio button.

f. Repeat steps d and e on PC2. When you finish returning both computers to normal, the router should give out the address infor-mation and you should be able to get back on the Internet.

Ipconfig and **ping** are extremely important for the Network+ exam. We will cover these in more depth in later chapters. For more information on these and other commands, check out Chapter 6 of the *Network+ Exam Prep 2e* and Chapter 5 of the *Network+ Exam Cram 2, 2e*.

Everything you have done so far has prepared you to learn a little more about the IEEE 802 networking technologies and some of the cabling standards. The IEEE 802 technologies are a set of ratified networking ideas that deal with data communications. This set of ideas is known as *802* because the first IEEE 802 convention met in February of 1980 to decide on guidelines for these technologies, thus 80 refers to the year, and 2 refers to the second month, February. The 802 convention is made up of the people who ratify the standards for Ethernet, Token Ring, and more. The 802 convention was developed by the IEEE (Institute of Electrical and Electronics Engineers) and is also represented in the U.S. by ANSI. Let's talk about a few of the 802 technologies, and give some examples.

First, the Ethernet technologies: 802.2 and 802.3. 802.2 is the standard for Ethernet Logical Link Control, a sublayer of the Data Link layer (See Chapter 2 for more information on the OSI layers). It builds on the ideas behind 802.1, which deals with internetworking in general and with the MAC address. 802.2 specifies the controlling of data between network adapters. It was ratified in the 1990s and reaffirmed in 2003, but the working group (that is, the group of people who convene to ratify the standard), has been disbanded. The problem with 802.2 is that computers transmit data whenever they want, which results in lots of collisions. Although most networks operate in 802.3 mode, some Novell systems still use 802.2.

On some cards, you can change the mode from 802.2 to 802.3 and vice versa. This would be done in the card's Properties dialog box in the Advanced tab.

Check out the following Internet links for more information on 802.2:

➤ http://grouper.ieee.org/groups/802/2/

➤ http://www.freesoft.org/CIE/RFC/1042/7.htm

➤ http://en.wikipedia.org/wiki/IEEE_802.2

802.3 is an advancement of Ethernet. It uses 802.1 MAC and 802.2 LLC technologies, but also combats the problem of chaotic collisions by enforcing what's called CSMA/CD (Carrier Sense Multiple Access/Collision Detection).

802.3 CSMA/CD is the most common type of Ethernet. Out of all the 802 technologies, the Network+ exam asks the most questions about 802.3.

This technology will sense if multiple computers have transmitted data simultaneously. It will also detect any collisions of that data. If it detects a collision, it will tell the network adapter to resend the corrupted data. This became the standard in the mid 1990s and still is today, mostly because it is non-proprietary; anyone can use it. Check out these Internet links for more information:

➤ http://standards.ieee.org/getieee802/802.3.html

➤ http://www.ieee802.org/3/

802.5 is known as the Token Ring technology. Developed by IBM and ratified by the IEEE, it is a proprietary technology, unlike Ethernet. This technology uses a physical star topology and a logical ring topology. Its central connecting device is normally known as an *MSAU* (multi-station access unit). You may still see it in the field and therefore it appears on the exam, but not to the extent that Ethernet does. Token ring uses an electrical impulse, known as a *token*, to move data across the network. There is only one token, and because of this, there are no collisions! A utopia! You may ask, "Why do we not use this technology across the board?" The answer is cost. Through the annals of time, cost has been the main factor in networking, and proprietary systems are almost always more expensive than those based on open-source technologies. But I digress! Back to the token. It is conceived by a master computer on the Token Ring network known as a *monitor*. It is then passed from computer to computer in order. So the token goes from a computer to the MSAU, then to the next computer, back to the MSAU, and so forth, until it completes the cycle. The monitor computer then regenerates the signal (that is, the token) and the whole thing starts again. This is illustrated in Figure 1.25.

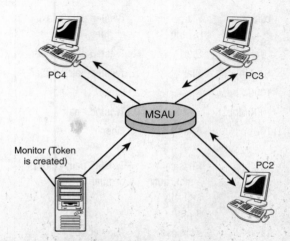

Figure 1.25   A Token Ring network.

Check out these links for more information:

➤ http://www.ieee802.org/5/www8025org/

➤ http://www.freesoft.org/CIE/RFC/1042/10.htm

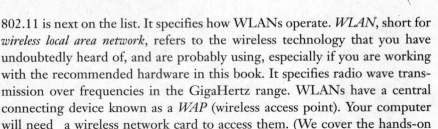

802.11 is next on the list. It specifies how WLANs operate. *WLAN*, short for *wireless local area network*, refers to the wireless technology that you have undoubtedly heard of, and are probably using, especially if you are working with the recommended hardware in this book. It specifies radio wave transmission over frequencies in the GigaHertz range. WLANs have a central connecting device known as a *WAP* (wireless access point). Your computer will need a wireless network card to access them. (We cover the hands-on portion of wireless later in this chapter.) The most common of the 802.11x technologies nowadays is 802.11g, which specifies that data is transmitted at 2.4GHz with a maximum data throughput of 54Mbps. Check out the following links for more information:

➤ http://grouper.ieee.org/groups/802/11/

➤ http://www.webopedia.com/TERM/8/802_11.html

There are a lot of discrepancies when referring to GH or GigaHertz. I think the best way is GigaHertz.

Let's wrap up these technologies by putting all the information you need to know for the exam in Table 1.2.

Table 1.2 IEEE technologies at a glance				
IEEE 802 Technology	**Name**	**Speed**	**Topology**	**Media**
802.2	Logical Link Control (LLC)	10Mbps	Star, bus, or ring	Twisted pair, coaxial, or fiber
802.3	CSMA/CD	10Mbps	Star	Twisted pair or fiber
802.3u	Fast Ethernet	100Mbps	Star	Twisted pair or fiber
802.3z	Gigabit Ethernet	1000Mbps	Star	Fiber
802.3ab	Gigabit Ethernet	1000Mbps	Star	Twisted pair
802.3ae	10 Gigabit Ethernet	10Gbps	Star	Fiber
802.5	Token ring	16Mbps	Physically a star, but logically a ring	Twisted pair, coaxial, or fiber
802.11	WLAN	11–54 Mbps	Wireless radio waves	Air, electro-magnetic waves

Table 1.2	IEEE technologies at a glance *(continued)*			
IEEE 802 Technology	**Name**	**Speed**	**Topology**	**Media**
802.11a	Orthogonal Frequency Division Multiplexing	54Mbps, 5GHz	Wireless radio waves	Air, electro-magnetic waves
802.11b	High rate or Wi-Fi	11Mbps, 2.4GHz	Wireless	Air
802.11g	Fast Wireless	54Mbps, 2.4 GHz	Wireless	Air

Finally, in this lab, I would like to talk a little bit about some of the cabling standards. The most common type of cable used is *twisted pair*. It will normally have eight wires, each with its own copper conductor. That said, you will also see fiber-optic cabling, which uses a glass or plastic conductor. Both are important for the exam. Although you need to be able to identify coaxial cabling (see http://www.technicalblog.com/labs/connectors and look for coax images), it has otherwise been phased out of almost all networks, and I am happy to say that it has been removed from the CompTIA Network+ objectives!

The most common cabling protocol by far is *100BaseT*. This is a hybrid protocol that dictates certain conditions on the physical and data link layers. The *100* tells us that we can transmit at a frequency of 100MHz. It also means that our maximum data throughput is 100Mbps. The *Base* stands for *baseband*. Simply put, it means that the LAN has one channel and one channel only. All computers will share this channel. The *T* stands for trouble. Just kidding, it stands for *twisted pair*. So this one protocol tells us how much data we can transfer, how many channels are on the network, and what type of cable we are using! You may also see this referred to as *100Base-T*. Either way is fine. There are also fiber-based cabling protocols that you need to know. Tables 1.3, 1.4, and 1.5 break down all of the technologies.

Table 1.3	100Mbps cabling standards			
Standard	**Cable Type**	**Segment Length**	**Connector**	**Topology**
100BaseTX	Category 5 UTP	100m	RJ-45	Physical star
100BaseT4	Category 3, 4, 5 UTP	100m	RJ-45	Physical star
100BaseFX	Multi-mode/ single-mode fiber-optic	412m multi-mode/ 10,000m single-mode	SC, ST, MIC	Physical star

Table 1.4   1000Mbps cabling standards

Standard	Cable Type	Segment Length	Connector
1000BaseLX	Multi-mode/ single-mode fiber	550m multi-mode/ 5,000m single-mode	Fiber connectors
1000BaseSX	Multi-mode fiber	550m using 50 micron multi-mode fiber	Fiber connectors
1000BaseCX	STP twisted pair	25m	9-pin shielded connector, 8-pin fiber channel type 2 connector
1000BaseT	Category 5 UTP	100m	RJ-45

Table 1.5   10Gbps cabling standards, 802.3ae

Standard	Transmission Method	Speed	Distance	Cable Type	Connector Type
10GBaseSR	Baseband	10,000Mbps	33m/300m	50 or 62.5 micron multi-mode fiber/ 50 micron multi-mode fiber	SC
10GBaseLR	Baseband	10,000Mbps	10,000m	fiber	SC
10GBaseER	Baseband	10,000Mbps	40,000m	single-mode fiber	SC

For more detailed theory and information on cabling standards, see Chapter 2 of the Que *Network+ Exam Prep, 2e* or Chapter 2 of the *Network+ Exam Cram 2, 2e.*

Well, that pretty much wraps it up for this lab. That was a good deal of information, so let's review!

What Did I Just Learn?

In the previous lab, you learned how to check for network adapter drivers and how to re-install if necessary. You were also educated on the basics of services and bindings of a NIC. In addition, you configured TCP/IP and tested it. Finally, you learned about 802 technologies and cabling standards. You practiced hands-on the skills you need to do the following:

➤ Verify and/or install NIC drivers

➤ Configure static IP addresses

➤ View NIC information with `ipconfig`

➤ Test your IP connection with `ping`

➤ Identify various networking technologies from 802.2 through 802.11

➤ Identify cabling standards from 10Mbps all the way to 10Gbps

Lab 3: Making a Patch Cable and Identifying Connectors

Orientation

In this procedure you will accomplish the following:

➤ Create a Category 5e straight-through patch cable.

➤ Test the cable for connectivity.

➤ Identify various media connectors.

➤ Recognize several types of media.

➤ Prepare for the Network+ sub domains 1.4 and 1.5.

The most common type of cable used in today's networks is twisted pair. The most common types of twisted pair are Category 5 and Cat5e. See Table 1.6 for their speeds.

Table 1.6 Category speeds	
Cable Type	Speed
Category 3	10Mbps
Category 5	100Mbps
Category 5e	350Mbps
Category 6	550Mbps (to a theoretical maximum of 1000Mbps)

All the cables in Table 1.6 are known as *UTP*, short for *unshielded twisted pair*. This type of cable is the favorite among network admins because of its flexibility, easy installation, and speed. There is, however, some research you must do first so you know what wiring standard to use, and what color sequence to work from. Most wiring standards are based on the original BOGB standard, which some call the AT&T standard. This specifies that wire colors go in the order blue, orange, green, brown. The 568A and B standards are based on this. Generally speaking, the most common standard you will see is the 568B standard. You should memorize the color sequence for that standard at the very least. Table 1.7 summarizes the various wiring standards you may see or use.

Table 1.7	Wiring Standards		
Original BOGB or AT&T Standard			
Pair 1	Pin 1.)	White/Blue	
	Pin 2.)	Blue	
Pair 2	Pin 3.)	White/Orange	
	Pin 4.)	Orange	
Pair 3	Pin 5.)	White/Green	
	Pin 6.)	Green	
Pair 4	Pin 7.)	White/Brown	
	Pin 8.)	Brown	
568A Standard		**568B Standard**	
Pin 1.)	White/Green	Pin 1.)	White/Orange
Pin 2.)	Green	Pin 2.)	Orange
Pin 3.)	White/Orange	Pin 3.)	White/Green
Pin 4.)	Blue	Pin 4.)	Blue
Pin 5.)	White/Blue	Pin 5.)	White/Blue
Pin 6.)	Orange	Pin 6.)	Green
Pin 7.)	White/Brown	Pin 7.)	White/Brown
Pin 8.)	Brown	Pin 8.)	Brown

Sometimes you will be called upon to make a patch cable. This may be either to connect a computer to a jack or to connect a port on a patch panel to a hub or switch. It could also be to make a custom link. Either way, it is an important skill to learn. The first thing we will do here is to make a straight-through patch cable. Let's start the lab!

Procedure

1. From your Category 5 cable, cut a 6-foot length. We will use this for our patch cable. Get two RJ-45 plugs ready as well.

2. With the wire stripper, remove about 2 inches of the PVC (plastic) jacket from one end of the cable.

3. When you remove the plastic jacket, you will see eight wires twisted together in pairs, as shown in Figure 1.26 (hence the name twisted pair). Unravel all these wires one by one, straightening them as you go.

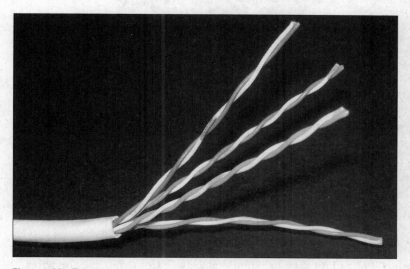

Figure 1.26   Twisted pair wires exposed.

4. As you straighten the wires, put them in order according to the 568B standard outlined in Table 1.7. Start with the white/orange wire and move down the line, as illustrated in Figure 1.27. As you work, hold the wires in place with your thumb.

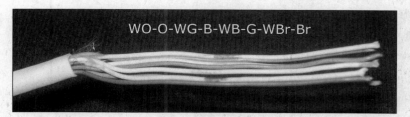

WO-O-WG-B-WB-G-WBr-Br

Figure 1.27   Wires in order according to the 568B standard.

5. Cut the wires to length and make sure they are flush. You will need about 1/4 inch to 1/2 inch of wire exposed after the cut is made, as illustrated in Figure 1.28. Keep your thumb on the wires after the cut is made to keep them in place.

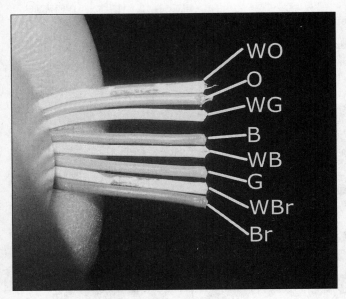

Figure 1.28 Wires after the cut has been made.

6. With your other hand, attach one of the RJ-45 plugs to the end of the cable. The tab on the plug should face away from you, and the wires should read from left to right, starting with white/orange and ending with brown.

7. Push the plug until the wires are fully inserted. The wires should go right to the end of the inside of the plug, as shown in Figure 1.29. Also, the plastic jacket should make it past the tooth inside the RJ-45 plug, as shown in Figure 1.30. This will prevent the plug from slipping off.

8. Now it's time to crimp. Fit the end of the cable with the plug inside the RJ-45 crimper.

9. Squeeze the crimper until the RJ-45 is fastened. You do not need too much pressure, but enough to keep it sturdy.

10. Repeat steps 2–9 on the other end of the cable.

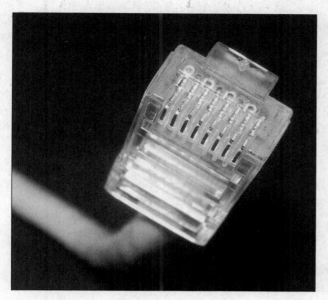

Figure 1.29 Flush wires on the front of the plug.

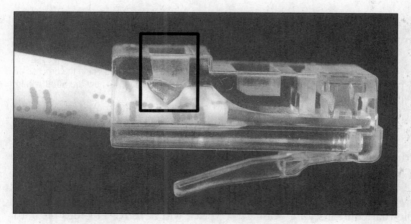

Figure 1.30 Inside tooth of the RJ-45 plug.

11. Test the cable.

    a. Place each end of the cable in your patch tester.

    b. Tap the button on the tester and cycle through all the wires. A light should come on for both ends for each wire—1 to 1, 2 to 2, and so on, through wire 8. If all correspond and all LEDs light up, your test has passed. An example of this is illustrated in Figure 1.31.

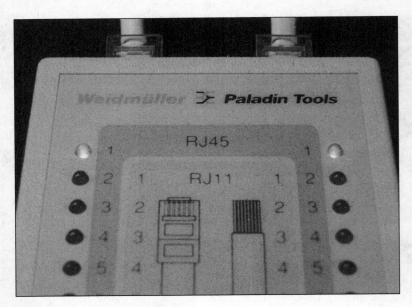

Figure 1.31 A tested patch cable.

12. Optionally, label the wire with a Brother P-touch or a similar tool as a straight-through cable, and you are finished! Great work!

Because you can buy straight-through and crossover cables, learning the process of making one is not that important. You do, however, need to know the 568B wiring order for the Network+ exam.

Now that we have made our patch cable, we need to identify some other media connectors and their uses:

► **RJ-11 connectors.** These are used for telephony applications. The cable that connects your phone to the jack will have RJ-11 plugs on both ends, as shown in Figure 1.32. RJ-11 connectors are capable of handling six wires but normally there are only four. This connector uses the GRBY (rhymes with *Herbie*) setup: green, red, black, and yellow.

If you look at the plugs with the tab facing away from you, you will see that one end is set up as BRGT, and the other end is set up in the opposite way, TGRB. When connecting to screw terminals or a punch block, however, the order is GRBY.

Figure 1.32 An RJ-11 connector.

The RJ in RJ-11 stands for *registered jack*. Query Google's Images page for the term **"RJ-11 Pictures"** and see what you get.

➤ **F-type connectors**. These are used for cable TV and cable Internet connections, as well as for satellite TV/Internet. They are screw-on connectors, the most common of which these days is the RG6.

➤ **Fiber connectors**. There are several types of fiber connectors, including the following:

➤ **ST**. The ST connector employs a rugged metal bayonet coupling ring with radial ramps that facilitate engagement to the studs of the mating adapter. Two ST connectors are available for jacketed fiber, one with a beige boot and one with a black boot. The two colors enable easy identification of the fibers when terminating individual connectors to form a duplex jumper.

➤ **SC**. The SC connector is designed for the most advanced fiber-optic systems and is available in single-mode and multi-mode utilizing epoxy adhesive and in multi-mode preloaded with hot melt adhesive.

➤ **Fiber LC**. This is another type of fiber connector that uses a push connecting end. Also referred to as *LC fiber*, this is fast becoming a staple in the industry.

➤ **USB**. *USB* stands for *universal serial bus* and is a mainstay in today's computers. It is used for cameras, printers, scanners, and even networking to a certain extent. A computer can handle anywhere from 1 to 127 devices on the USB—though a USB hub would be needed to go beyond two devices, because most computers have only two USB interfaces. Figure 1.33 shows an example of a USB cable.

Figure 1.33   A USB cable.

➤ **IEEE 1394**. The IEEE1394 interface, also known as FireWire (as originally created by Apple), is more commonly associated with the attachment of peripheral devices such as digital cameras or printers than with network connections. However, it is possible to create small networks with IEEE1394 cables. The IEEE1394 interface comes in a 4- or 6-pin version.

Go to the Internet and point your browser tohttp://www.technicalblog.com/labs/connectors. There, you will find many more examples of all the media connectors described here. Spend some time examining the various connectors. Then try to quiz yourself when you are finished!

Finally, we need to describe the different cable media you need to know about for the exam. Table 1.8 sums up the various cable media that are out there.

Table 1.8 Cable media	
Type	**Usage**
UTP (unshielded twisted pair)	Local area networks, telephony
STP (shielded twisted pair)	Secure LANs
Coaxial	Cable Internet, cable TV, legacy LANs, satellite TV
SMF (single-mode fiber optic)	Long-distance data communications
MMF (multi-mode fiber optic)	Shorter-distance data communications, but can go farther than UTP or STP

For more information on the various types of cabling media, reference Chapter 2 of the Que *Network+ Exam Prep, 2e* and Chapter 2 of the *Network+ Exam Cram, 2e*.

That about wraps up this lab. Let's discuss what has taken place.

What Did I Just Learn?

After completing this hands-on lab, you examined many different types of connections and learned about several cable media. Of course, you were also educated on how to create a computer patch cable. Specifically, you learned about the following:

➤ Twisted pair connectors such as RJ-11 and RJ-45

➤ Fiber connectors like ST, SC, and more

➤ USB and FireWire (IEEE 1394)

➤ Cable media including UTP, STP, coax, and fiber

➤ Wiring standards such as 568B

➤ How to create a 568B straight-through patch cable

Lab 4: Research and Identify Network Components

Orientation

There are a dozen network components that you need to be able to identify on the Network+ exam. In this short lab, we will research these on the Internet and sum up the qualities of each component. This will prepare you for the Network+ subdomain 1.6.

Procedure

There are several physical devices that you will see in the networking field. Take care to know the following devices:

➤ **Hubs.** A *hub* is a central connecting device used in a physical star topology. It is used in Ethernet networks only. Other network technologies have a different name for this type of device. A hub is actually a simple device, connecting multiple computers together and amplifying and passing on the electrical signal. Internally, the hub just has one trunk circuit to which all of the ports connect. It resides on the Physical layer of the OSI model.

Examine Figure 1.34. When you are finished, go to the Internet and use Google's Images page to run a search for "Ethernet hub". Examine the images that that query returns. Notice the smaller workgroup hubs and the larger rack mount hubs. Finally, visit http://www.technicalblog.com/labs/components to see more Ethernet hubs.

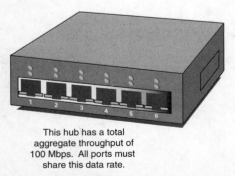

This hub has a total aggregate throughput of 100 Mbps. All ports must share this data rate.

Figure 1.34   An illustration of a hub.

Aside from Google, another good technical search engine is http://www.teoma.com.

➤ **Switches**. Ethernet switching was developed in 1996 and quickly took hold as the preferred method of networking. Like a hub, a *switch* is a central connecting device to which all computers on the network connect. Again, like a hub, a switch will regenerate the signal. That's where the similarity ends, however. Unlike a hub, a switch sends the signal to the correct computer instead of broadcasting it out to every port. This can effectively make every port an individual entity in addition to exponentially increasing data throughput. Switches employ a matrix of copper wiring instead of the standard trunk circuit, as well as intelligence to pass information to the correct port. Although there are layer 1 through layer 4 switches, the type that you will usually see, which is covered in the Network+ exam, is the layer 2 switch. This switch sends information to each computer via MAC addresses.

Take a look at Figure 1.35. When you are finished, go to the Internet and use Google's Images page to run a search for "Ethernet switch." Examine the images that that query returns. Finally, visit http://www.technicalblog.com/labs/components to see more Ethernet switches.

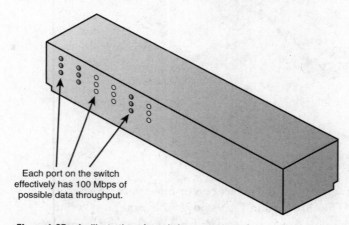

Each port on the switch effectively has 100 Mbps of possible data throughput.

Figure 1.35 An illustration of a switch.

➤ **Bridges.** A *bridge* is used to separate a physical LAN into two logical
  LANs. You do this by physically connecting the device to separate the
  LAN. The device will then seek out all MAC addresses on both sides of
  the LAN and keep that information stored in a table. If a person on one
  side of the bridge wants to communicate on the network, the bridge will
  decide whether the information should cross to the other side. This
  eliminates anywhere from 20–50 percent of broadcasts. You can also use
  a bridge to connect two LANs. This device resides on the Data Link
  layer. Note that since the advent of switching, bridges have become
  much less commonplace.

  Examine Figure 1.36. This shows a bridge connecting two physical
  LANs, making a logical LAN. When you are finished, go to the Internet
  and use Google's Images page to run a search for "network bridge."
  Examine the images that that query returns. Finally, visit
  http://www.technicalblog.com/labs/components to see more bridges.

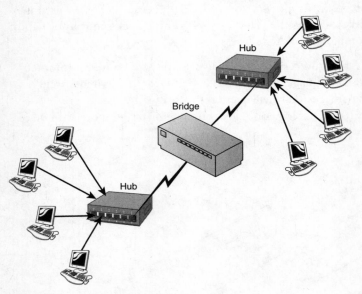

Figure 1.36 How a bridge works.

➤ **Routers.** A *router* is used to connect two or more networks to form an
  internetwork. They are used in LANs, in WANs, and most commonly
  on the Internet. This device routes data from one location to another,
  usually by way of IP address and IP network numbers. Routers function
  on the Network layer of the OSI model. They are intelligent and even
  have their own text-based system known as an *IOS* (*Internetwork
  Operating System*).

Take a look at Figure 1.37. Then go to the Internet and use Google's Images page to run a search for "network router." Examine the images that that query returns. Finally, go to http://www.technicalblog.com/labs/components to see more routers.

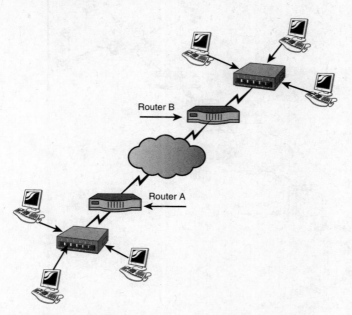

Figure 1.37 Two routers in action.

➤ **Gateway.** A *gateway* is a device or computer that translates between two different types of networks or protocols. An example of this would be an SNA gateway, which translates between IBM mainframes and Ethernet LANs with PCs. The gateway resides on the application layer of the OSI model. This is not to be confused with a router, although routers are sometimes referred to as gateways.

➤ **CSU/DSU.** CSU/DSU, short for *channel service unit/data service unit*, refers to the modems for your entire LAN. They are known as data communication equipment (DCE) devices. If you bring a T-1 line into your office for high-speed Internet access, you will need to connect that line to a CSU/DSU. That then connects to your router, and finally to your LAN, as illustrated in Figure 1.38. There is normally a master CSU/DSU that sets the timing. Nowadays, the CSU/DSU is built right into the router device, or can be added as a card.

Go to the Internet and use Google's Images page to run a search for "CSU/DSU." Examine the images that that query returns. Finally, go to http://www.technicalblog.com/labs/components to see more CSU/DSU devices.

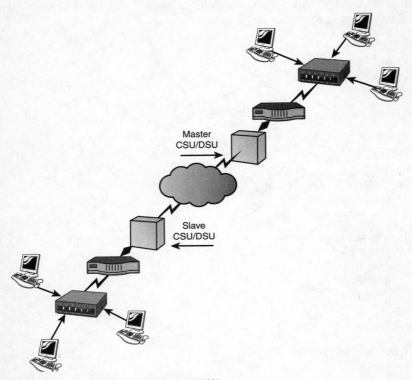

Figure 1.38 The CSU/DSU completes our WAN.

➤ **NIC.** Short for *network interface card*, a NIC is installed inside your computer to allow communication over the network. NICs reformats the parallel information that the OS sends to them for the LAN in a serial configuration. They reside on the data link layer of the OSI model. For more information on NICs, visit http://www.technicalblog.com/labs.

➤ **ISDN adapters.** Short for *Integrated Services Digital Network*, ISDN was the only choice in the 1990s for people who wanted faster Internet access than dial-up, but it has since been phased out in the home by cable and DSL. That said, businesses still use ISDN for various reasons, including fault tolerance and streaming media applications. Companies can purchase a BRI or PRI line. BRI can handle 128Kbps and PRI bumps that up to 1.544Mbps. Either way, you will need some type of ISDN device to connect you to the Internet. Some technicians and manufacturers refer to these as ISDN routers, but they are all actually ISDN terminal adapters. These allow the communication between computers and the Internet through an ISDN line. They could be a single card or a black box that you rack-mount.

Go to the Internet and use Google's Images page to run a search for "ISDN adapter" and "ISDN router." Examine the images that those queries return. Finally, visit http://www.technicalblog.com/labs/components to see more ISDN devices.

➤ **WAPs**. Short for *wireless access points*, these allow data communications over the air as long as your computer is equipped with a wireless networking card. They transmit their data over radio waves either on the 2.4GHz or 5GHz frequency. This brings mobility to a whole new level. Some WAPs also have a router built in, like the Linksys router we are using in this chapter. This allows wireless computers to not only communicate with each other, but to access the Internet as well! A few WAPs are shown at the following link: http://www.technicalblog.com/labs/components. An example of wireless communications is illustrated in Figure 1.39.

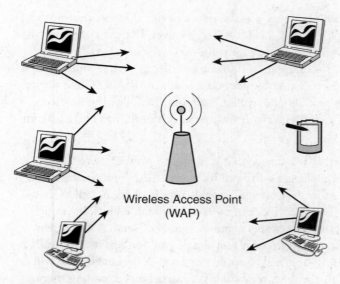

Figure 1.39   Wireless communications.

➤ **Modems**. *Modems* are devices that take care of communications for us. Technically, they modulate and demodulate signals from digital to analog and back. The dial-up modem is the best known, allowing users to access the Internet with a regular POTS phone line. Modems do much more, however. They convert data that is sent from the processor from parallel mode to serial mode. Also, they add a stop bit onto every set of 8 bits to allow for asynchronous data transmission. In addition, they encode data. Encoding allows more than one bit per cycle. In the case of a V.90 modem, you will have 24 bits per cycle on a 2400-Baud line. This allows for a mathematical 57,600 bps. Of course, there are also cable modems. Although these are not actually modems in the common technical sense, we still use the terminology; therefore, you need to be able to identify them on the exam. A few modems are shown at the following link: http://www.technicalblog.com/labs/components. An example of dial-up modem communications is illustrated in Figure 1.40.

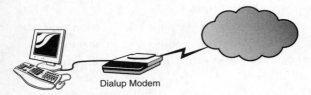

Dialup Modem

Figure 1.40   Dial-up modem communications.

➤ **Transceivers.** Simply put, a *transceiver* is a device that can transmit and receive data. So, in reality, a NIC is a transceiver, but the transceiver has come to be known as a device that will usually connect two different types of media—for example, a 100BaseT transceiver that connects to a router to convert the Ethernet port on a router to RJ-45. These devices quite often have link lights as well. Check out the following link for more examples of transceivers: http://www.technicalblog.com/labs/components.

➤ **Firewalls.** A *firewall* is a device that is meant to protect users from external attack. By placing a firewall between a LAN and the Internet, you add a layer of protection against malicious hackers as well as inadvertent attacks. These devices can be rack-mountable black boxes or computers. Trojans, port scans, zombies, denial of service, and other attacks can be deadly; in this day and age, if you don't have a firewall, you will most likely be attacked sooner or later. A decent firewall will watch all layers of the OSI, read packet headers before sending them through, filter packets, and filter ports. A firewall can also be used to create a DMZ, or de-militarized zone. This way, computers on the LAN are fully protected, but systems on the DMZ can provide valuable services to clients on the Internet. An example is illustrated in Figure 1.41.

Go to the Internet and use Google's Images page to run a search for "firewall". Examine the images that that query returns.

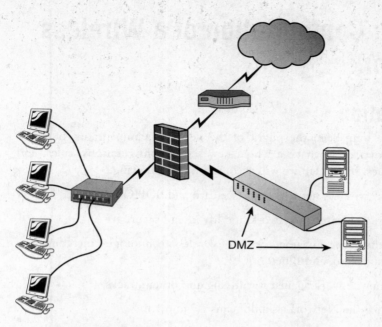

Figure 1.41   A firewall and a DMZ.

And there you have it. That was some basic information on the 12 network components on the Network+ exam. Let's go ahead and talk about what was covered.

What Did I Just Learn?

This lab dealt more with researching on the Internet than anything else. You learned how to find information and images of just about anything related to networking. You also learned about the main 12 network components on which you will be tested. We documented and illustrated how routers, WAPs, firewalls, and other devices function. You learned the following:

➤ Hubs and switches are central connecting devices on the LAN

➤ Routers and CSU/DSUs offer communications over the WAN

➤ WAPs allow data communications over the air using radio waves

➤ Firewalls protect single computers or entire LANs from external attack

Lab 5: Configuration of a Wireless Network

Orientation

Cables have long been the plight of the network administrator, but with wireless networks, we have a whole new set of configurations, rules, and security issues. In this lab we will accomplish the following:

➤ Install our wireless network interface card and SOHO router.

➤ Configure our wireless network, modify it, and secure it.

➤ Discuss the general characteristics of wireless technologies including 802.11x, infrared, and Bluetooth.

➤ Protect our network against wardriving and other attacks.

➤ Prepare for the Network+ subdomains 1.7 and 1.8.

Wireless networks have emerged as a real presence in the networking field. Indeed, it is now common for a family to have a SOHO (small office/home office) router at home. Wireless means portability, ease of use, and easy installation. There is a trade off, however, of speed and security. In this lab we will set up a simple home-based wireless network and show how to combat the security and speed issues. Let's get started!

Procedure

1. Install the wireless NIC in the computer. For this exercise, install the PCI wireless NIC into PC1.

    a. With your computer turned off and unplugged, open the case.

    b. Make sure you have an anti-static strap attached, and select a PCI slot to install your wireless NIC.

    c. Touch the chassis with both hands to further discharge yourself.

    d. Remove the PCI card from the anti-static bag and install it in the chosen PCI slot.

    e. Screw the card into the slot and close the case.

    f. On the back of the computer screw on the antenna, making sure that it is firmly attached to the card.

Installing adapter cards is also an A+ topic. For more information on installing adapter cards, refer to the *Exam Cram 2 A+ Lab Manual.*

2. Boot both computers.

3. Install the driver for the wireless NIC.

   a. On PC1, insert the CD that came with the NIC. The Welcome to Setup Wizard window should appear. If for some reason you do not have a CD, the NIC driver can be downloaded from Linksys's Web site. In that case, you will most likely need to install the driver through the Device Manager. Refer to this chapter's Lab 2, "Configuration of the NIC and TCP/IP," Section 1g, for more information.

   b. Click Install.

   c. Agree to the license by clicking Next.

   d. You are asked whether you would like to use Infrastructure mode or Ad-Hoc mode. Choose Infrastructure mode, which essentially means that you have a WAP to which you want to connect. Ad-Hoc means that you would be communicating with other wireless network cards without the use of a WAP.

   e. You are asked for an SSID (service set identifier). Leave this as "linksys," which is how the router is set by default. That is the name of the wireless network that the card will look for once installed. Click Next.

   f. The next screen deals with security. Because we have not yet configured security on the router, leave this screen's default setting intact click Next.

   g. Review the settings and click Next if they are correct. Files will then be copied to your machine.

   h. If you get a pop-up window from Windows 2000 that tells you that a digital signature could not be found, click Yes to continue the installation.

   i. When the file-copy operation is complete, you will see the screen shown in Figure 1.42. Click Exit. The driver installation is complete.

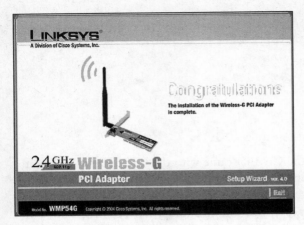

Figure 1.42 Wireless NIC completion screen.

4. Test the wireless connection.

  a. Disable the original wired network adapter to avoid any confusion, and then rename both adapters.

  i. Right-click My Network Places and select Properties.

  ii. Right-click Local Area Connection and choose Rename. Rename the connection "LAN Card" and press Enter.

  iii. Right-click Local Area Connection again, but this time select Disable. After a few seconds, the card's icon on the screen should turn to gray, as shown in Figure 1.43.

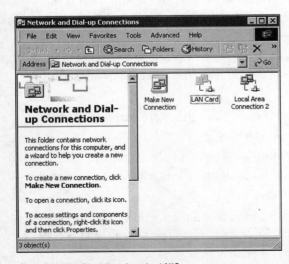

Figure 1.43 Disabling the wired NIC.

iv. Rename the other card. Currently, it's called "Local Area Connection 2"; change it to "Wireless LAN Card."

b. Test the wireless card.

i. Open a command prompt by clicking the Start button, choosing Run, and typing `cmd.exe` in the window that appears.

ii. Type `ipconfig`. You should see information showing that the wireless router automatically gave your wireless NIC an IP address, as shown in Figure 1.44.

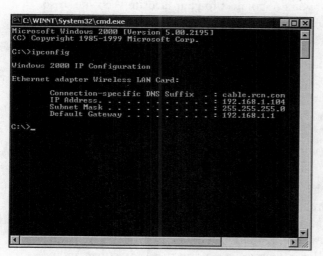

Figure 1.44   Viewing the wireless IP address with **ipconfig**.

NOTE   We received 192.168.1.104 as the IP address. This could be different for you because the addresses from 100–150 are handed out dynamically by the router.

iv. In the command prompt, type `ping 192.168.1.1`. You should get replies! Great work!

c. View your wireless connection details.

i. You may have noticed that after the installation, a green icon appeared in your system tray in the lower-right portion of the screen. Hover your mouse icon on top of the green wireless icon now to view the details for your wireless connection, as shown in Figure 1.45.

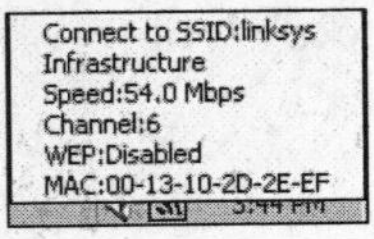

```
Connect to SSID:linksys
Infrastructure
Speed:54.0 Mbps
Channel:6
WEP:Disabled
MAC:00-13-10-2D-2E-EF
```

Figure 1.45   Details of the wireless connection.

d. Test with data.

    i. Now that we you tested the card from a networking stand-point, go ahead and do a real test. Open up Internet Explorer and see if you can connect to your favorite Web site. If so, great job! Now you can use the wireless NIC just as you would a wired network adapter.

5. Connect to and configure the router.

> The SOHO wireless router is a great device. It acts as a hub, router, IP proxy, NAT device, WAP, encryption device, and Firewall! That's a lot of bang for your buck. It can also handle 253 wired connections and as many wireless connections concurrently.

a. Your router has a ROM chip that you can access to change the way your wireless network behaves. We will connect to this now. This is also known as "ROMing into the router." You do this with a simple browser like Internet Explorer! Easy! To begin, open Internet Explorer, type 192.168.1.1 in the Address bar, and press Enter.

> The numbers you typed represent the default IP address for all Linksys routers. Other manufacturer's routers will use different IPs, for example Belkin uses **192.168.2.1**. Always refer to the manufacturer's directions or website for this important information.

b. The Enter Network Password dialog box, shown in Figure 1.46, asks you for a login. By default, Linksys sets the username blank, and sets the password to admin. Type admin in the password field now. (If you changed the login during setup, type the password you supplied instead.)

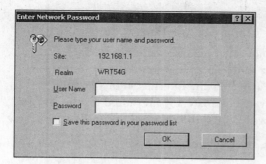

Figure 1.46   The router login screen.

c. Notice that the screen that appears features a main menu comprised of the options Setup, Wireless, Security, and so on, as shown in Figure 1.47. Underneath each entry in this main menu are secondary menus. Take a few minutes to navigate through these menus and familiarize yourself with them, but don't make any changes as of yet.

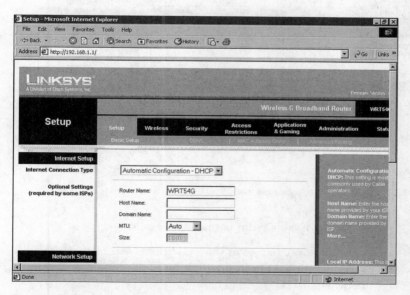

Figure 1.47   The router configuration screen.

d. There are a slew of configuration options, but for now, we will modify only a couple—starting with the time zone, which you can access by scrolling down on the main screen. By default, this is set to Pacific time; change it to reflect your time zone.

e. The moment your router was up and running, it started broadcasting over the air waves—and the transmission can go a good distance. There is a possibility that people next door or on the street could get access to your router; people who do this on purpose are known as *wardrivers*. Fortunately, by filtering who your router accepts, you can effectively eliminate any unwanted people on your network. This is done with MAC filtering.

    i. On the main menu, select Wireless.

    ii. On the secondary menu, select Wireless MAC Filter. You'll see a window like the one in Figure 1.48.

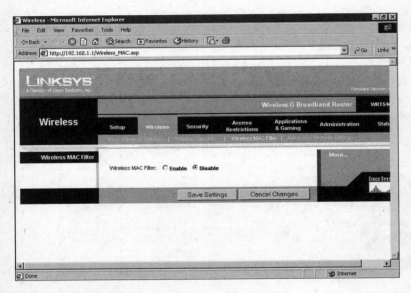

Figure 1.48 The MAC Filter configuration screen

    iii. Click the Enable radio button.

    iv. The window enlarges to show additional settings. Click the second option, Permit only PCs listed to access the wireless network.

Be very sure that you select the second option and not the first one or you may lose connectivity. In that case, you might have to reinstall the ROM (Read Only Memory) from a wired computer with the CD.

Although it is not necessary, most technicians set all the configurations on the router from a wired PC before putting the router into action.

v. Click the Edit MAC Filter List button. This opens another window, where we will add the MAC addresses of each machine.

New to MAC addresses? Don't worry. A MAC address is simply a physical address that is part of your NIC. What we will do here is locate the MAC address for each computer and add that to the MAC filter table.

vi. Leave the current window open and open your command prompt.

vii. Type `ipconfig/all`. As shown in Figure 1.49, this will display detailed information about your wireless NIC including the MAC address, which is referred to as the physical address.

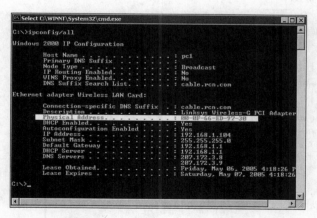

Figure 1.49   The ipconfig/all screen.

viii. Jot down the hexadecimal MAC address for your computer.

ix. Enter the MAC address for every wireless NIC on your network into the router's MAC filter list. You can easily add the MAC address for the computers that already have wireless NICs by clicking the Wireless Client MAC List button and clicking the check box next to each computer you want to add.

(Make sure there are no other unwanted computers using your router when you view this window!) In addition, this filter will not affect wired computers because the filter is only for wireless connections. When you're finished, it will look something like Figure 1.50. Make sure that every octet is separated by a colon—for example, 00:60:08.

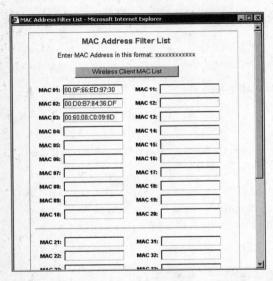

Figure 1.50 The edited MAC Filter table.

x. Scroll to the bottom and click the Save Settings button to save the changes for the MAC filter list.

You may lose your wireless connection at times when you save the information, but it should come back in a few seconds. (You can always reconnect to the router through the browser if you have to.) If you have any other problems, enable your wired NIC and reconnect to the router with that card.

xi. Save the changes on the main screen; you should see a screen that tells you the changes were successful. Again, you may lose the connection to the router for a moment or two. If you have to, log back in.

f. When you are finished with the MAC filtering, you want to do one more thing: change the password.

i. Go back to the router configuration screen and click Administration in the main menu.

ii. You will see that the first option is the password. Type a new complex password that no one will be able to guess, and type it a second time to confirm it. Write it down for now, until you are sure you have memorized it.

iii. Click the Save Settings button at the bottom of the screen.

iv. Close the router configuration window.

6. Re-enable the wired NIC.

    a. Right-click My Network Places.

    b. Right-click the LAN card and select Enable.

    c. Close all windows.

7. One of the great things about these devices is that they come with a built-in firewall that runs automatically after you set up the router. Before you move on, you must test this built-in firewall.

    a. Go to the Internet and access http://www.grc.com. This website offers a free firewall checker. It is not the best in the industry, and we will cover other scanning programs in later chapters, but it is free and easy to use and access. It gives you a basic idea of whether or not your firewall is functioning properly.

    b. Select the Shield's Up option.

    c. Scroll down about halfway and click the Shield's Up link.

    d. Click OK in the security pop-up window, if it is displayed.

    e. Click the Proceed button.

    f. Scroll down and select the Common Ports option. The firewall checker will verify your IP address and check your connection and its ports. There are three possible outcomes: open (which is bad), closed (which is not so bad), and stealth. Stealth is what you want down the line. If you are using the Linksys router, the firewall checker should return "stealth" for all ports on the list. That means that your LAN has a decent firewall protecting it. If for some reason you have ports that are open or closed, you'll need to troubleshoot them; we cover this in Chapter 4.

    g. Close Internet Explorer.

You need to know how to work with a wireless router for the exam and for the field.

Great work! As you saw, there were many other configurations and settings in the router. For example, you can change the frequency (channel) of the router so as not to conflict with other devices like cordless phones. Just make sure that your wireless NIC finds the new frequency, or set that in the wireless NIC properties if need be. You can also change the name of the network and add security features like WEP or WPA. In addition, you can filter by computer name as well as by the aforementioned MAC address. You can allow certain applications to work through the Internet so that users outside of your LAN can connect to you. You can enable VPN so that you can connect to your home network from outside the home. There is a lot more. We will cover a few of these features in future chapters.

I'd like to touch on a few more wireless technologies:

► **802.11 frequency-hopping spread spectrum**. *Frequency hopping* is one of two basic modulation techniques used in spread-spectrum signal transmission. It is the repeated switching of frequencies during radio transmission, often to minimize the effectiveness of electronic warfare— that is, the unauthorized interception or jamming of telecommunications.

► **802.11 direct-sequence spread spectrum**. *Direct-sequence spread spectrum*, also known as *direct-sequence code division multiple access* (DS-CDMA), is one of two approaches to spread-spectrum modulation for digital-signal transmission over the airwaves. In direct-sequence spread spectrum, the stream of information to be transmitted is divided into small pieces, each of which is allocated to a frequency channel across the spectrum.

► **Bluetooth**. This is a short-range radio technology aimed at simplifying communications among Internet devices and between devices and the Internet. It also aims to simplify data synchronization between Internet devices and other computers. Bluetooth is divided into three classes. Class I has a maximum transmission range of 100 meters, Class II (the most common) has a range of 10 meters, and Class III is very short range and hardly used. An example of Bluetooth technologies would be the common Motorola Bluetooth wireless headsets. These need to be *paired* with your cellular phone. Figure 1.51 shows a PDA/cell phone and Bluetooth headset in the pairing mode.

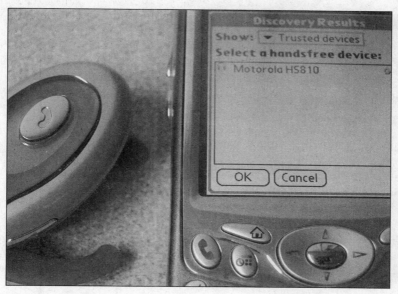

Figure 1.51 Bluetooth in action.

➤ **Infrared**. This is another type of data-transmission technique, and is higher in frequency than radio waves and microwaves. Usually used as a line of sight technology, it is standardized by the Infrared Data Association (IrDA).

➤ **Interference**. There are all kinds of interference in this world, from electrical interference to electromagnetic interference (EMI). One of your jobs as a network administrator is to avoid it. For example, an electrical panel will give off a lot of EMI, so it would be wise to keep your WAP away from the panel. The same applies to fluorescent lights, outlets, and any electrical devices with magnets. There is also interference from other air-based media. Radio interference (RFI) is common because so many devices use radio waves nowadays—cordless phones, remote-control cars, garage-door openers, the list goes on! Try to keep your wireless network on an unused frequency. Linksys uses channel 6 by default, and Belkin uses channel 10. Usually the default will work, but if you get sporadic connections with your wireless card, try changing the channel. Also, direct the antennae at a 45-degree angle for best reception.

For more information on wireless technologies, refer to Chapters 3 and 6 of the *Network+ Exam Cram 2, 2e*.

What Did I Just Learn?

In this final lab of Chapter 1, you learned how to configure a wireless router and wireless NIC. You also verified that your devices were working, and made sure that you had an active firewall. Specifically, you learned how to do the following:

➤ Install a wireless NIC and driver.

➤ Set up and configure a wireless router.

➤ Use tools to verify your network connection and firewall.

➤ Identify Bluetooth and other wireless technologies.

Domain 1 Practice Questions

Objective 1.1

1.1 Recognize the following logical or physical network topologies given a diagram, schematic or description: Star, Bus, Mesh, & Ring.

1. Which of these is the most common type of topology?
   - ❑ a. Bus
   - ❑ b. Star
   - ❑ c. Ring
   - ❑ d. Mesh

2. Which of these devices can be used as a central connecting device in a star topology?
   - ❑ a. Bridge
   - ❑ b. Gateway
   - ❑ c. NIC
   - ❑ d. Hub

3. Which physical network topologies are used with coaxial Ethernet networks? (Select two.)
   - ❑ a. Bus
   - ❑ b. Mesh
   - ❑ c. Ring
   - ❑ d. Star

4. Which physical network topology is used with twisted pair Ethernet networks?
   - ❑ a. Bus
   - ❑ b. RJ-45
   - ❑ c. Ring
   - ❑ d. Star

Objectives 1.2 and 1.3

1.2 Specify the main features of 802.2 (Logical Link Control), 802.3 (Ethernet), 802.5 (token ring), 802.11 (wireless), and FDDI (Fiber Distributed Data Interface) networking technologies.

1.3 Specify the characteristics (for example, speed, length, topology, and cable type) of cable standards.

1. Which of these cabling standards uses twisted pair cable?
   - ❏ a. 100BaseFX
   - ❏ b. 10Base2
   - ❏ c. 1000BaseLX
   - ❏ d. 100BaseT

2. 100BaseTx uses what category cable?
   - ❏ a. Category 3
   - ❏ b. Category 5
   - ❏ c. Category 2
   - ❏ d. 802.3u

3. Which wireless standards can transmit data at up to 54Mbps? (Select the best two answers.)
   - ❏ a. 802.11b
   - ❏ b. 802.11ae
   - ❏ c. 802.11g
   - ❏ d. 802.11a

4. Which Ethernet standard can transmit data at 100Mbps?
   - ❏ a. 802.2
   - ❏ b. 802.3
   - ❏ c. 802.3b
   - ❏ d. 802.3u

5. What command is used to view your IP settings?
   - ❏ a. **ping**
   - ❏ b. **nbtstat**
   - ❏ c. **ipconfig**
   - ❏ d. **tracert**

Objectives 1.4 and 1.5

1.4 Recognize media connectors and describe their uses.

1.5 Recognize media types and describe their uses.

1. What type of connector would a computer's UTP patch cable use?
   - ❏   a. RJ-11
   - ❏   b. RJ-45
   - ❏   c. F-type
   - ❏   d. ST

2. What is the maximum data throughput of a Category 5e cable?
   - ❏   a. 350Mbps
   - ❏   b. 100Mbps
   - ❏   c. 1.4Gbps
   - ❏   d. 350Kbps

3. Which pins (wires) are used to transmit Ethernet data in a CAT5 cable?
   - ❏   a. 1, 2, 4, and 5
   - ❏   b. 1, 3, and 6
   - ❏   c. 1, 2, 7, and 8
   - ❏   d. 1, 2, 3, and 6

4. What is the most commonly used wiring standard in LANs today?
   - ❏   a. 568A
   - ❏   b. 619B
   - ❏   c. USOC
   - ❏   d. 568B

5. What is the device that connects the RJ-45 plug to the CAT5 cable?
   - ❏   a. Wire stripper
   - ❏   b. Patch tester
   - ❏   c. RJ-45 crimper
   - ❏   d. TDR

Objective 1.6

1.6 Identify the purposes, features, and functions of network components.

1. Ethernet networks use what two types of central connecting devices within the LAN? (Select two.)
   - ❏   a. Hub
   - ❏   b. MSAU
   - ❏   c. ISDN adapter
   - ❏   d. Switch

2. Which device will protect a LAN from a hacker?

   ❏ a. Hub

   ❏ b. Router

   ❏ c. Gateway

   ❏ d. Firewall

3. An example of a DCE device would be what?

   ❏ a. Router

   ❏ b. CSU/DSU

   ❏ c. Cloud

   ❏ d. DMZ

4. Which of the following is an area with limited access from users on the Internet?

   ❏ a. CSU/DSU

   ❏ b. DMZ

   ❏ c. ISDN

   ❏ d. POTS

5. What device connects two LANs to form a WAN?

   ❏ a. Router

   ❏ b. Hub

   ❏ c. Switch

   ❏ d. Mainframe

Objective 1.7 and 1.8

1.7 Specify the general characteristics (for example: carrier speed, frequency, transmission type and topology) of the following wireless technologies: 802.11 (Frequency hopping spread spectrum), 802.11x (Direct sequence spread spectrum), Infrared, & Bluetooth.

1.8 Identify factors that affect the range and speed of wireless service (for example, interference, antenna type, and environmental factors).

1. Bluetooth can normally transmit up to how far?

   ❏ a. 30 meters

   ❏ b. 10 meters

   ❏ c. 100 meters

   ❏ d. 185 meters

2. MAC filtering will filter out which type of address?

   ❏ a. IP address

   ❏ b. Computer name

   ❏ c. Physical address

   ❏ d. Router address

3. What are two types of interference? (Select the best two.)

- ❏ a. RFI
- ❏ b. Static electricity
- ❏ c. Hurricane
- ❏ d. EMI

4. How many channels are available to you in the 2.4GHz frequency range?

- ❏ a. 10
- ❏ b. 6
- ❏ c. 11
- ❏ d. 2.4

5. Which networks do most SOHO routers offer their clients? (Select two.)

- ❏ a. 10.10.1.0
- ❏ b. 10.0.0.0
- ❏ c. 192.168.1.0
- ❏ d. 192.168.2.0

Answers and Explanations

Objective 1.1

1. Answer b is correct. The star is by far the most common topology. Bus and ring are older types of physical topologies that are rarely in use today. Mesh is uncommon but may be seen in exceptional situations.

2. Answer d is correct. The hub connects multiple computers to create the star topology. A bridge is used to dissect a LAN or to connect two LANs. A gateway allows access to the Internet for an entire LAN. A NIC is a network interface card, which is installed inside a computer to allow access to the network or LAN.

3. Answers a and c are correct. Bus and ring topologies commonly use coaxial cable. Star topologies use twisted pair cabling; mesh topologies normally use twisted pair as well.

4. Answer d is correct. Star topologies normally use twisted pair cabling, whereas bus and ring topologies use coaxial. RJ-45 is a type of connector or plug for the twisted pair network.

Objectives 1.2 and 1.3

1. Answer d is correct. FX and LX are fiber standards, and 10Base2 is an outdated coaxial standard.

2. Answer b is correct. Category 3 is limited to 10Mbps, while Category 2 is an old type of cabling that you really shouldn't see anymore. 802.3u isn't a cable at all; it's a network technology.

3. Answers c and d are correct. 802.11b transmits only at 11Mbps, and 802.11ae is not used in America.

4. Answer d is correct. All other answers can only transmit 10Mbps.

5. Answer c is correct. ping tests the connection, nbtstat gives network statistics, and tracert checks routes on your network.

Objective 1.4 and 1.5

1. Answer b is correct. RJ-11 would be for a phone cable, F-type is for cable Internet and TV, and ST is a type of fiber-optic connector.

2. Answer a is correct. All other answers are the wrong data throughput.

3. Answer d is correct. Pins (wires) 1, 2, 3, and 6 are part of the orange and green pairs. Those are the two pairs that deal with Ethernet.

4. Answer d is correct. 568B is the most common and has for the most part replaced 568A. 619 is a completely different electrical wiring standard. Although USOC is another viable option, it is not nearly as common as 568B.

5. Answer c is correct. To crimp plugs onto the end of a cable, you need an RJ-45 crimper. The wire stripper removes the plastic jacket, the patch tester tests the cable after you have made it, and a TDR, short for time domain reflectometer, is a different device altogether that checks for breaks in a long-distance cable run.

Objective 1.6

1. Answers a and d are correct. An MSAU is a central connecting device for a Token Ring network and an ISDN adapter will offer a connection for a computer (or more than one) to the Internet.

2. Answer d is correct. A hub is a central connecting device, a router offers a LAN the capability to connect to the outside world, and a gateway translates between two different types of systems or protocols.

3. Answer b is correct. A router would be an example of a DTE, the cloud is the technical term for the Internet or anything beyond your building's network, and the DMZ is a gray area. It is not quite your LAN and not quite the Internet, more a mixture of both.

4. Answer b is correct. A CSU/DSU is the modem or communications device for your entire LAN. ISDN is a different type of WAN technology altogether, and POTS is the Plain Old Telephone System, used by dial-up connections.

5. Answer a is correct. A hub is a central connecting device, as is a switch; both deal with the LAN only. A mainframe is a computer and works in a different environment known as *centralized computing*.

Objective 1.7 and 1.8

1. Answer b is correct. 30 meters is for other types of wireless technologies. 100 meters would be the limit on Category 5 twisted pair Ethernet networks (10BaseT, 100BaseT), and 185 meters is the limit on coax thinnet networks (10Base2).

2. Answer c is correct. The MAC is the physical address that is burned into the PROM (Programmable Read Only Memory) chip of the NIC at the manufacturer's plant. Each one is unique. IP addresses are logical and are assigned by the OS.

3. Answers a and d are correct. Although static electricity can damage a component, it is not considered interference per se. And although a hurricane could interfere with your daily life, what the Network+ exam will be looking for is interference from AC electricity and RFI.

4. Answer c is correct. All other answers are the wrong amount.

5. Answers c and d are correct. In fact, on most of the SOHO routers, you cannot change the network number. You will, however, see the 10 network in larger companies.

Need to Know More?

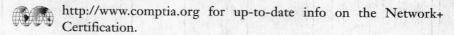 http://www.comptia.org for up-to-date info on the Network+ Certification.

Bird, Drew and Mike Harwood. *Network+ Exam Prep 2*. Indianapolis: Que Publishing. ISBN: 0-7897-3255-6.

Bird, Drew and Mike Harwood. *Network+ Exam Cram 2, 2e*. Indianapolis: Que Publishing. ISBN: 0-7897-3254-8.

Brooks, Charles. *Network+ Exam Cram 2 Practice Questions (Exam NIO-003)*. Que Publishing. ISBN: 0-7897-3352-8.

Protocols and Standards

This chapter delves into TCP/IP, the OSI model, remote access, and WAN technologies. You are sure to get plenty of questions pertaining to this chapter on the Network+ exam, and for good reason. This chapter is comprised of the stuff that makes a good network admin great! This chapter has 10 labs in total with lots of exercises, making it a power-packed chapter. Let's break down the subdomains you need to know for this chapter and then we'll get the labs started.

Domain 2.0: Protocols and Standards

The following is a list of the exam objectives covered in this chapter:

➤ 2.1 Identify a MAC (Media Access Control) address and its parts.

➤ 2.2 Identify the seven layers of the OSI (Open Systems Interconnect) model and their functions.

➤ 2.3 Identify the OSI (Open Systems Interconnect) layers at which the following network components operate: Hubs, Switches, Bridges, Routers, NICs (Network Interface Card), WAPs (Wireless Access Point).

➤ 2.4 Differentiate between the following network protocols in terms of routing, addressing schemes, interoperability and naming conventions: IPX / SPX (Internetwork Packet Exchange / Sequence Packet Exchange), NetBEUI (Network Basic Input / Output System Extended User Interface), AppleTalk / AppleTalk over IP (Internet Protocol)and TCP / IP (Transmission Control Protocol / Internet Protocol).

➤ 2.5 Identify the components and structure of IP (Internet Protocol) addresses (IPv4, IPv6) and the required setting for connections across the Internet.

➤ 2.6 Identify classful IP (Internet Protocol) ranges and their subnet masks (For example: Class A, B and C).

➤ 2.7 Identify the purpose of subnetting.

➤ 2.8 Identify the differences between private and public network addressing schemes.

➤ 2.9 Identify and differentiate between the following IP (Internet Protocol) addressing methods: Static, Dynamic, Self-assigned (APIPA (Automatic Private Internet Protocol Addressing)).

➤ 2.10 Define the purpose, function and use of the following protocols used in the TCP / IP (Transmission Control Protocol / Internet Protocol) suite: TCP (Transmission Control Protocol), UDP (User Datagram Protocol), FTP (File Transfer Protocol), SFTP (Secure File Transfer Protocol), TFTP (Trivial File Transfer Protocol), SMTP (Simple Mail Transfer Protocol), HTTP (Hypertext Transfer Protocol), HTTPS (Hypertext Transfer Protocol Secure), POP3 / IMAP4 (Post Office Protocol version 3 / Internet Message Access Protocol version 4), Telnet, SSH (Secure Shell), ICMP (Internet Control Message Protocol), ARP / RARP (Address Resolution Protocol / Reverse Address Resolution Protocol), NTP (Network Time Protocol), NNTP (Network News Transport Protocol), SCP (Secure Copy Protocol), LDAP (Lightweight Directory Access Protocol), IGMP (Internet Group Multicast Protocol), LPR (Line Printer Remote).

➤ 2.11 Define the function of TCP / UDP (Transmission Control Protocol / User Datagram Protocol) ports.

➤ 2.12 Identify the well-known ports associated with the following commonly used services and protocols: 20 FTP (File Transfer Protocol), 21 FTP (File Transfer Protocol), 22 SSH (Secure Shell), 23 Telnet, 25 SMTP (Simple Mail Transfer Protocol), 53 DNS (Domain Name Service), 69 TFTP (Trivial File Transfer Protocol), 80 HTTP (Hypertext Transfer Protocol), 110 POP3 (Post Office Protocol version 3), 119 NNTP (Network News Transport Protocol), 123 NTP (Network Time Protocol), 143 IMAP4 (Internet Message Access Protocol version 4), 443 HTTPS (Hypertext Transfer Protocol Secure).

➤ 2.13 Identify the purpose of network services and protocols (For example: DNS (Domain Name Service), NAT (Network Address Translation), ICS (Internet Connection Sharing), WINS (Windows

Internet Name Service), SNMP (Simple Network Management Protocol), NFS (Network File System), Zeroconf (Zero configuration), SMB (Server Message Block), AFP (Apple File Protocol), LPD (Line Printer Daemon) and Samba).

➤ 2.14 Identify the basic characteristics (For example: speed, capacity, and media) of the following WAN (Wide Area Networks) technologies: Packet switching, Circuit switching, ISDN (Integrated Services Digital Network), FDDI (Fiber Distributed Data Interface), T1 (T Carrier level 1) / E1 / J1, T3 (T Carrier level 3) / E3 / J3, OCx (Optical Carrier), X.25.

➤ 2.15 Identify the basic characteristics of the following internet access technologies: xDSL (Digital Subscriber Line), Broadband Cable (Cable modem), POTS / PSTN (Plain Old Telephone Service / Public Switched Telephone Network), Satellite, Wireless.

➤ 2.16 Define the function of the following remote access protocols and services: RAS (Remote Access Service), PPP (Point-to-Point Protocol), SLIP (Serial Line Internet Protocol), PPPoE (Point-to-Point Protocol over Ethernet), PPTP (Point-to-Point Tunneling Protocol), VPN (Virtual Private Network), RDP (Remote Desktop Protocol).

➤ 2.17 Identify the following security protocols and describe their purpose and function: IPSec (Internet Protocol Security), L2TP (Layer 2 Tunneling Protocol), SSL (Secure Sockets Layer), WEP (Wired Equivalent Privacy), WPA (Wi-Fi Protected Access), 802.1x.

➤ 2.18 Identify authentication protocols (For example: CHAP (Challenge Handshake Authentication Protocol), MS-CHAP (Microsoft Challenge Handshake Authentication Protocol), PAP (Password Authentication Protocol), RADIUS (Remote Authentication Dial-In User Service), Kerberos and EAP (Extensible Authentication Protocol)).

What You Will Need

The following is a list of the components and their minimum recommended requirements that you will need for the Chapter 2 labs:

➤ A PII 266MHz PC with 64MB RAM, 2GB HDD, CD-ROM, and network interface card (installed with Windows 2000 Professional). This will be known as PC1.

➤ A PII 266MHz PC with 128MB RAM, 2GB HDD, CD-ROM, and network interface card (installed with Windows 2000 Professional or Server). This will be known as PC2.

➤ A four-port wireless/wired router with built-in firewall.

➤ A wireless NIC.

➤ Access to Windows 2000 Professional software.

➤ Access to Windows 2000 Server software.

➤ Access to the Internet.

➤ (Optional) A two- or four-port KVM switch.

For these labs, we will be referring to the following:

➤ Compaq Deskpro PIII 533MHz computers with 256MB RAM and 3Com 3C905 XL 10/100 PCI TX network interface cards. (These cards will automatically be recognized by Windows 2000 during the OS install.)

➤ Linksys wireless router model WRT54G.

➤ Linksys PCI wireless NIC model WMP54G.

➤ Belkin four-port KVM switch bundled with cables, PS/2, part #F1DJ104P.

➤ Cable Internet access.

Lab 1: Upgrading to a Client/Server Domain

Orientation

In this procedure you will accomplish the following:

➤ Upgrade your Windows 2000 member server to a domain controller.

➤ Install a Domain Naming System (DNS) server.

➤ Join your Windows 2000 Professional computer to the domain.

➤ Copy the CD information that you will need for the rest of this book.

➤ Prepare as a prelude to the Domain 2 objectives.

Up until now, we have been running what we refer to as a peer-to-peer network. Microsoft calls this a *workgroup*. In this type of network, there is little or no centralized administration and you are extremely limited as far as the number of sessions you can have. Although a workgroup is fine for a small home network or a small office, it is time to transcend this and move into the client/server environment. The client/server network scenario is the most common in the IT workplace. It provides a central location for people to log on, save their work, and rely on fault tolerance and strong systems support. Microsoft refers to their client/server network as a *domain*. The domain includes all the computers, users, accounts, data, and resources on the entire network. It is run by a special computer known as a *domain controller*, which takes care of synchronizing all logons, time, accounts, and more.

What you need to remember when working with client/server environments is to configure the server first. Then move on to the client. So, we will upgrade our Windows 2000 Server to domain controller status first, and then connect to the new domain with our Windows 2000 Professional client. Let's go.

Procedure

This lab will guide you through the Promotion process, the installation of Active Directory and the installation of the DNS Service as well as connecting clients to the domain.

1. Upgrade the Windows 2000 Server to a domain controller.

   a. Go to PC2, your Windows 2000 Server.

   b. Be doubly sure that you have a working NIC that has IP configured properly. Also, if you had connected your server to a router or other DHCP device, you will undoubtedly have a DNS setting in your NIC's Internet Protocol (TCP/IP) Properties dialog box. Remove it and any other DNS settings; otherwise, they will interfere with our installation of DNS. Even if you don't think you have one, check anyway to be sure. Now go ahead and give your Windows 2000 Server a *static* IP, 192.168.1.200; a subnet mask, 255.255.255.0; and a preferred DNS server of 192.168.1.200 (yourself). Leave the gateway address blank. Click OK for both the Internet Protocol (TCP/IP) Properties dialog box and the Local Area Connection window and close all other open windows.

   c. Click Start button, choose Run, and type dcpromo. This launches the Active Directory Installation Wizard screen, shown in Figure 2.1. Click Next.

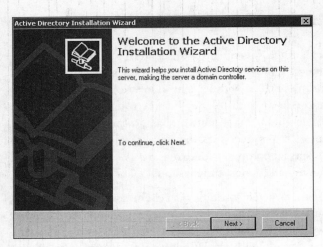

Figure 2.1 The Active Directory Installation Wizard screen.

    d. In the Domain Controller Type screen, click the Domain controller for a new domain option button, as shown in Figure 2.2. Then click Next.

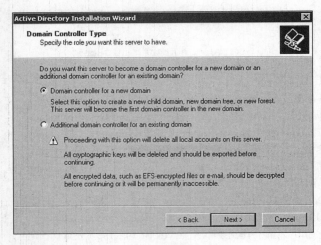

Figure 2.2 The Domain Controller Type screen.

    e. In the Create Tree or Child Domain screen, click the Create a new domain tree option button, as shown in Figure 2.3. Then click Next.

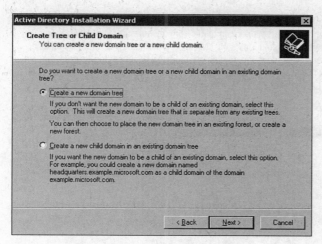

Figure 2.3 The Create Tree or Child Domain screen.

f. In the Create or Join Forest screen, click the Create a new forest of domain trees option button, as shown in Figure 2.4. Then click Next.

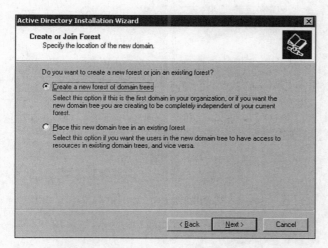

Figure 2.4 The Create or Join Forest screen.

g. The New Domain Name screen is where you name your domain. It works just like the Internet, but for now, will only be internal to your home LAN. Choose a name that you will want to work with for your entire network. For example, we are using TESTLAB.COM, as shown in Figure 2.5. If you do not plan to ever connect your home domain to the Internet, type whatever domain name you want. When you're finished, click Next.

If you plan to connect this domain directly to the Internet sometime in the future, then you should reserve a domain name from a wholesaler like Network Solutions (http://www.networksolutions.com). Make sure the name you want is available, and register it. Use the same domain on your LAN when setting up your domain controller. That way, when the time comes to go global, you will be able to connect your LAN domain name to your Internet presence, and they will be one and the same.

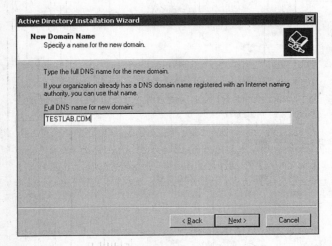

Figure 2.5 The New Domain Name screen.

> **h.** Type the NetBIOS domain name in the NetBIOS Domain Name screen. This should be the same name as your domain name, minus the .com, as shown in Figure 2.6. Click Next.

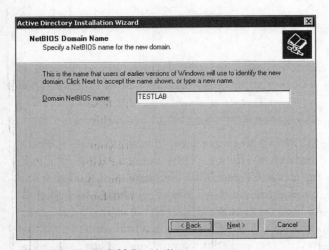

Figure 2.6 The NetBIOS Domain Name screen.

i. In the Database and Log Locations screen, type the database and log locations. Although you can put them in different locations, we are using the default path, as shown in Figure 2.7. Click Next.

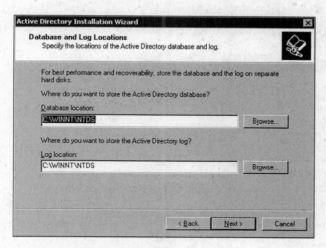

Figure 2.7   The Database and Log locations screen.

j. In the Shared System Volume screen, use the default path and click Next.

k. A pop-up window appears, stating that a DNS server could not be located. This is okay, because we will be installing DNS ourselves. Click OK.

 If this pop-up screen does not appear, make sure that you removed all DNS settings from your NIC's IP Properties dialog box.

l. In the Configure DNS screen, shown in Figure 2.8, select the default option: Yes, install and configure DNS on this computer.

m. The Permissions screen enables you to configure your domain controller to work with Windows 2000 Servers, or with a hybrid network (the default). Because there may be a time when you have other types of servers on the network, select the default, as illustrated in Figure 2.9, and click Next.

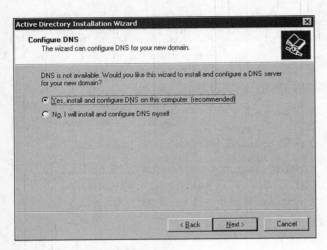

Figure 2.8 The Configure DNS screen.

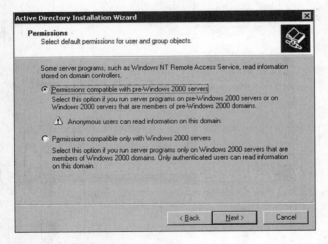

Figure 2.9 The Permissions screen.

    n. Enter a password to be used in conjunction with Directory Services Restore Mode in the event the Active Directory database fails. (You recover the Active Directory database by pressing F8 during bootup, choosing Directory Services Restore Mode, and entering the password you set here.) Select a password that you will remember. When you're finished, click Next.

    o. The Summary screen appears, as shown in Figure 2.10. Click Next, and the Directory Services promotion will begin, as shown in Figure 2.11.

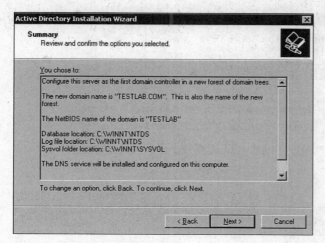

Figure 2.10   The Summary screen.

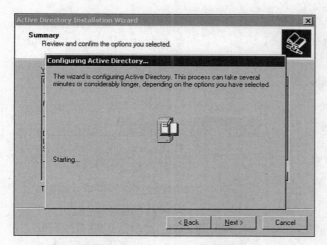

Figure 2.11   The Configuring Active Directory window.

p. When asked for the CD-ROM, place it in the drive, and press Enter.

q. This installation will most likely take a few minutes. When it is complete, you will see a screen like the one shown in Figure 2.12. Click Finish.

r. When prompted to restart the system, remove the CD from the drive and restart as directed, keeping in mind that the initial restart after DCPROMO can be very slow.

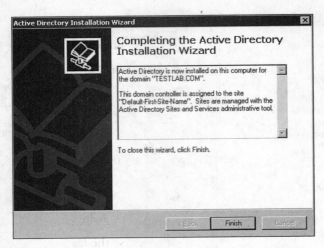

Figure 2.12 The Completing the Active Directory Installation Wizard screen.

    s. Log on to the domain with the same logon that you were using before. Great job! You now have a domain controller and a brand new domain.

2. Copy the Windows 2000 Server CD contents to your hard drive.

    a. Insert the Windows 2000 Server CD into your CD-ROM drive.

    b. Exit from the autorun splash screen that appears.

    c. Close the Configure Your Server window.

    d. Open Windows Explorer.

    e. Navigate to your CD-ROM drive.

    f. Copy the I386 folder to the root of your C drive. The file copy may take a few minutes to complete because you're moving hundreds of megabytes of data.

Alternatively, you can use the command prompt. The syntax is **copy D:\I386 C:**

Quite often, administrators also copy the Bootdisk, Clients, and Support folders to the C drive. In fact, you can copy the entire CD if you want. We are doing this I386 file copy because the OS will ask us for the CD a lot in the upcoming labs. Because you've copied the whole CD to the C drive, when installing new services, you can just redirect to the hard drive instead of having to find the CD, put it in the drive, wait for it to spin up, and so on. This makes things much easier on the network as well, especially if the server room is far away or inaccessible.

3. Connect your Windows 2000 Professional computer to the domain.

    a. Go to PC1, your Windows 2000 Professional computer.

    b. Right-click My Network Places and select Properties from the menu that appears.

    c. Disable the Wireless LAN card.

    d. Make sure your LAN card is enabled.

    e. Right-click the LAN card and select Properties from the menu that appears.

    f. Select Internet Protocol, and click the Properties button. This opens the Internet Protocol (TCP/IP) Properties dialog box.

    g. Change the DNS setting. To begin, click the Use the following DNS server addresses option button. Type the IP address of your Windows 2000 Server, which should be 192.168.1.200, as shown in Figure 2.13. (Leave the Obtain an IP address automatically option button selected.)

One of the most common mistakes made by technicians is to forget to configure the DNS server address in the client computer's Internet Protocol (TCP/IP) Properties dialog box. Always do this first before connecting to a domain.

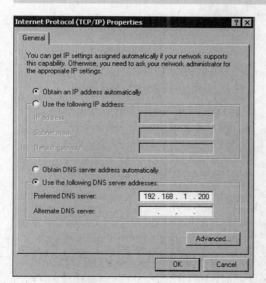

Figure 2.13   The Internet Protocol (TCP/IP) Properties dialog box.

h. Click OK in both dialog boxes.

i. Restart the computer.

j. Right-click My Computer and select Properties from the menu that appears to open the System Properties dialog box.

k. Click the Network Identification tab. The resulting dialog box should look like the one shown in Figure 2.14.

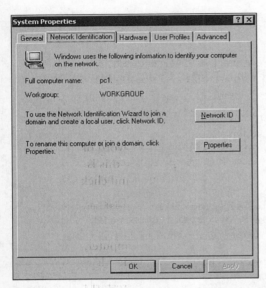

Figure 2.14 The Network Identification tab of the System Properties dialog box.

l. Click the Properties button to open the Identification Changes dialog box.

m. On the bottom half of the dialog box, click the Domain option button and type TESTLAB.COM, as shown in Figure 2.15. (If you chose a different name for your lab's domain in the first section of this lab, type that name instead.) When you're finished, click OK.

There are many possible problems that could occur at this stage. If you followed all the steps exactly, you should be fine, but you just never know with computers. If you do have any issues, start troubleshooting. Check to make sure that the IP settings are correct, that the router is functioning, and that the cables are properly connected. Also, make sure that the client's wireless NIC is disabled. If the MAC filtering on the router is giving you any problems, disable it for now. Be sure to post any further issues on my support site, http://www.technicalblog.com.

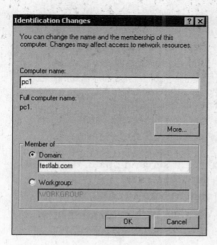

Figure 2.15   Changing the domain name.

n. The system will ask for the user name and password of someone with administrative rights on the server. For us, this is Administrator and password. Type those in now and click OK.

o. After a minute you should be welcomed to the testlab.com domain. Click OK.

p. When the system informs you to restart the computer, click OK, and then click OK again in the System Properties dialog box.

q. When the computer asks whether you want to restart the computer now, click Yes.

r. The computer restarts. When you see the Ctrl+Alt+Del logon screen, press Ctrl+Alt+Del.

s. Click the Options button. This uncovers a third line item that you need to change. Currently, it says "PC1 (this computer)," otherwise known as the local machine. Open the drop-down menu to change it to testlab.com.

t. Type your user name and password (administrator and password) and click OK. You are now logged on to the domain. Even though you are logging on with the same user name and password as when you logged into the old workgroup network, this is actually a whole new user account. We will be using it a lot throughout the rest of the book.

u. Close the Getting started with Windows 2000 screen.

v. Copy the I386 folder from the Windows 2000 *Professional* CD to your hard drive.

 If you ever want to check whether you are logged on to the domain or the local machine, or who is logged on, just press Ctrl+Alt+Del. This opens the Windows Security dialog box, which gives you all that information.

Well, there you have it! A fully functional client/server domain. Great work! Now that we have this running, we can do all kinds of client/server-based labs like WINS, DHCP, DNS, terminal services, RRAS, and more! So now it's going to get exciting. Let's wrap up what we have accomplished in this lab.

What Did I Just Learn?

In this lab you learned how to set up a Microsoft domain. This allows you to centralize administration, resources, and synchronization. You also learned how to get past relying on CDs all the time. Finally, you logged on to the domain with a second computer. Specifically, you learned how to do the following:

➤ Upgrade your server to a domain controller with DCPROMO.

➤ Install a DNS server.

➤ Modify your client so that it can log on to the domain.

➤ Log on with Ctrl+Alt+Del.

Lab 2: Working with the OSI Model

Orientation

In this lab you will accomplish the following:

➤ Learn about the seven layers of the OSI model in a hands-on fashion.

➤ Identify which devices work at which layers of the OSI model.

➤ Identify a MAC address and its parts.

➤ Prepare for the Network+ subdomains 2.1, 2.2, and 2.3.

Although everything we have completed in this book so far can be described by the OSI model, you need to remember that computer networks were developed first. The OSI model was created afterward to explain how computers sent data to each other via communications protocols. The people who created the first networks were top-level technicians. Because it was hard for others to understand the technology, an orderly structure that could explain how computer networks operate was created. This structure is known as the *Open Systems Interconnection (OSI) reference model*. First I'd like to talk about the model and the seven layers, and then we will show hands-on examples of each layer in action.

The OSI Reference Model

The Open Systems Interconnection model was created and ratified by the International Organization for Standardization (ISO), and is represented in the U.S. by the American National Standards Institute (ANSI). This model was created to do the following:

➤ Explain network communications between hosts on the LAN or WAN.

➤ Present a categorization system for communication protocol suites.

➤ Show how different protocol suites can communicate with each other.

Remember, network communications existed before the model was created. This model is an abstract way of categorizing the communications that already exist. The model was created to help engineers understand what is happening with communication protocols behind the scenes. Let's go ahead and break down the OSI into its distinct layers and functions.

OSI: The Layers

The model was created as a set of seven layers, or levels, each of which houses different protocols within a protocol suite. Sometimes a protocol suite such as TCP/IP is referred to as a *protocol stack*. The model shows how the protocol stack works on different levels of transmission (that is, how it stacks up against the model).

Because you have worked with physical networks already, let's start with the bottom layers. Later, when you view the model, it will be from seventh layer on top to first layer on bottom.

➤ **Layer 1: Physical layer.** Unit of measurement: bits. This is the physical and electrical medium for data transfer. It includes but is not limited to cables, jacks, patch panels, punch blocks, hubs, and MAUs. It is also known as the *physical plant*. Concepts related to the physical layer include topologies, analog versus digital/encoding, bit synchronization, baseband versus broadband, multiplexing, and serial (5-volt logic) data transfer.

► **Layer 2: Data Link layer.** Unit of measurement: frames. This layer establishes, maintains, and decides how transfer is accomplished over the physical layer. Devices that exist on the DLL are network interface cards and bridges. This layer also ensures error-free transmission over the physical layer under LAN transmissions. It does this through physical addresses (the hexadecimal address that is burned into the ROM of the NIC), otherwise known as the MAC address.

► **Layer 3: Network layer.** Unit of measurement: packets. The Network layer is dedicated to routing and switching information to different networks, LANs, or internetworks. This can be on the LAN or WAN. Devices that exist on the network layer are routers and IP switches. Now we are getting into the logical addressing of hosts. Instead of physical addresses, the addressing system of the computer is stored in the OS—for example, IP addresses.

Until now we have been working in what is known as the communications subnetwork, or com subnet.

► **Layer 4: Transport layer.** Unit of measurement: messages. This layer ensures error-free transmission between hosts through logical addressing. Therefore, it manages the transmission of messages through the com subnet. The protocols that are categorized by this layer break up messages, send them through the subnet, and ensure correct reassembly at the receiving end, making sure there are no duplicates or lost messages. This layer contains both connection-oriented and connectionless systems, which we will cover later in the book.

► **Layer 5: Session layer.** Unit of measurement: messages. This layer governs the establishment, termination, and synchronization of sessions within the OS over the network and between hosts—for example, when you log on and log off. It is the layer that controls the name and address database for the OS or NOS. NetBIOS (Network Basic Input Output System) works on this layer.

► **Layer 6: Presentation layer.** Unit of measurement: messages. This layer translates the data format from sender to receiver in the various OSes that may be used. Concepts include code conversion, data compression, and file encryption. For example, suppose a UNIX host uses TCP/IP as its primary communications protocol, and it is sending information to a PC running TCP/IP. Although the same communications protocol is used, the two machines use different languages, so the code must be converted from one to the other. Redirectors work on this layer.

➤ **Layer 7: Application layer.** Unit of measurement: messages. This is where message-creation—and, therefore packet–creation—begins. DB access is on this level. End-user protocols like FTP, SMTP, Telnet, and RAS work at this layer. For example, suppose you are using Outlook Express. You type a message and click Send. This initiates SMTP (Simple Mail Transfer Protocol) and other protocols, which send the mail message down through the other layers, breaking it down into packets at the network layer and so on. This layer is not the application itself, but the protocols that are initiated by this layer.

It is imperative that you know the seven layers for the Network+ exam.

Sound like a lot of information? Well, it is, but you need to get into the habit of picturing the model whenever you are doing data transfer. An example is illustrated in Figure 2.16. The more you imagine the data transfer through the levels, the more you will be able to memorize and understand how the OSI model works. In addition, it will be invaluable to you in the future when troubleshooting network problems.

To help memorize the layers, some people use mnemonic devices, such as associating the first letter of each layer name with a different word—for example, All People Seem To Need Data Processing. That was from layer 7 to layer 1. Or how about the opposite direction? Please Do Not Throw Sausage Pizza Away. Or just memorize the real names! It's up to you.

In Figure 2.16, the message is created in Outlook Express, the Send button is clicked, and the message goes down the layers of the OSI model to the physical medium. It then crosses the medium (probably cables) and climbs the OSI model at the receiving machine. This happens every time two computers communicate.

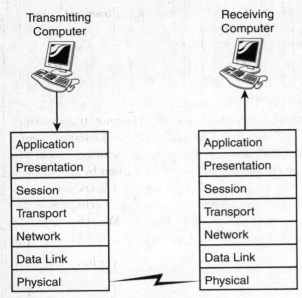

Figure 2.16 An illustration of the OSI model.

NOTE

Although the OSI model is always in place, all the levels may not be involved with every communication. It depends on the type of communication and the number of protocols being used for that specific transmission.

Different devices operate on different layers of the OSI. Check out Figure 2.17 to see a list of those now.

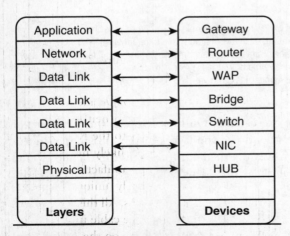

Figure 2.17 Devices and their layers on the OSI.

You need to know these devices and their corresponding layers for the Network+ exam.

The Data Link Layer Revisited

The Data Link layer (DLL) is responsible for Ethernet transmissions. Ethernet was originally formulated by Xerox, which was joined by Digital and Intel to create the DIX foundation. The network structure was a success and the companies worked to have the architecture ratified by the Institute of Electrical and Electronics Engineers (IEEE). The IEEE created a committee called the 802 convention, and every type of LAN architecture (and some WAN architectures) was given an 802 notation. We refer to this as 802.*x*.

To make things a little more interesting, the Data Link layer has two sublayers.

► **Media Access Control (MAC).** This layer, which is closest to the Physical layer, controls how multiple devices (usually NICs) share a media channel, like twisted pair cable on the LAN. This is where MAC addresses come into play. These are also known as *physical addresses*, *hexadecimal addresses*, and *Ethernet IDs*. A typical address might be 0A:FF:72:3F:2B:00. The octets can also be separated by hyphens, as is the Microsoft way.

► **Logical Link Control (LLC).** This layer, which is closer to the network layer, establishes and maintains the link between devices and governs how the media channel will be used.

On PC1, open the command prompt and type ipconfig/all. You should get a hexadecimal address like the one highlighted in Figure 2.18, although yours will be a different number.

In order for NICs to communicate, they must have *unique* addresses. Two NICs with the same address would cause a conflict, and neither would be able to communicate. Because this address is burned into the ROM chip of the NIC by the manufacturer, however, you will most likely never see this occur. The IEEE allots a range of addresses to each manufacturer; in addition, every manufacturer gets its own organizationally unique identifier (OUI), which is the first three octets of the MAC address. All this is to ensure that each NIC has a unique address. When you plug the cable into the card, the card has all the information it needs to communicate on the subnet. The address is hard-wired into the chip as firmware, as is the version of Ethernet that the card will use.

```
C:\Select C:\WINNT\System32\cmd.exe                                    _ [] X
    Host Name . . . . . . . . . . . . : pc1
    Primary DNS Suffix  . . . . . . . : testlab.com
    Node Type . . . . . . . . . . . . : Broadcast
    IP Routing Enabled. . . . . . . . : No
    WINS Proxy Enabled. . . . . . . . : No
    DNS Suffix Search List. . . . . . : testlab.com
                                         cable.rcn.com

Ethernet adapter LAN Card:

    Connection-specific DNS Suffix  . : cable.rcn.com
    Description . . . . . . . . . . . : 3Com EtherLink XL 10/10
(3C905B-TX)
    Physical Address. . . . . . . . . : 00-01-02-3D-5F-5D
    DHCP Enabled. . . . . . . . . . . : Yes
    Autoconfiguration Enabled . . . . : Yes
    IP Address. . . . . . . . . . . . : 192.168.1.102
    Subnet Mask . . . . . . . . . . . : 255.255.255.0
    Default Gateway . . . . . . . . . : 192.168.1.1
    DHCP Server . . . . . . . . . . . : 192.168.1.1
    DNS Servers . . . . . . . . . . . : 192.168.1.200
    Lease Obtained. . . . . . . . . . : Sunday, May 08, 2005 12
    Lease Expires . . . . . . . . . . : Monday, May 09, 2005 12

C:\>_
```

Figure 2.18 The physical MAC address.

From now on, we will refer to this address as the *MAC address*, but do remember the other names that other technicians may call it.

To locate the manufacturer of any NIC, visit http://standards.ieee.org/regauth/oui/index.shtml and plug in the first three octets of the MAC on the NIC. The site should respond with the manufacturer of the NIC. For example, when you enter our NIC's first three octets, 00-01-02, the site responds by indicating that the NIC was manufactured by 3Com Corporation. Of course, we knew that already, but this may be a very valuable tool for you in the future.

Procedure

In the following procedure, you will discover each of the OSI layers from a hands-on perspective. Before this, however, you must configure your Windows 2000 Professional client for Internet access because you are logging on with a whole new profile and user account. You must also install Service Pack 4 so that all of your software-based labs will run correctly. You will also create and share a Downloads folder on your client to enable your server to access the service pack.

1. Configure PC1 (the Windows 2000 Professional client) for the Internet and for higher-resolution video.

   a. Re-enable the wireless NIC.

      i. Right-click My Network Places and select Properties.

      ii. Right-click the Wireless LAN card and select Enable.

      iii. Close the Network and Dial-up Connections window.

   b. Change your video settings so that you can fit a little more on your screen.

      i. Minimize all windows.

      ii. Right-click anywhere on the open area of the desktop and select Properties to open the Display Properties dialog box.

      iii. Click the Settings tab.

      iv. Under Screen Area, drag the slider until the resolution is 800×600.

> Your resolution should be at least 800×600 minimum with 16-bit color; feel free to run at a higher resolution if you wish.

   c. Launch Internet Explorer. The Welcome to the Internet Connection Wizard screen appears, as illustrated in Figure 2.19.

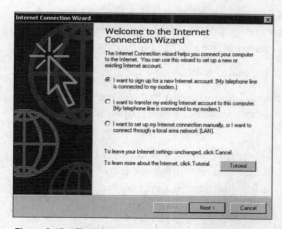

Figure 2.19   The Welcome to the Internet Connection Wizard screen.

    d. Click the I want to set up my Internet connection manually option button and then click Next.

    e. When asked how you will be connecting to the Internet, choose LAN, and click Next.

    f. In the Local Area Network Internet Configuration screen, click Next.

    g. When asked whether you want to set up an Internet mail account, select No and click Next.

    h. The wizard is complete. Click Finish. The Internet Explorer window opens by default to http://www.msn.com.

You will need to initially configure your Internet connection the first time you want to connect to the Internet with any new user account.

2. Download and upgrade to Service Pack 4 on both computers.

> You should always run the latest service packs for your OSes.

    a. In Internet Explorer, type the following URL in the address bar: http://www.microsoft.com/windows2000/downloads/servicepacks/sp4/default.asp.

    b. Click the Go button on the right side of the Web page.

    c. If you have a dial-up Internet connection, click the SP4 Express Version button. If you are on a high-speed connection (DSL, or cable), click the SP4 Network Installation button.

    d. A pop-up window opens, asking you to save the file. Click OK.

    e. When asked to specify where you would like to save the file, create a new folder in your C drive called Downloads, open it, and click Save to save the file there.

    f. The download will take approximately 6–8 minutes on a cable Internet connection. While you're waiting for it to complete, let's configure the Downloads folder you just created for sharing.

        i. Open Windows Explorer.

A quick way to open Windows Explorer is by pressing the Windows+E shortcut key.

ii. Locate the Downloads folder.

iii. Right-click the Downloads folder and select Sharing from the menu that appears to open the Downloads Folder Properties dialog box.

iv. Click the Share this folder option button and then click OK. A small hand will appear under the Downloads folder, indicating that the folder is now shared. That's how easy it is to share data on the network!

v. Close Windows Explorer. We will use that shared folder later by connecting to it from the server.

vi. Open the command prompt and type `ipconfig/all`. Make a note of your Windows 2000 Professional IP addresses.

g. When your download finishes, a pop-up window will let you know. When it does, click Open to extract the service pack file and start the installation.

h. The Welcome screen opens, prompting you to close any other open programs. Do so, and then click Next.

i. Agree to the license and click Next.

j. On the next screen, select the Do not archive files option button, and click Next. The service pack upgrade will begin.

k. When the completion screen appears, Click Finish. The computer will restart.

l. Switch to PC2 (Windows 2000 Server) and open Windows Explorer.

m. Open the Tools menu and select Map Network Drive.

n. Map a drive from the server to your Windows 2000 Professional machine. To begin, assign a drive letter to the mapping; the default is fine for now. The path should be `\\ipaddress\downloads`, where *ipaddress* is the IP of your Windows 2000 Professional machine; type that path now. For example, our path is `\\192.168.1.102\down-loads`.

> The preceding path is known as a universal naming convention (UNC) and can be used with a computer name (for example, *computername\sharename*) or with an IP address (for example, **192.168.1.102*sharename*).

o. Click Finish. The drive will be mapped to your shared resource on the Windows 2000 Professional machine.

p. Inside the shared resource on your Windows 2000 Professional machine, you will see the service pack file. Double-click it to start the service pack installation and proceed with the install just like before. When you're finished, restart the server. Now your entire network is upgraded to Service Pack 4, the latest from Microsoft as of the publishing of this book.

> All systems on the network need to run the same service pack (preferably the latest) in order to have proper network communications.

3. Access DSL Reports to find out your Physical layer data-transfer rate.

a. Go back to PC1 (Windows 2000 Professional).

b. In the Internet Explorer address bar, type http://www.dslreports.com, and press Enter.

c. On the left side, click the Tests+Tools link.

d. Scroll down until you find the Speed Tests link and click it. This test uses a Java plug-in, as shown in Figure 2.20. Don't worry, it's safe.

e. Click the verify your Java version link.

f. The site reports what version of Java you are running and whether that version will work with this test. Most likely you are running version 1.1.4 and are not compatible. That's okay because we are about to install the Java client.

g. Click the Get Java button. This will open another browser window.

h. Click the Begin Download button.

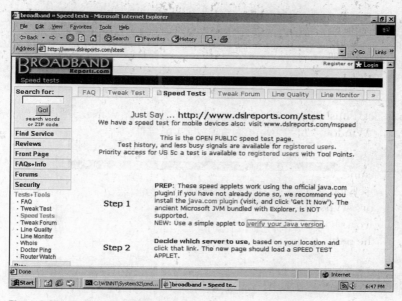

Figure 2.20   The DSL Reports speed test.

i. A pop-up window appears, asking whether you want to install and run the program. Click Yes.

j. Accept the terms and click Next.

k. Choose the Typical Installation option and click Next. The installation of the J2SE Runtime Environment will begin.

l. When the installation is complete, click Finish to exit.

m. Check out all the cool things Java has to offer on the Web site. When you're finished, return to http://www.dslreports.com.

n. Navigate back to the Speed Test section.

o. Instead of verifying your version, scroll down and click a server near your geographical location to start the test. If the server is too busy, try another server.

p. When you find a server with availability, scroll down and click the Start button.

q. After a minute or two, you should get results for the physical speed of your Internet connection; ours are shown in Figure 2.21. The download and upload speeds are shown in either Mbps or Kbps.

> **NOTE**
>
> Notice that you can compare your connection speed with other users locally and around the country. Also, you can use this test from any computer. It's a great way to test a customer's data transfer rate.

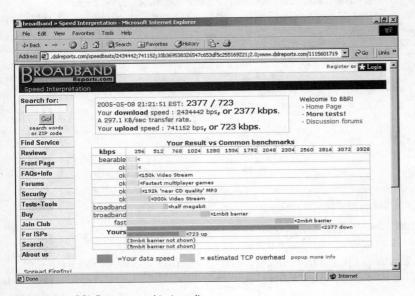

Figure 2.21 DSL Reports speed test results.

4. Use Ethereal to view data on the Data Link, Network and Transport layers.

> **NOTE**
>
> Ethereal is a free, open-source program used to capture data on all different platforms. This will help you to visualize data transfer on these layers. WinPcap is a program that runs in association with, and in the background of, Ethereal as well as other applications. It allows the actual capture of packets.

a. Access the Internet.

b. Download Version 10.11 of the Ethereal network sniffer and Version 3.0 of WinPcap at http://www.ethereal.com/distribution/win32 to your Downloads folder.

c. Install WinPcap first and Ethereal second, both with the default options.

d. When the installations are finished, close all windows.

e. An icon for Ethereal appears on your desktop. Double-click it to open the program. You'll see an application window like the one shown in Figure 2.22.

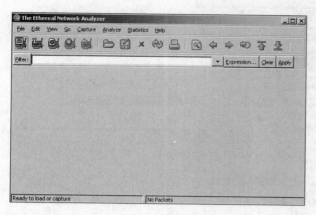

Figure 2.22   The Ethereal program window.

f. Before you continue with the capture, you need to send some data over the network. To do so, open your command prompt and type `ping -t 192.168.1.1`. This will run a continuous `ping` to the router, with plenty of juicy data you can capture. Leave it running while you do the next steps.

g. Because you have two NICs, you need to decide which card to capture data on. Let's use the wired 3Com card.

    i. Open the Capture menu bar and select Options.

    ii. Open the Interface drop-down list and select your wireless card, as shown in Figure 2.23. If the 3Com card is already selected, move to the next step.

h. Click the Capture button. After a few moments, a Capture window will open, although it may hide behind other windows. If so, simply click its button on the taskbar. You should see data being captured, as in Figure 2.24.

i. While capturing data, access the Web and point your browser to http://www.technicalblog.com. This will create additional traffic that you can view later.

j. Click Stop in the Capture window to drop all the captured frames of data into the main window for analysis, as shown in Figure 2.25.

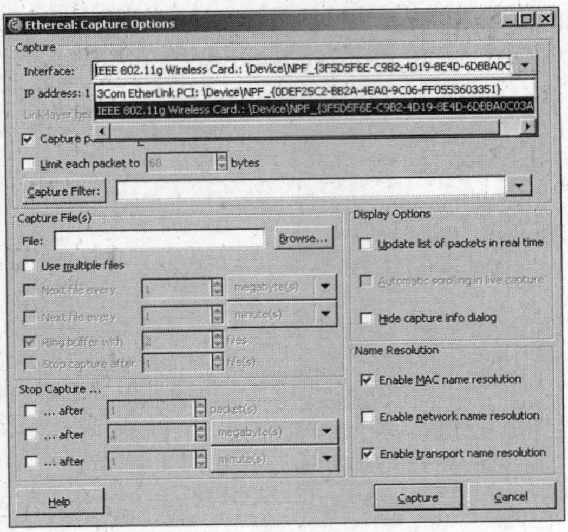

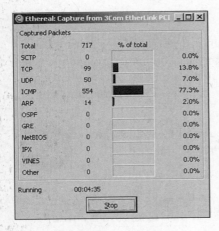

Figure 2.23 Selecting the NIC for capturing.

Figure 2.24 The Capture window.

 k. Maximize the window to show the details of each frame, as illustrated in Figure 2.26.

 l. You can sort the various columns by their column headers. Sort the Protocol column alphabetically.

 m. Scroll down until you find an entry with an ICMP protocol. Look for one that says Echo (ping) Request in the Information column. There should be many.

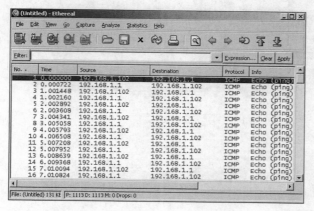

Figure 2.25 Captured data.

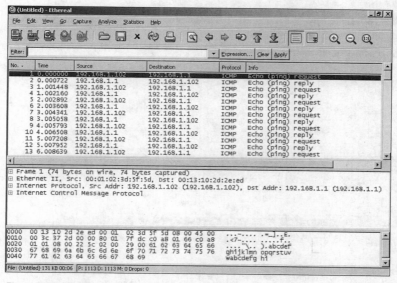

Figure 2.26 Details of a frame of data.

    n. Click an `Echo (ping) Request` entry to select it. When you do, the data area at the bottom of the window should display several lines of information, as shown in Figure 2.27.

    o. Now let's examine that information.

        i. The first two lines deal with the Data Link layer, with the first line showing the frame number. Click the plus (+) sign next to this line to drill down into the details, as shown in Figure 2.28. Here you can find out the size of the frame in bytes, the time it was sent, and lots more.

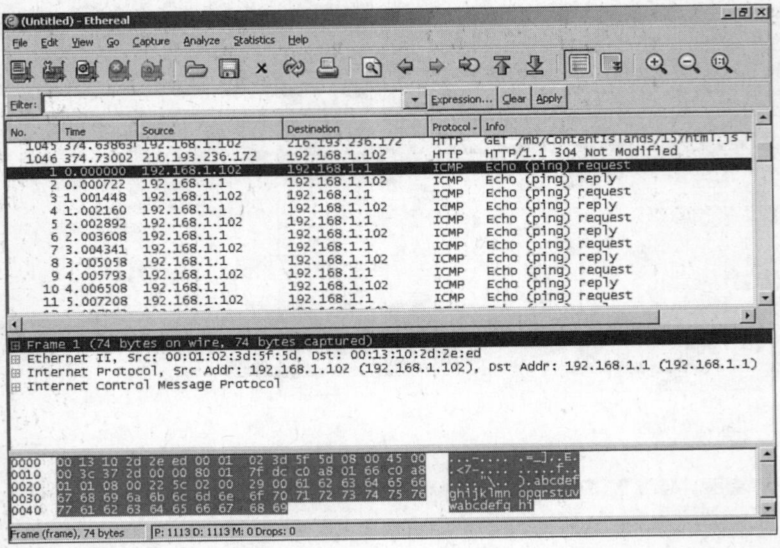

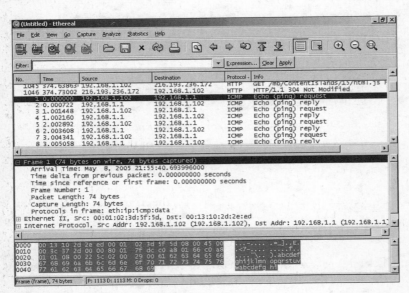

Figure 2.27 Captured ICMP echo.

Figure 2.28 Drilling down into a frame of data.

ii. Click the plus (+) sign next to the Ethernet II entry. Here you can see the destination and source MAC addresses. (Recognize our 3Com card?) This proves that MAC addresses send Ethernet frames on the Data Link layer.

iii. Click the plus (+) sign next to the Internet Protocol entry to view information about the Network layer. (You may have to scroll down to see it.) You'll see the size of the IP packet that was sent, as well as the source and destination IP addresses, as shown in Figure 2.29.

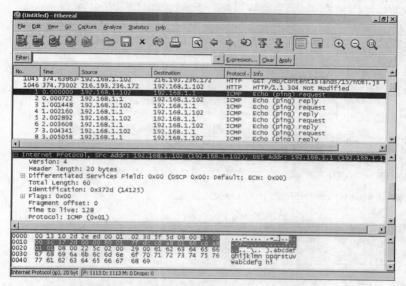

Figure 2.29   Drilling down into a packet of data.

iv. Click the plus (+) sign next to the Internet Message Control Protocol entry to view the actual size of the ICMP Echo (ping) sent, its checksum, and sequence number. Nice work so far.

v. To see information that deals with the Transport layer, scroll down in the window's top data area until you find the first HTTP-type frame. It should say something like Get / HTTP/1.1. Click the frame to select it, as shown in Figure 2.30.

vi. In data area at the bottom of the window, scroll down to the Transmission Control Protocol section and click that entry's plus (+) sign to see the port number used, the size of the overhead, and sequence information (see Figure 2.31).

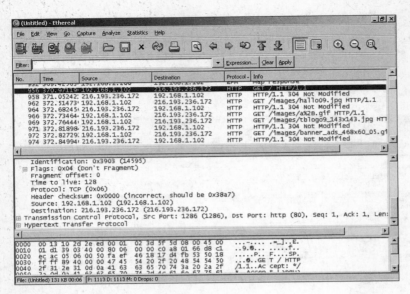

Figure 2.30 A frame with an embedded HTTP protocol.

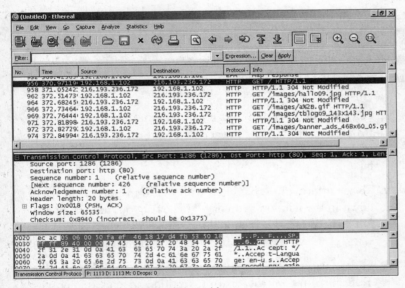

Figure 2.31 The TCP portion of our captured frame.

vii. To view information about the Application layer, click the + sign next to the HTTP entry. You will see the site that you went to, the browser that was used, even cookies of information that could hold user names and passwords.

This simple-to-use, free program could be very helpful or detrimental, depending on your disposition. Network administrators will use it to gather legitimate data about network performance and security, whereas a hacker might use it to steal your password!

p. Great job. You are finished with Ethereal for now, so go ahead and close it. You'll be asked you if you want to save the capture. Click Yes, and save the capture as `Capture1`.

q. Close all other windows. When you get to the command prompt, the `ping` should still be running; end that by pressing the Ctrl+C shortcut key. Then type CLS to clear the command prompt.

5. Examine the Session layer with `netstat`.

a. Type `netstat` and press Enter to view any sessions (connections) that you may have to other computers. You'll see a screen like the one shown in Figure 2.32, probably with only two line items in the results.

Figure 2.32 **netstat** in the Command Prompt window.

netstat and many other TCP/IP command-prompt utilities are extremely important to master for the Network+ exam.

b. Leaving the command prompt open, connect to the Internet and point your browser to http://www.insecure.org.

c. Return to the command prompt and type `netstat` again. You should see additional information, as shown in Figure 2.33.

Every time you run a session—that is, connect to a computer—a random port on your machine (the local address) is opened and is connected to a specific port on the destination computer (the foreign address).

Figure 2.33 **netstat** with additional line items.

6. Identify the Presentation layer with compression.

a. Open Windows Explorer.

b. Locate your C:\Downloads folder.

c. Find Service Pack 4. It should be named W2KSP4_EN.

d. Right-click the file and select Properties from the menu that appears.

e. On the General tab, click the Advanced button.

f. Click the Compress contents to save disk space check box to select it, and click OK. The file will take a few minutes to compress.

g. Open the Tools menu and select Folder Options.

h. Click the View tab.

i. Click the Display compressed files and folders with alternate color check box to select it.

j. If you haven't done so already, click the Show hidden files and folders option button to select it, and look two more lines down to the Hide protected operating system files checkbox. Click that checkbox to *deselect* it. This will enable you to see all files on the machine, regardless of their attributes.

k. Click OK. The service pack file should show up as blue, indicating that it is compressed. It now takes up less space on the drive than before.

Compressing a file is kind of like stuffing a 5-inch Nerf ball into a 2 inch–wide PVC pipe. It works, but how will your Nerf ball look when it comes out the other side? The answer is, usually fine, but you increase your chances of corrupting data when you compress it. This also applies to WinZip and Winrar, all of which work on the Presenstation layer.

7. Examine the Application layer with HTTP in the URL.

a. Switch to Internet Explorer.

b. In the address bar, type http://www.speedguide.net.

c. This directs you to the Web site, but what happens behind the scenes? Let's examine the process.

   i. The act of typing the Web site name (http://www.speedguide.net) and pressing Enter initiates the HTTP protocol.

   ii. The HTTP message travels down the OSI model, checking for special code and encryption, starting a session with the Web server, and sending the message as TCP. It then enters the communications subnet.

   iii. TCP breaks up the message into many IP packets on the Network layer. These packets are then encapsulated inside Ethernet frames on the Data Link layer, and finally converted from parallel data to serial data on the Physical Layer.

   iv. At the Physical layer, the data is sent on to the physical cabling and through your Internet connection.

   v. When the data gets to the receiving computer, it ascends through the layers to the top.

   vi. The reply is then sent back to your computer in the same fashion, down the layers, across the Internet, and up the layers until Hypertext is displayed on your screen.

As you can see, HTTP is not an application. Instead, it is an application-layer protocol, something that works behind the scenes when you initiate it—for example, by clicking the Go button next to the address bar in Internet Explorer or by pressing Enter.

What Did I Just Learn?

In this lab you learned that data communications is an in-depth process with many levels. An HTTP message is actually encapsulated as a TCP message, which is in turn encapsulated inside an IP packet, which is in turn encapsulated inside of an Ethernet frame. You also learned how to view the physical address of your computer and how to use various TCP/IP utilities and third-party programs. You were educated on how to do the following:

➤ Upgrade to Service Pack 4.

➤ Share folders and map drives.

➤ Use Ethereal, a network-analysis program.

➤ Test your Internet connection speed from http://www.dslreports.com.

➤ Use several TCP/IP utilities.

➤ Identify the seven OSI layers and their corresponding devices.

Lab 3: Identifying the Various Network Protocol Suites

Orientation

In this lab you will accomplish the following:

➤ Discover and identify the three main protocol suites that work within the OSI model.

➤ Learn about and install NetBEUI.

➤ Install and configure protocols on the computers.

This lab is a short, albeit important, one. (Aren't they all?) There are various systems out there, some of which do not use TCP/IP. You need to know how to work with these other protocol suites, and how to configure them so that they can interoperate with each other. Let's make this happen.

Procedure

Take a look at Table 2.1 and spend a few minutes analyzing the different protocols. After you do, we will begin installing the various protocols and compliant connectors.

Table 2.1	The three routable protocol suites of the OSI	
TCP/IP and the OSI Model		
Layer Number	**Layer Name**	**Supported Protocols**
7	Application	FTP, Telnet, SMTP, POP3, HTTP
6	Presentation	FTP, Telnet, SMTP, POP3, HTTP
5	Session	FTP, Telnet, SMTP, POP3, HTTP
4	Transport	TCP, UDP, DNS
3	Network	ARP, IP, ICMP, RIP, OSPF
2	Data link	802.3, 802.5, 10BASET, 100BASET
1	Physical	Hub, MSAU
IPX/SPX and the OSI		
Layer Number	**Layer Name**	**Supported Protocols**
7	Application	SAP, NCP
6	Presentation	SAP, NCP
5	Session	SAP, NCP
4	Transport	SPX
3	Network	IPX, RIP, NLSP
2	Data link	802.2, 802.3
1	Physical	Hubs, MSAUs, and so on
AppleTalk and the OSI		
Layer Number	**Layer Name**	**Supported Protocols**
7	Application	AppleTalk, AFP
6	Presentation	AFP
5	Session	ADSP, ZIP, PAP, AFP, ASP
4	Transport	ADSP, ATP, NBP, RTMP, AEP
3	Network	DDP, NBP, RTMP, AARP
2	Data link	Local Talk, AARP, Ether Talk, Token Talk, SNAP
1	Physical	Local Talk, Ether Talk, Token Talk

1.   Install NWLink to enable connections with IPX/SPX networks.

NOTE   Short for Internetwork Packet Exchange/Sequenced Packet Exchange, IPX/SPX was created by Novell, and fashioned after XNS (Xerox Networking System). It dominated LANs for a decade until about 1995. If you want to connect your Windows 2000 Professional client to an IPX/SPX network, you will need to install Microsoft's compliant version, which is known as NWLink.

a. Right-click My Network Places and select Properties.

b. Right-click your LAN card and select Properties.

c. In the LAN Card Properties dialog box, click the Install button. The Select Network Component Type dialog box opens, as shown in Figure 2.34.

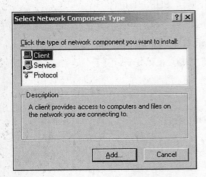

Figure 2.34 The Select Network Component Type dialog box.

d. Click Protocol and click Add.

e. You'll see a dialog box containing the various protocols that you can install. Click the NWLink entry, as shown in Figure 2.35, and click OK. The LAN Card Properties dialog box shows NWLink as being installed.

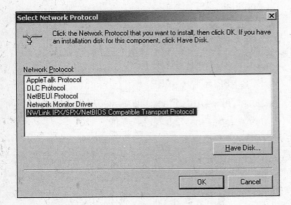

Figure 2.35 Installing NWLink.

2. Install NetBEUI.

NOTE

Short for Network BIOS Extended User Interface, NetBEUI was developed by IBM and taken on by Microsoft as its main protocol in the early 1990s. It is a small and quick protocol but used only on the LAN. That means it is not routable. There is no logical numbering system involved, so you cannot traverse to other networks or the Internet. NetBEUI uses NetBIOS names only.

    a. In the LAN Card Properties dialog box, click the Install button.

    b. Click Protocol and click Add.

    c. In the dialog box that contains the various protocols that you can install, click the NetBEUI entry and click OK.

    d. If you get a message indicating that a duplicate name exists on the network, click OK.

3. Install AppleTalk, which is Apple's main protocol suite.

    a. In the LAN Card Properties dialog box, click the Install button.

    b. Click Protocol and click Add.

    c. In the dialog box that contains the various protocols that you can install, click the AppleTalk entry and click OK.

4. Notice all the protocols listed in the LAN Card Properties dialog box.

    a. While you are here, click the Show icon in taskbar while connected check box. Your NIC will now show up in your system tray.

    b. Click OK.

5. Investigate how the multiple protocols are bound to your LAN card.

    a. Right-click My Network Places and select Properties.

    b. Open the Advanced menu and select Advanced Settings to open the Advanced Settings dialog box, as shown in Figure 2.36.

    c. The protocol order in this dialog box dictates how quickly protocols are initiated. Notice that TCP/IP is at the bottom of the list for the Wireless Card. You need to fix this.

        i. In the Bindings section, find the File and Printer Sharing for Microsoft Networks entry. Underneath that entry is an Internet Protocol subentry. Click the Internet Protocol entry to select it, and then click the up arrow button to the right twice to bring IP to the top of the File and Printer Sharing for Microsoft Networks list.

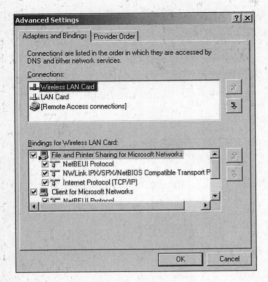

Figure 2.36   The Adapters and Bindings tab of the Advanced Settings dialog box.

    ii. Click the Internet Protocol subentry under the Client for Microsoft Networks entry to select it, and then click the up arrow button to the right twice to bring IP to the top of the Client for Microsoft Networks list.

    iii. Change the order of NIC cards to make sure your wired LAN card is first. To do so, click the LAN card in the Connections section, and click the up arrow to the right once to move the wired LAN card to the top position on the list.

  d. Verify that IP is the top protocol for all services for *both* cards. Your Advanced Settings dialog box should look like the one in Figure 2.37 when you are finished.

  e. Click OK. You must restart when any bindings are changed; do so when the computer prompts you.

6. You are finished with the added protocols, so let's uninstall them.

  a. Go back to PC1 and again access the LAN Card Properties dialog box.

  b. Select the AppleTalk protocol and click the Uninstall button. This will take a minute.

  c. Click No when prompted to restart.

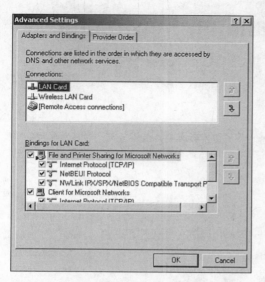

Figure 2.37   The Adapters and Bindings tab, with IP as the first binding.

> **d.** Repeat the uninstall process for NetBEUI and NWLink IPX/SPX compatible transport.
>
> **e.** Restart the computer. Now you will be back to using TCP/IP only.

 Remember that when you install or remove protocols on one card, it adds or removes them from all the cards due to bindings. That means your wireless LAN card should also now be using TCP/IP only.

What Did I Just Learn?

In this lab you learned how to install protocols, change binding orders, and were educated on the various protocol suites available to you. You learned how to do the following:

➤ Identify protocols and their corresponding layers.

➤ Install protocol suites like AppleTalk, NWLink, and NetBEUI.

➤ Configure the binding order for both NICs.

Lab 4: Understanding IP Structure and Classes

Orientation

In the lab you will accomplish the following:

➤ Configure IP Version 4.

➤ Identify IP Version 6.

➤ Identify the gateway setting.

➤ Work with the different IP classes and their subnet masks.

➤ Learn the Network+ subdomains 2.5 and 2.6.

For the Network+ exam you need to be able to configure IP settings and to understand their meaning on the network. You also need to know how to classify the different IP categories, and why those classifications exist.

TCP/IP was originally developed by ARPANet in the early 1970s. It was not really meant for billions of computers, which is what we are nearing today. As a result, the IP version that has been in use is running out of available IP addresses. The new version, IP Version 6, will combat this problem by offering a slew more addresses, perhaps more than we will ever need. Let's show some of these concepts at work.

Procedure

IP addresses are 32-bit, dotted decimal addresses. That's because an IP address consists of four numbers (for example, 192.168.1.1) separated by dots, or periods. Each number has a possible value of 0–255—that's 256 possible values in all, each of which is known as an *octet*. The binary representation of 0–255 is 00000000–11111111. Every value has 8 bits; what differs for each value is how those bits are arranged. For example, the decimal number 192 is shown in binary as 1100000. Each octet has 8 bits, and four octets make up the IP address; 4 octets × 8 bits = 32. There you have it: our 32-bit dotted decimal address.

The first number in the IP address dictates what class the address is part of. For example, suppose you are using the IP address 192.168.1.104. In that case, the first number is 192, which means the IP address is part of a Class C network. Table 2.2 shows the various classes and their associated IP address ranges. Table 2.3 shows the IP classes and their associated subnet masks, which identify which portion of the IP address is the network portion, and which is the host portion.

There are many tutorials on the Web to help you convert between decimal and binary. If you need more help on this, your best bet is to Google using the following query: **"Converting decimal to binary"**.

Table 2.2 IP classifications

IP Class/Structure	Range	Number of Networks	Number of Hosts Per Network	Total Hosts Worldwide	Who Uses It?
A/net.node.node.node	**1–126**	126	16,777,214	2,113,928,964	Large corps, ISPs
B/net.net.node.node	**128–191**	16,384	65,534	1,073,709,056	Corps, universities, ISPs
C/net.net.net.node	**192–223**	2,097,152	254	532,676,608	Small companies and organizations
D/net.net.net.net	**224–239**	NA	NA	NA	Multicast testing
E/NA	**240–255**	NA	NA	NA	Future use

When you look at Table 2.2 and try to get a feel for the different IP classes available, you will likely realize that this classification system was created to appease different organizations of different sizes. In this lab manual, because you have a small office at home, it is simplest and most common to use Class C.

The total hosts, for all classes combined, is 3,720,314,628. That's just under four billion—and we are getting very close to that number today. You may have also noticed that there are only 254 possible hosts per network in Class C instead of 256. This is because you can never use the first or the last. More on that later.

Table 2.3	Binary and the default subnet masks	
IP Class	**Binary Equivalent**	**Default Subnet Masks**
A: 1–126	00000001–01111110	255.0.0.0 net.node.node.node
B: 128–191	10000000–10111111	255.255.0.0 net.net.node.node
C: 192–223	11000000–11011111	255.255.255.0 net.net.net.node
D: 224–239	11100000–11101111	255.255.255.255 net.net.net.net
E: 240–255	11110000–11111111	N/A

 You need to memorize the class structure of IP Version 4 for the Network+ exam. Pay strict attention to Class A, B, and C.

Now that you know about the 32-bit dotted decimal IP addresses, the classes, and the default subnet masks, it should all fall into place fairly easily.

Notice how the number 255 in a subnet mask coincides with the name "net." Also, notice the 0 coincides with the name "node." "Net" is the network portion of the IP address, whereas "node" is the host or computer portion of the address. The IP address our PC1 is using is 192.168.1.104. This would mean that the network we are on is considered 192.168.1 or 192.168.1.0, and the host portion of the address or the computer number would be 104. It was really classified as such by the subnet mask 255.255.255.0. The three 255s coincide with 192.168.1 and the 0 in the subnet mask coincides with 104.

In this lab we are going to change the network that our two computers are on. First we will choose a Class A network, then a Class B, and finally switch back to Class C.

1. Modify the IP settings to Class B.

   a. Go to PC1.

   b. Access the Internet Protocol (TCP/IP) Properties dialog box for the LAN card. Right now, this card will most likely be obtaining an IP address from the router but has a static DNS address configured.

c. Change your IP settings so they reflect the following:

   i. IP address: 172.16.1.1.

   ii. Subnet mask: 255.255.0.0.

   iii. Leave the gateway and DNS IP addresses blank. The correct settings are shown in Figure 2.38.

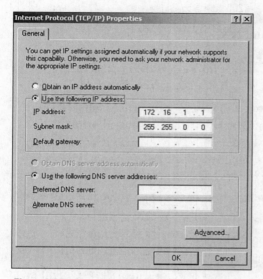

Figure 2.38 Class B IP configuration.

d. Click OK in both the Internet Protocol (TCP/IP) Properties dialog box and the LAN Card Properties dialog box.

e. Switch to PC2.

f. Access the Internet Protocol (TCP/IP) Properties dialog box for the NIC on PC2. Change the IP settings to the following:

   i. IP address: 172.16.1.2.

   ii. Subnet mask: 255.255.0.0.

   iii. Leave the gateway blank, but set the DNS server IP address to 172.16.1.2 (itself).

   iv. Click OK in both dialog boxes.

g. Return to PC1 and test the connection.

   i. Open the command prompt.

   ii. Type ping 172.16.1.2. You should get replies.

2. Modify the IP settings to Class A.

    a. Access the Internet Protocol (TCP/IP) Properties dialog box for the LAN card.

    b. Change the IP settings so they reflect the following:

        i. IP address: 10.1.1.1.

        ii. Subnet mask: 255.0.0.0.

        iii. Leave the gateway and DNS IP addresses blank.

    c. Click OK in both dialog boxes.

    d. Switch to PC2.

    e. Access the Internet Protocol (TCP/IP) Properties dialog box for the NIC on PC2. Change the IP settings to the following:

        i. IP address: 10.1.1.2.

        ii. Subnet mask: 255.0.0.0.

        iii. Leave the gateway blank, but set the DNS server IP address to 10.1.1.2 (itself).

        iv. Click OK in both dialog boxes.

    f. Return to PC1 and test the connection.

        i. Open the command prompt.

        ii. Type ping 10.1.1.2. You should get replies.

3. Return all IP settings to the original.

    a. Go to PC1 and change the IP settings to Automatic.

        i. In the Internet Protocol (TCP/IP) Properties dialog box, select the Obtain an IP address automatically option button.

        ii. Select the Obtain DNS server address automatically option button, as shown in Figure 2.39.

        iii. Click OK in both dialog boxes to close them.

    b. Go to PC2 and change the IP settings to the following configuration, as shown in Figure 2.40:

        i. IP address: 192.168.1.200.

        ii. Subnet mask: 255.255.255.0.

        iii. Gateway: 192.168.1.1.

        iv. DNS server: 192.168.1.200.

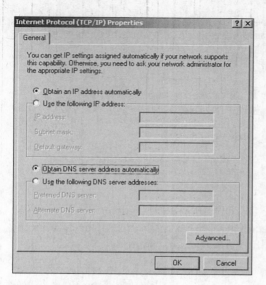

Figure 2.39 Original IP settings.

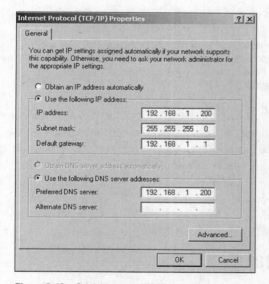

Figure 2.40 Original server (PC2) IP settings.

Notice that we added a gateway address—**192.168.1.1**, which is the address of our router—to the server's IP properties this time. Why? Because it is the device that allows us access to the Internet. In essence, it is a gateway to the rest of the world. To complete the scenario, we could change the DNS server address to reflect our external DNS on the Internet; for us, it's **207.172.3.8**, which is the DNS server provided by our ISP for cable Internet. This would allow the server (PC2) to access the Internet. We don't want to do that, however. First, we really don't need

> Internet access on a server; people are not meant to work off of that machine locally. Second, it will cause conflicts in our DNS resolutions. So we will stick with our LAN DNS server as the IP, **192.168.1.200**, which is PC2. This will ensure proper resolution between all PCs in our domain.

c. Make note of the server IP information because you will be using that as the default for most of the labs.

d. Click OK in both dialog boxes to close them.

IPv6

The upcoming IP Version 6, or IPv6 for short, will combat the shortage of IP addresses worldwide. Some companies are actually already using it internally, although it is not fully ratified as of the publishing of this book.

IP Version 6 is a 128-bit system, as opposed to the 32-bit system in place now. This is exponentially bigger. In fact, it will allow for somewhere in the neighborhood of 340 undecillion addresses—340 with 36 zeroes after it. That's a phenomenal number; it should last us a while.

 Actually, the number of available IP addresses will be somewhat less because some will be reserved for testing, multicasting, and so on. For more information on the ranges see http://www.iana.org/assignments/ipv6-address-space. Also check out http://www.ipv6.org/.

Here's an example of an IP address in Version 6: `3ffe:ffff:0100:f101:0210:a4ff:fee3:9566`, which will often be abbreviated as `3ffe:ffff:100:f101:210:a4ff:fee3:9566` (the leading zeroes can be omitted). This is obviously a big deal and will be very important for you in the future. For now, however, the Network+ exam only requires you to be able to spot an IP Version 6 address, and explain the reasoning for it.

What Did I Just Learn?

In this lab you learned about IP Versions 4 and 6 and were taught how to configure IP for various classes. You learned the value of a gateway, and reviewed the binary equivalents of the various IP ranges. You also were educated on the various default subnet masks. Great work so far! Specifically you learned the following:

➤ Class A, B, and C ranges and configurations.

➤ How to configure for each of the major classes and subnet masks.

➤ How to recognize a Version 6 IP address.

➤ How many networks and hosts the various classifications can offer.

Lab 5: Identifying the Purpose of Subnetting

In this lab you will learn the basics of subnetting and create a basic working subnet. You will also prepare for subdomain 2.7.

Subnetting IP Networks

Until now you have used default subnet masks. However, one of the reasons for having a subnet mask is to have the ability to create subnetworks logically by IP. You may be wondering, what is a *subnet*? Simple. It is a subdivision of your logical IP network. And…what is a *mask*? Even easier. It is any binary number that is a 1. If the binary digit is a 1, then the digit is masked. If the binary digit is a 0, then the digit is unmasked.

Let's review the Standard default subnet masks, as shown in Table 2.4.

Table 2.4	Standard subnet masks	
Type	**Decimal**	**Binary**
Class A	255.0.0.0	11111111.00000000.00000000.00000000
Class B	255.255.0.0	11111111.11111111.00000000.00000000
Class C	255.255.255.0	11111111.11111111.11111111.00000000

For this exercise you will use a Class C network, 192.168.1.0, to show how it can be divided into smaller subnetworks. By default, the subnet mask would be 255.255.255.0. But what if you wanted to divide the network into four distinct IP subnetworks? You could use something like this: 255.255.255.240. This is also known as 192.168.1.0 /28 because the subnet mask has 28 masked bits and 4 unmasked bits. The first three 255s are the same, and you can pretty much ignore them. the fourth octet (240), however, tells you how many subnetworks (subnet IDs) and how many hosts you can have per subnetwork. All you need is some know-how on basic math, converting to binary, and remembering one good rule: $2^n - 2 = x$.

Here's how you do it:

1. Convert 240 to binary. It equals 11110000.

2. Break it up like this: 1111   0000. Use the parts that are ones for the subnet IDs and the parts that are zeroes for the host IDs.

There are four ones. In decimal, this means the maximum number of subnets is 16. There are also four zeroes, and in decimal this means the maximum number of hosts per subnet is, again, 16. But—there's always a but—you can never use the first and the last for a host ID. All ones and all zeroes cannot be used because they are for identifying the subnetwork and for doing broadcasting. So now you have 14 possible subnets and 14 possible hosts per subnet. That gives you a total of 196 hosts on your whole network. An example of the math is listed in Table 2.5.

Table 2.5 Example for both the subnets and the hosts			
Subnet ID	#	Host IP	Host IP in Decimal
0000 (unusable)	0	0000–1111	0–15
0001	1	0000–1111	16–31
0010	2	0000–1111	32–47
0011	3	0000–1111	48–63
0100	4	0000–1111	64–79
0101	5		80–95
0110	6		96–111
0111	7		112–127
1000	8		128–143
1001	9		144–159
1010	10		160–175
1011	11		176–191
1100	12		192–207
1101	13		208–223
1110	14		224–239
1111 (unusable)	15		240–255

As you can see, there are 16 numbers, but you can't use the first and last because they are all zeros and all ones respectively.

Getting back to the equation: $2^n - 2 = x$. X is what we are trying to calculate for, and N is equal to the number of ones or zeroes in binary—that is, the number of digits in the binary number. So, 2 to the power of 4 = 16, and 16–2 = 14. You can do this for any subnet mask. Try it! Use Table 2.6 to calculate.

Table 2.6			
Subnet Mask	**Subnets**	**Hosts per Subnet**	**Total Hosts**
255.255.255.192			
255.255.255.224			
255.255.255.240			
255.255.255.248			

Procedure

Use the following information to create a working subnetwork:

➤ Network: 192.168.50.0.

➤ Subnet mask: 255.255.255.240.

➤ Subnet ID: 7.

1. Go to PC1.

2. Right-click My Network Places and select Properties to display the Network Connections window.

3. Disable the wireless LAN card.

4. Access the Internet Protocol (TCP/IP) Properties dialog box and change your IP settings to reflect the subnet information provided above. For the sake of simplicity, we chose the first valid IP for PC1, as shown in Figure 2.41.

If you refer to Table 2.5, you will notice that subnet ID 7 dictates that you can use IP addresses between 192.168.50.112 and 192.168.50.127. However, you cannot use the first and last of those IP addresses. That leaves you with 113–126. You can use any of the IPs in that range that you wish, but make sure that no two computers get the *same* IP address.

5. Click OK in both dialog boxes to close them.

6. Go to PC2.

7. Access PC2's Internet Protocol (TCP/IP) Properties dialog box and give the next valid IP address—here, 192.168.50.114. Make sure to use the proper subnet mask! DNS and gateway addresses are not needed.

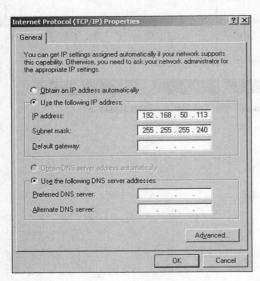

Figure 2.41 The Internet Protocol (TCP/IP) Properties dialog box.

8. Click OK in both dialog boxes to close them.

9. Return to PC1 and open the command prompt.

10. Type `ipconfig/all` and verify that your settings are as they should be.

11. Type `ping 192.168.50.114`. You should get replies.

12. Try pinging the router by typing `ping 192.168.1.1`. It should *not* reply, and you should get the message "Destination host unreachable," as shown in Figure 2.42.

```
C:\WINNT\system32\cmd.exe                                      _ □ ×
        Connection-specific DNS Suffix  . :
        Description . . . . . . . . . . : 3Com EtherLink XL
(3C905B-TX)
        Physical Address. . . . . . . . : 00-01-02-3D-5F-5D
        DHCP Enabled. . . . . . . . . . : No
        IP Address. . . . . . . . . . . : 192.168.50.113
        Subnet Mask . . . . . . . . . . : 255.255.255.240
        Default Gateway . . . . . . . . :
        DNS Servers . . . . . . . . . . :

C:\>ping 192.168.1.1

Pinging 192.168.1.1 with 32 bytes of data:

Destination host unreachable.
Destination host unreachable.
Destination host unreachable.
Destination host unreachable.

Ping statistics for 192.168.1.1:
    Packets: Sent = 4, Received = 0, Lost = 4 (100% loss),
Approximate round trip times in milli-seconds:
    Minimum = 0ms, Maximum = 0ms, Average = 0ms

C:\>
```

Figure 2.42 Pinging a device not on the subnet.

13. You now have a working subnet that shields the two computers from everything else, including the router.

14. Change all IP informtion on both PCs back to normal. This information is listed in Lab 4, Step 3.

 More information about subnetting is available on the Web at http://www. learntosubnet.com.

And there you have it! You create subnets to compartmentalize your network. This could be to decrease broadcasts, increase data throughput, add security, limit access, and use your IP addresses more wisely. It is common in the field, and although the Network+ exam probably won't test you on how to subnet, it will at the very least ask you how it works—and now you know.

What Did I Just Learn?

You learned how to create a functional subnetwork, discovered that communications will be limited to the hosts on that particular subnet, learned the various configurations for subnetworking, and tested your configurations.

Lab 6: Private Versus Public, and Static Versus Dynamic

Orientation

In this lab you will accomplish the following:

➤ Set up a private and public network range.

➤ Identify APIPA and disable it.

➤ Show the differences between a static and a dynamic IP network.

➤ Prepare for the Network+ subdomains 2.8 and 2.9.

In the TCP/IP suite, certain IP network numbers have been classified for internal use. These are known as *private network numbers*. Usually, you will find these inside companies behind a firewall. Everything else, and any IP number that can connect *directly* to the Internet, is considered a public IP. Table 2.7 shows the different private IP ranges that are accessible to you.

Table 2.7	Private IP networks
Class	**IP Network**
Class A	**10.0.0.0**
Class B	**172.16.0.0–172.31.0.0**
Class C	**192.168.1.0–192.168.255.0**
APIPA (Class B)	**169.254.0.0**

As you have seen, your router has been handing out addresses to your computers all along on the 192.168.1.0 network. That is the standard Class C private network. Remember that these addresses cannot connect directly to the Internet; they are for internal use between computers on your LAN. The limitation of this choice is that you can only have 254 hosts maximum. If you need up to 65,000 addresses, then you want a Class B private network. If you need even more addresses than that (or more flexibility), then you need a Class A private network, which has the ability to add as many as 16,000,000 addresses. The 10.0.0.0 network is a standard choice for large companies today.

In reality, you can use whatever IP network number you want as long as you are behind a firewall, because these IP addresses will not be able to communicate *directly* with other systems on the Internet. You should, however, stick to the standard private IP ranges.

The difference between static and dynamic has already been shown, but not quite explained. Simply put, a static IP address is one that you, the tech, manually enter. A dynamic address is one that is given to your computer automatically, usually by a DHCP server. It is called *dynamic* because the IP address has a lease that may only last for a week, four days, even one day. It all depends on how the DHCP server is set. In our scenario, when you select the Obtain IP address automatically option button in the Internet Protocol (TCP/IP) Properties dialog box, you get the dynamic IP from the Linksys router. When you type in the IP address, it is considered manual.

There is one more way to get an automatic IP address, however. That is to obtain an APIPA address. APIPA stands for *Automatic Private IP Addressing*, and it is built into Windows 2000 and XP, which gives *itself* an IP address. This type of address isn't quite dynamic, because it doesn't change; instead, we call it *self-assigned*. With APIPA, there's no need to be connected to a network, or to have access to a DHCP server. The only problem with APIPA is that sometimes it can get in the way of true DHCP. Let's go ahead and start the lab.

Procedure

In this lab we will show you how to bind a secondary IP address to your NIC. You will also create a public Class A network, and learn how to turn off APIPA.

1. Create the Class A network.

   a. Go to PC1.

   b. Access the Internet Protocol (TCP/IP) Properties dialog box for the LAN card.

   c. Click the Advanced button.

   d. The IP tab is displayed by default. Notice the one address that is already there; that is the address from Lab 5, "Identifying the purpose of subnetting." Click Add.

   e. Enter the following information, as shown in Figure 2.43.

      i. IP address: 65.88.25.154.

After you enter the IP address, press the Tab key. The following subnet mask should be filled in automatically. If it isn't, you'll have to type it manually.

      ii. Subnet mask: 255.0.0.0.

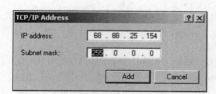

Figure 2.43   Binding a secondary IP address to the NIC.

   f. Click Add.

   g. Click OK in all three dialog boxes to close them.

   h. Switch to PC2.

   i. Access the Internet Protocol (TCP/IP) Properties dialog box for the NIC.

   j. Click the Advanced button.

k. Click the Add button.

l. Just as you did on PC1, add another IP address to the NIC:

    i. IP address: 65.215.128.12.

    ii. Subnet mask: 255.0.0.0.

m. Click Add.

n. Click OK in all three dialog boxes to close them.

o. Still on PC2, access your command prompt and type ping 65.88.25.154 to try to ping PC1's new IP address. You should get replies from the Class A public IP address, as shown in Figure 2.44.

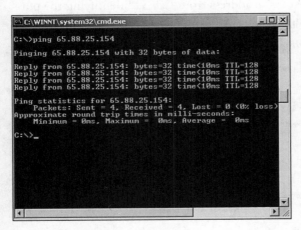

Figure 2.44 Testing the Class A network.

As mentioned previously, APIPA can give your computer an IP automatically, even if you are not connected to a network. The address will look like something like this: 169.254.102.25. Regardless of the last two octets, the network will be 169.254. That tells you that APIPA is in force! It uses an algorithm to decide on the IP you get. The chances of getting the same APIPA IP as another computer on the network are somewhere around one in 65,000. Sometimes, APIPA can get in the way of your DHCP server. If it is the first time you are requesting a DHCP address, there may be complications, or the DHCP may take a little too long to answer. This could happen on the LAN or at home on your Internet connection. If the DHCP takes too long to respond, then APIPA might kick in, giving you an address on the 169.254 network and rendering your computer incommunicable. The next steps show how to turn off APIPA so it does not get in the way.

1. Identify APIPA and disable it.

   a. Go to PC1.

   b. Access your LAN card's Internet Protocol (TCP/IP) Properties dialog box.

   c. Select the Obtain an IP address automatically and Obtain DNS server address automatically option buttons.

   d. Click the Start button, select Run, and type `regedit` to launch the Registry Editor. (See Figure 2.45.)

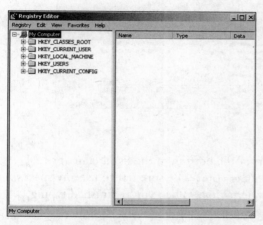

Figure 2.45 The Registry Editor.

   e. Maximize the window.

   f. Click the plus (+) signs next to the following entries, in order: HKEY_LOCAL_MACHINE, System, CurrentControlSet, Services, TCP/IP, Parameters, Interfaces.

   g. Look through the Interfaces subkeys (folders) until you find the subkey with the IP address you are using now, `192.168.1.x`. For us, it's the first Interfaces subkey, as shown in Figure 2.46.

   h. Shut off APIPA.

      i. In the right pane, right-click anywhere on the white area to open the New context menu.

      ii. Choose New and then select Dword from the drop-down list that appears.

Figure 2.46 The Interfaces subkey.

   iii. A new entry appears at the bottom of the list. Name it as follows: `ipautoconfigurationenabled`. Be sure not to use any spaces, periods, or other punctuation. When you're finished typing, press Enter. The new entry is automatically set to 0, so APIPA is disabled! Hooray.

   i. Close the Registry Editor. The changes will be saved automatically.

That about does it for this lab. Let's take it to the bridge!

What Did I Just Learn?

In this lab you used a public network number on your private home network, proving that it is *possible* to use whatever number you want. You also learned that the accepted proper way is to use one of the assigned private network numbers or ranges. In addition, you learned how to identify and remove an APIPA address. To wrap it up, you specifically learned the following:

➤ The Class A, B, and C private network numbers.

➤ The APIPA `169.254` network number.

➤ How to create a public network.

➤ How to disable APIPA.

Lab 7: Identifying TCP/IP Protocols

Orientation

The TCP/IP protocols are a big part of the Network+ exam, so you need to be able to identify and define them. For a true network administrator, this is second nature.

In this lab you will accomplish the following:

➤ Identify 19 TCP/IP protocols.

➤ Use various programs and TCP/IP utilities to define the protocols.

➤ Identify the common TCP/IP port numbers.

➤ Prepare for the Network+ subdomains 2.10, 2.11, and 2.12.

Procedure

In this lab you will use NetStat, Internet Explorer, and other TCP/IP command prompt utilities to visualize the protocols. We will also give basic definitions of the various protocols and their location on the OSI model.

1. Explore Transport layer protocols.

   ➤ **TCP: Transmission Control Protocol**. This transport layer protocol governs connection-oriented data transmissions. It takes any kind of message (HTTP, SMTP, POP3), encapsulates it, and guarantees its transmission over the communication subnetwork.

   ➤ **UDP: User Datagram Protocol**. Like TCP, this protocol is on the transport layer, and governs data transmissions. Unlike TCP, however, it is for connectionless, non-guaranteed data. These will normally be real-time connections like streaming media.

   a. Go to PC1 and open up the command prompt.

   b. Type netstat -a. The left column of results should show all sessions that are using TCP and UDP ports, as shown in Figure 2.47.

2. Explore Network layer protocols.

   ➤ **ICMP: Internet Control Message Protocol**. This is a Network layer protocol, and ICMP is the type of packets that are sent when you initiate a ping. They are referred to as *ICMP echoes*.

Figure 2.47 TCP and UDP sessions.

➤ **ARP: Address Resolution Protocol**. This protocol converts (resolves) between IP addresses on the network layer and MAC addresses on the Data Link layer. This allows the IP network and the Ethernet networks to communicate seamlessly.

a. In the command prompt on PC1, type ping PC2. You should get replies from your server, each one an ICMP echo packet. If not, check your IP settings.

b. In the command prompt, type arp -a. You should get information like that shown in Figure 2.48. If you don't, try pinging PC2 again and then run arp -a again immediately afterward.

Figure 2.48 The *arp –a* command.

 Notice that the displayed test shows you the server's IP address and its corresponding MAC address. You can also view these packets with Ethereal, as shown in Chapter 1, "Media and Topologies."

3. Explore Application layer protocols.

➤ **HTTP: Hyper Text Transfer Protocol.** This is the most commonly used application layer protocol in the TCP/IP suite. Whenever you open your Web browser and type http://www.*whatever*.com, the HTTP protocol and port 80 are used.

➤ **HTTPS: Hyper Text Transfer Protocol Secure.** This uses SSL (Secure Sockets Layer) to encrypt the session at the Web site. This protocol uses port 443.

➤ **FTP (File Transfer Protocol):** This is another Application layer protocol that is used to move files from a remote server to your local computer and vice-versa. It is a great way to connect to disparate systems and access files.

a. Access HTTP and HTTPS sites.

  i. In the Internet Explorer address bar, type http://www.technicalblog.com.

  ii. Press Alt+Tab to access your command prompt, and type `net-stat -a`. You should see connections to the Web site. (Our server name is `krypton.lunarpages.com`; you can't miss it!) The results are displayed in Figure 2.49.

If you don't see these connections, return to the browser and press F5 to refresh the page. Then return to the command prompt, press the up arrow key on your keyboard to display the last command issued (here, **netstat –a**) and press Enter.

Figure 2.49 An HTTP session.

  iii. Return to Internet Explorer and type a new URL: http://www.affinityfcu.org.

    iv. A pop-up window appears, telling you that you are about to enter a *secure* connection. Click OK.

    v. The Web site opens. Notice that the URL has changed to https://www.affinityfcu.org and that a small padlock has appeared in the bottom-right portion of the browser window, as shown in Figure 2.50.

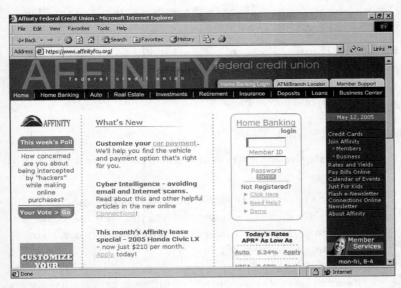

Figure 2.50 An HTTPS Web site.

    vi. Return to the command prompt and type netstat -a. You should see the secure connections, as shown in Figure 2.51.

Figure 2.51 An HTTPS session.

  b. Access an FTP site and download a file.

We will be using our Windows XP computer for this exercise, but you can use any system as long as you can connect to the Internet. PC1 with Windows 2000 Professional will be fine.

i. Go to PC1 and open your browser.

ii. Access the following Web site: http://www.smartftp.com/ download/.

iii. Download the Smart FTP program.

iv. Install this evaluation version to your computer.

v. Run the Smart FTP program.

vi. In the address bar, type the following: ftp.technicalblog.com.

vii. In the login section, type anonymous@technicalblog.com.

viii. Do not type a password.

ix. If it is not already entered, add 21 to the Port field.

x. Click the leftmost icon on the toolbar to connect.

xi. A window like the one shown in Figure 2.52 will open. Click OK to log in to our FTP server.

Figure 2.52 The Enter Login Information dialog box.

xii. If you have a window pane in your FTP program called "Transfers," close it now.

xiii. Open the FTP menu and select Local Browser to open a window that displays your computer's file system.

xiv. Open the Window menu and select Tile Horizontally. (See Figure 2.53.)

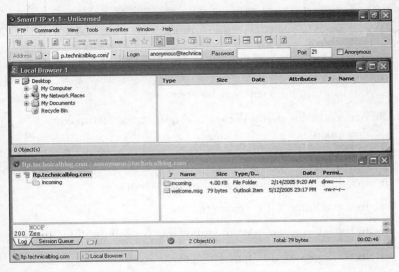

Figure 2.53 The FTP server and the local browser.

xv. Right-click the Welcome.msg file and choose View.

xvi. Click and drag that file to your local machine, in whatever folder you want. That is how you move files from an FTP server to your home computer! You can FTP to government servers, libraries, work FTP servers, and Web servers as well.

xvii. Close the FTP program.

c. Use the Network Time Protocol (NTP) to view, modify, and synchronize the network time.

➤ **NTP: Network Time Protocol.** This protocol is used to synchronize time across the network, be it a LAN or the Internet. Without time syncing, you could have problems browsing or connecting to other computers.

i. Go to PC1 and open the command prompt.

ii. Type net time. As shown in Figure 2.54, you should see the time on your domain, which is shown as the time at PC2, your Windows 2000 Server domain controller.

iii. Change the time server that you synchronize to. To do so, type net time /set \\PC1 and press Enter. When asked whether you want to make the change, type Y for yes, as shown in Figure 2.55.

C:\WINNT\system32\cmd.exe
C:\>net time
Current time at \\PC2 is 5/13/2005 3:24 AM
The command completed successfully.
C:\>

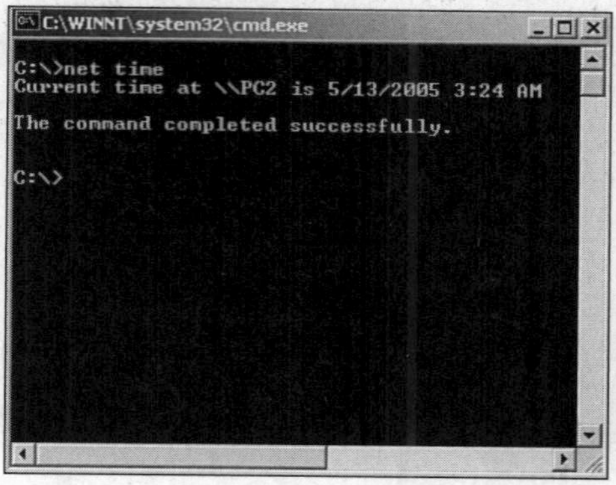

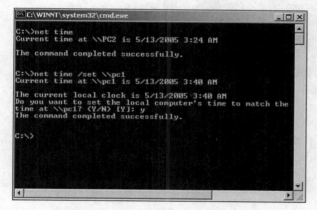

Figure 2.54 The ***net time*** command.

C:\WINNT\system32\cmd.exe
C:\>net time
Current time at \\PC2 is 5/13/2005 3:24 AM
The command completed successfully.
C:\>net time /set \\pc1
Current time at \\pc1 is 5/13/2005 3:40 AM
The current local clock is 5/13/2005 3:40 AM
Do you want to set the local computer's time to match the
time at \\pc1? (Y/N) [Y]: y
The command completed successfully.
C:\>

Figure 2.55 Changing ***net time*** to the local machine.

iv. To see NTP in action double-click the clock in the bottom-right portion of your screen.

v. Change the time to two hours ahead.

vi. Return to the command prompt and resynchronize to the server by typing `net time /set \\PC2`. Once again, when prompted, type `Y` to agree. See how the clock on the bottom right is automatically adjusted.

vii. Now let's sync up to Internet time. Once again, double-click the clock on the bottom right and move it ahead by two hours.

viii. Return to the command prompt, type `net time /setsntp:time.windows.com`, and press Enter. You'll see a message indicating that the command was successful. You just added the Internet time server known as `time.windows.com` to your list of possible time servers.

ix. Type `w32tm` and press Enter to change your clock to Internet time, as it is given to you by time.windows.com. (See Figure 2.56.)

Figure 2.56 Configuring Internet time.

x. Notice that the command hovers and doesn't bring you back to the prompt. To end this loop, press Ctrl+C.

xi. Now let's resynchronize back to our domain controller. Type `net time /set \\PC2` and press Enter, and then type `Y` for yes to agree. Everything is now back to normal. As you can see, configuring Internet time is as easy as 1, 2, 3!

Great work so far! Table 2.8 describes the various protocols, how they fit into the OSI model, and their purpose in this model.

Table 2.8	Protocols, their purpose, and their place on the OSI		
Protocol	**Name**	**Purpose**	**OSI Layer**
FTP	File Transfer Protocol	Used to move files between computers	Application
HTTP	Hyper Text Transfer Protocol	Used to view regular Web pages	Application
HTTPS	Hyper Text Transfer Protocol over Secure Socket Layer	Used to view encrypted Web pages	Application and (over) presentation

Table 2.8	Protocols, their purpose, and their place on the OSI *(continued)*		
Protocol	**Name**	**Purpose**	**OSI Layer**
POP3	Post Office Protocol 3	Used to download or receive mail	Application
SMTP	Simple Mail Transfer Protocol	Used to send mail to people	Application
Telnet	Terminal Emulation	Used to connect via text to other hosts	Application
TFTP	Trivial File Transfer Protocol	Simpler to use than FTP but less capable	Application
SFTP	Secure File Transfer Protocol	FTP with encrypted SSH transport	Application
DNS	Domain Naming System	Resolves domain names (and host names) to IP addresses	Transport, also considered all the way to application
TCP	Transmission Control Protocol	Guaranteed connection oriented delivery system	Transport
UDP	User Datagram Protocol	Non-guaranteed connectionless delivery system	Transport
IP	Internet Protocol	IP addressing system	Network
ARP	Address Resolution Protocol	Resolves between IP addresses and MAC addresses	Network
ICMP	Internet Control Message Protocol	Sends ping packets, known as *ICMP echoes*, for testing	Network

Here are a few more protocols that you should be able to describe:

➤ **Secure Shell (SSH).** This is a protocol that allows someone using one computer to remotely operate another computer, normally by text. Unlike Telnet, it uses encrypted sessions.

➤ **Network News Transfer Protocol (NNTP).** This is a protocol to allow Usenet news to be read by news readers on the Internet.

➤ **Secure CoPy (SCP).** This is a protocol and a program that copies files between hosts on a network. It uses SSH for authentication and data transfer, thus gaining the features of strong authentication and encrypted sessions.

➤ **Lightweight Directory Access Protocol (LDAP).** This protocol is used to access many different types of directory listings. It is now being implemented in Web browsers and e-mail programs to enable lookup queries in addition to being used with directories on network controllers.

➤ **Internet Group Management Protocol (IGMP).** This protocol is used by hosts to keep local routers informed of their membership in multicasting.

➤ **Line Printer Daemon/Line Printer Remote (LPD/LPR).** This is a printer protocol that uses TCP/IP to establish connections between printers and computers on the network.

Finally, you should memorize the assigned ports for the following applications/services as shown in Table 2.9. The most important for the Network+ exam are in bold.

Table 2.9 Services and their assigned port numbers	
Port Number	**Service**
20	**FTP**
21	**FTP**
22	**SSH**
23	**Telnet**
25	**SMTP**
53	**DNS**
69	**TFTP**
70	Gopher
79	Finger
80	**HTTP (also 8080)**
88	Kerberos
110	**POP3**
119	**NNTP**
123	**NTP**
135	RPC
137	NetBIOS Naming Service
139	NetBIOS Session Service
143	**IMAP: Internet Message Access Protocol**
161	SNMP: Simple Network Management Protocol

Table 2.9 Services and their assigned port numbers *(continued)*	
Port Number	**Service**
443	**HTTPS (SSL)**
1723	PPTP: Point to Point Tunneling Protocol
3389	RDP: Remote Desktop Protocol

What Did I Just Learn?

In this heavy-duty lab you learned the importance of protocols and services and their impact on network communications. You also took a hands-on approach to several of the most commonly used services to explain their connection to the OSI and to each other. Specifically, you learned how to do the following:

➤ Connect to and identify secure Web sites.

➤ Utilize an FTP program to download and view files.

➤ Work with the command prompt to show address resolution, ping echoes, sessions, and Internet time.

➤ Identify many different protocols and services and their corresponding ports.

Lab 8: Configuring Common TCP/IP Services

Orientation

In this lab you will accomplish the following:

➤ Identify some common network services and protocols.

➤ Configure WINS and DNS.

➤ Set up NAT in the form of a working router.

➤ Prepare for the Network+ subdomain 2.13.

Procedure

This lab builds on what you learned in the previous one. A few of the most common things you will see used in a networked environment are DNS and NAT (Network Address Translation). We will show these using a hands-on approach. You will also discover how to configure WINS. The first exercise in routing requires additional systems and network cards to work properly.

The purpose of this procedure is internetworking with NAT and Static Routing. This will be used to connect two separate networks (LANs) together over a simulated WAN (Wide Area Network). This is known as *internetworking*. Normally, a client on one IP network cannot connect to or ping a client on the other IP network. The goal is to have the clients on both networks pinging each other through a routed connection. In this scenario, imagine that you have two LANs, each consisting of a server and client. Each LAN is in a separate city—Sydney and NYC—with its own network number. You will simulate the WAN by connecting the two cities to each other. Table 2.10 shows the IP addresses and network numbers you will use. You will need the following at your disposal:

➤ Two servers with two NICs each. Because these will have two network connections, they will be known as *multi-homed machines*.

➤ Two client computers.

➤ Crossover cable.

1. Change the IP addresses on all machines.

    a. Servers' LAN Cards should be set up as IP .1, and client IP addresses should ascend from there.

    b. Set the gateway address to the server's LAN IP.

    c. When all IPs are configured, make sure that all clients can ping the server on the LAN.

Table 2.10 IP chart		
City	**LAN Networks**	**WAN IP (2nd NIC)**
NYC	192.168.21.0	65.43.18.1
Sydney	192.168.22.0	65.43.18.2

2. Let's say that you are working on a computer in the NYC LAN. Try to ping any host on the Sydney LAN. You should not be able to do so; instead, you'll see a "Destination host unreachable" or "Request timed

out" message. You should, however, be able to ping all hosts—including the server—in the NYC LAN.

3. Verify that your servers have the second NIC set up and functioning with the proper IP address as shown in Table 2.10. Label the second NIC "WAN card."

4. Connect your crossover cable from the WAN card on the NYC server to the WAN card on the Sydney server.

You can make a crossover cable yourself. Just make sure to use the 568A wiring standard on one end and the 568B standard on the other.

5. Configure RRAS (Routing and Remote Access) servers step by step. Set up each server to act as a network router.

   a. Go to PC2. RRAS is installed automatically during the OS installation.

   b. Click the Start button, choose Programs, select Administrative Tools, and choose Routing and Remote Access to open the RRAS Configuration Console.

   c. Right-click the PC2 computer and select Configure Routing and Remote Access, as shown in Figure 2.57.

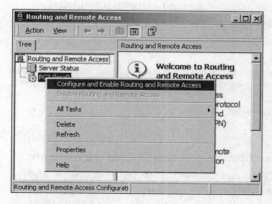

Figure 2.57 Turning on and configuring RRAS.

   d. The Routing and Remote Access Server Setup wizard launches. Read the contents of the Welcome screen and click Next.

e. Click the Network router option button, as shown in Figure 2.58, and then click Next.

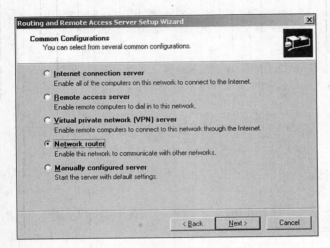

Figure 2.58   Selecting the Network router option button.

f. Verify that TCP/IP is installed and on the list, and click Next.

g. The next screen asks about demand dial options. Leave the default answer of No and click Next.

h. Click Finish to complete the wizard and return to the Routing and Remote Access Console, where your server should be listed with additional information alongside a green arrow pointing up (see Figure 2.59). Make sure to configure RRAS on both the NYC and the Sydney servers. The final network is illustrated in Figure 2.60.

> **NOTE**
>
> The green arrow means that the service is now running. If this arrow ever appears red, it means the service is not running and needs to be restarted or reconfigured.

i. Open the command prompt on the server and run the route print command in order to view the network-routing information and look at the networks available on the server.

j. Run the following syntax filling in your information in the brackets: route add [destination LAN] mask 255.255.255.0 [destination server's WAN IP]. For example, if NYC wanted to connect to Sydney, the command would be as follows: route add 192.168.22.0 mask 255.255.255.0 65.43.18.2.

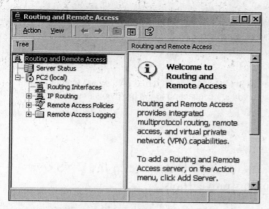

Figure 2.59 Completed RRAS console.

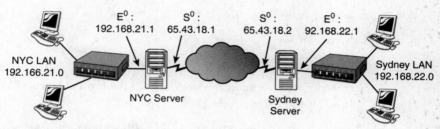

Figure 2.60 Internetwork diagram.

k. To enable routing in both directions, repeat the command in step j, but for the other city. Only the network numbers and IP addresses will change. If all is correct, clients from both cities should be able to ping each other.

l. Run tracert from one city's client to another city's client and view the hops over the network. An example from a NYC client command line would be `tracert 192.168.22.2`. It should show three hops in total.

m. Congratulations, you have just created a fully functional internetwork! Great work! Now it's time to change all the IP addresses on the servers and clients back to their original settings.

6. Configure Domain Naming System (DNS). DNS resolves between host names and IP addresses. It can also resolve between domain names and IP or FQDNs and IP. Nowadays, it is centralized, automated, and can be dynamic. It takes the place of the flat text file `HOSTS.TXT`.

a. DNS should be running already because you have a Windows 2000 domain that requires it. Regardless, verify that DNS is installed and has a forward lookup zone.

> On the clients, you may need to change the preferred DNS server to your LAN DNS server—especially if you are connecting to the Internet with an ISP-supplied DNS server.

   i. Add the DNS snap-in to your MMC or open the DNS console from your Administrative Tools.

   ii. Expand DNS, expand the server, and look at the forward lookup zones to make sure your domain is listed.

b. Click your domain name to select it.

c. Add a static entry.

   i. Open the domain so you can see the Hosts list.

   ii. Right-click anywhere in the work area in the right side window pane and choose New Host.

   iii. Add the name of the computer. (DNS will automatically use the parent domain name if you only enter a NetBIOS name, which is actually known as a host name!) It doesn't have to be a real computer; you can imagine that you have another system on your network named PC4 with an IP address of 192.168.1.140.

   iv. Add the computer's IP address, as shown in Figure 2.61.

   v. Click Add Host. You have now a static entry. Well done.

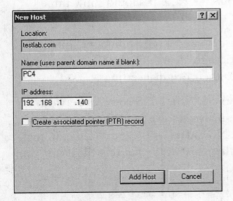

Figure 2.61 Adding a host.

7. The FQDN (Fully Qualified Domain Name) of this host is actually PC4.testlab.com. You can modify this with an alias so that if users want to connect (often for FTP purposes) to this client, they don't have to type the entire name. The alias could simply be something like FTP1. Add an alias now.

   a. Right-click in the white work area on the right side window pane and select New Alias.

   b. Add the alias name, FTP1, and the FQDN, pc4.testlab.com, as shown in Figure 2.62.

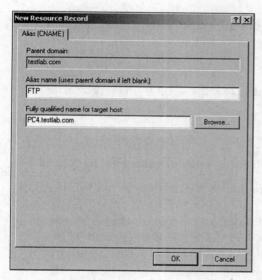

Figure 2.62 Adding an alias.

   c. Click OK. You should now have an alias (FTP1) that resolves to PC4.testlab.com, which in turn resolves to 192.168.1.140.

In the following steps you will now configure WINS.

8. Configure Windows Internet Naming Service (WINS) in a client/server environment. WINS is used to resolve between NetBIOS names and IP addresses. It is centralized and automated and takes the place of the flat text file LMHOSTS.TXT.

   a. Install the WINS service to the domain controllers.

      i. Open the Control Panel, choose Add Remove Programs, select Windows Components, choose Networking Services (Details), and select WINS.

    ii. Snap the WINS console into your MMC on the domain controller or open it from the administrative tools. WINS will automatically run! No other configuration is necessary on the server.

  b. Configure WINS on the Windows 2000 Professional client.

    i. Open the client's Internet Protocol (TCP/IP) Properties dialog box.

    ii. Click the Advanced button.

    iii. Click the WINS tab.

    iv. Enter the IP address of the WINS server (PC2), leaving the rest of the settings as their default configuration.

    v. Restart the Client.

  c. View the new WINS entries for the client in the server's database.

    i. Open WINS.

    ii. Open the server.

    iii. Right-click Active Registrations and select Find by Name.

    iv. Add an asterisk (*) to find all registrations in the WINS.MDB.

 You may have to click Active Registrations again to get the info. You may also have to close the MMC, re-open it, and then view the Active Registrations.

  d. Notice the three unique entries for the three main services: Workstation <00>, Messenger <03>, and Server <20>. These will be shown per computer.

That was excellent work. Let's go over some other terminology:

➤ **Network Address Translation (NAT).** This is an Internet standard that lets LANs use a set of IP addresses for internal traffic and a second set of addresses for external traffic. It will translate between the two networks. Usually the internal network will be a private IP network and any IP addresses displayed to the Internet will be public.

➤ **Internet Connection Sharing (ICS).** This is a method for connecting multiple computers in a LAN to the Internet through a single c onnection utilizing a single IP address. It usually incorporates NAT to translate between the LAN and the Internet connection.

➤ **Simple Network Management Protocol (SNMP).** SNMP is the standard protocol for remote monitoring and management of hosts, routers, and devices on a network.

➤ **Network File System (NFS).** This is a client/server application designed by Sun Microsystems that allows all network users to access shared files stored on computers of different types.

➤ **Zero Configuration Networking (Zeroconf).** This set of technologies allows two or more computers to communicate with each other without any external configuration.

➤ **Server Message Block (SMB).** This is the communications protocol used by Windows-based operating systems to support resource sharing across a network.

➤ **AppleTalk Filing Protocol (AFP).** Non-Apple networks use this in order to access data on an AppleTalk server.

What Did I Just Learn?

In this lab you learned how to configure some more client/server applications and were educated on some additional services and protocols. You also set up an internetwork all your own! Specifically you did the following:

➤ Configured static routes to form a simulated WAN.

➤ Set up additional hosts and aliases in DNS.

➤ Configured WINS and verified computers' services.

Lab 9: Identifying WAN Services

Orientation

In this lab you will accomplish the following:

➤ Identify, set up, purchase, and configure X.25 and frame relay.

➤ Define WAN technologies such as T-1, OCx, FDDI, and ISDN.

➤ Identify and define Internet access methods such as broadband cable, DSL, satellite, wireless, and PSTN.

Procedure

This lab discusses and illustrates packet-switching services including X.25 and Frame Relay. Then it talks about the various other WAN technologies in use today. So relax, sit back and read carefully; we will be getting heavily into the theory! Be ready to access the Internet as well. This lab is based on the Network+ subdomains 2.14 and 2.15.

Understanding the Technology that Pre-Dated Packet Switching

Until the early 1970s, data transfer was analog with much static and noise. It also was primarily asynchronous and conducted by regular modems. Data transfer could be as much as 40% overhead and only 60% actual information. Overhead included the allowance for noise, error checking, flagging, stop/start bits, parity, and so on. Longer transfers (files containing megabytes of information) could be disconnected for many reasons, including the following:

➤ Poor connection

➤ Network degradation

➤ Loss of circuits

If there was a disconnect, the entire message (file) would have to be re-sent, usually after the person re-dialed out.

Packet Switching Arrives with the Advent of the X.25 Communications Protocol

Packet switching was originally created to break down large messages into smaller, more manageable segments for transmission over a WAN. With packet switching, a sending computer sends its message over the LAN to the hardware/software component known as the *router*. The router would break down the file into more manageable pieces (known as *packets*).

Every packet gets a portion of the original message. Every packet also gets a segmentation number and address info. The packet is then transmitted over the physical link to the switching system (Telco), which picks a wire for transmission from the header information of the packet. This establishes a virtual connection or virtual circuit. Packets are re-assembled at the receiving router.

Understanding X.25 Packet-Switching Steps

A computer sends data, as normal, through the OSI model over the LAN to the router. Data, in the form of a message, is gathered by the router (also known as a PAD, short for *packet assembler/disassembler*), which disassembles the entire lot into jumbled packets. Packets are then sent by the PAD to a CSU/DSU (high-speed digital data interchange device) as serial information. Packets are sent by the CSU/DSU to the demarcation point in the office or company. This then leads to the central office (C.O.) of the phone company that is supporting the X.25 service.

The central office picks (switches to) a wire and transmits to the switching office, power lines, and so on. When the central office does this, it is known as a *virtual circuit*. The information ends up at the receiving central office, which sends the data over another virtual circuit to the correct line, which leads to another office in another city, and finally to the destination network.

This leads to the demarcation point (D-mark) and to a CSU/DSU, and then to their receiving router (PAD). The receiving PAD buffers the info, checks it, recounts, and puts the packets in sequence. The receiving PAD sends the message over the LAN in regular OSI model fashion to the receiving and correct computer.

Understanding X.25

X.25 is the following:

➤ Usually digital.

➤ Usually synchronous.

➤ 56K or 64K max line.

➤ Known as variable length packet switching.

The idea behind packet switching is that a PAD decides which circuit the information is going to take. Usually packets have 128 bytes of actual data, although some configurations go up to 512 bytes. Regardless, packet data is always of variable length. In fact, some packets have no data at all; they are informational only to the X.25 system.

Discovering X.25 Components—Overhead (Header and Trailer) and Data

If asked what the two parts of a packet are, you would answer the *overhead* and the *data*. The overhead consists of a header and a trailer. If someone asked what the three parts of a packet are, you would say the *header*, the *data*, and the *trailer*.

Overhead is the packet's header and trailer information. Overhead is not real data. It is information sent as electrical impulses, but it is not part of the original message. The *header* information includes the following:

➤ Packet flag, which is 8 bits of information used for start/stop purposes.

➤ HDLC (High Level Data Link Control) which is used for the framing format.

➤ 16 (or 32) bits, this displays the from address.

➤ 8 bits for the type of HDLC, which could be one of the following:

   ➤ **I**. Information. This HDLC includes error detection.

   ➤ **S**. Supervisory. This determines the ready state of devices. Options include RR (receiver ready), RNR(receiver not ready), and Rej (reject).

   ➤ **U**. Unnumbered. This HDLC option dictates parameters and modes.

➤Packet-specific information in the header, which includes the following:

   ➤ **GFI: General Format Identifier**. This is comprised of 4 bits and is concerned with how the packet is being used—incoming, outgoing, VC, PVC, and so on.

   ➤ **LGN: Logical Channel Group Number**. This number ranges from 0–7 and is comprised of 4 bits. There are eight combinations of channels.

   ➤ **LCN: Logical Channel Numbers**. This number ranges from 1–2047 and is comprised of 8 bits. Usually this number is 255, maximum. But if multiply 255 by the eight channel groups, and you get a maximum of 2,048 ports. These ports are the actual channel or port that is being used on the WAN connection. As a result, the value can go to 2048.

   ➤ **PTI: Packet Type Identifier**. X.25 uses six different types of packets: incoming call, clear, data, interrupt, reset, and restart. This value is comprised of 8 bits.

After the overhead is inserted, the data is inserted—usually 128 bytes maximum per packet. Following the data is the *trailer*. It includes the following:

➤ **CRC:** CRC stands for *Cyclic Redundancy Check*. It is 16 bits long and includes error detection and correction data. A 16-bit CRC has a 99.999995% rate of detection.

➤ **End flag.** The End flag is 8 bits often represented as a 126 or 01111110 in binary. This represents the *stop* byte and signals the end of the packet.

An example of the entire X.25 packet is illustrated in Figure 2.63.

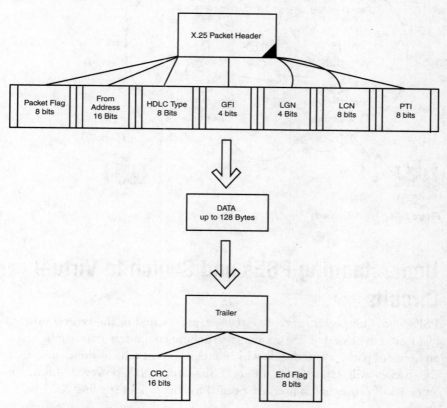

Figure 2.63   X.25 packet diagram.

Discovering the Cloud and its Impact on X.25

The *cloud* is the area of the telephone company's infrastructure that is between the demarcation point of your office and the receiving office. All central offices, switching offices, telephone poles, and lines are part of the cloud, which is represented in Figure 2.64.

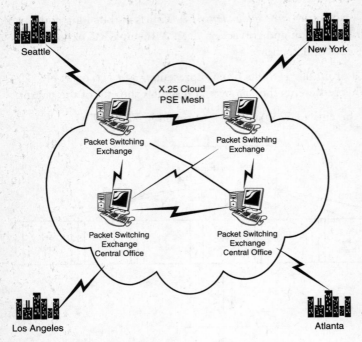

Figure 2.64 The X.25 cloud.

Understanding PSEs and Switch to Virtual Circuits

PSEs, short for *packet switching exchanges*, are located in the central offices, just inside the cloud. They are mega-switching computers that handle huge amounts of packets and decide which circuit (out of tens of thousands) that the packet will take. Quite often, PSEs are UNIX-powered. Immense amounts of processing power are needed for the task of sending X.25 packets.

The PSE reads the address and framing information of the packet and then *routes* it in the correct direction. So you see, computers can be routers as well; in fact, they are the original routers. They act as routers because they can decide multiple paths for the packet, as you saw in Figure 2.64.

The PSE chooses the circuit (out of tens of thousands) that is used least, is most direct, or is most available. The PSE then orders a leased line from the local exchange carrier (LEC). It uses this line as the circuit for the packets. In the old days this was an analog line (2,400bps) which some administrators still refer to as 9,600bps. Now it is a digital line, usually at the speed of 64Kbps. It is also synchronous.

Remember, the PSE has thousands of circuits to choose from. These circuits are known as a *circuit set*. The chances of all the packets from the entire message using one circuit are slim because so many different users and companies are using the bandwidth. Therefore, a typical message of 10 packets could be spread over five circuits. Because multiple circuits are being used, the entire circuit set is known as the *virtual circuit*.

There could be several PSE stops along the way. These PSEs are also PADs. They disassemble and reassemble the packets. These stops are also known as *hops*. For every hop along the way, the PSE buffers the packets into RAM and holds them there until the next PSE along the way gets the packet and acknowledges it. This way, if a packet is lost between two PSEs, the first will resend it.

At the receiving office, the PAD (router) reassembles the packets and the overhead (header and trailer) is discarded. The router then sends the information in the regular OSI format to the receiving computer on the LAN.

The Advantages of X.25 as Compared to Dial-up Analog Lines

If any data fails, X.25 automatically recovers and resends—assuming that there are circuits available in the virtual circuit. If this is not the case and all the circuits are being used by others, then other arrangements are made. There is a TTL (time to live) for the packets to be buffered in the PSE, but if a virtual circuit is not available past the TTL, then the PSE will notify the previous PSE or sending router.

X.25 allows shared access among multiple users on the LAN. They share access through the LAN via the router and the CSU/DSU out to a 64Kbps line, as opposed to each user having a separate dial-up line.

X.25 also has full error and flow control. X.25 offers protection from intermediate link failure. It is not completely fault tolerant, but is 70% effective. This is thanks to the virtual circuit; in contrast, on a dial-up line, you use the same circuit to move a file through the whole transfer. If that circuit is lost, then the whole message must be resent.

Pricing is per shared packet sent, not per minute. X.25 is a synchronous, digital transmission. Digital is inherently better and faster than analog because there is less noise, and because the information does not have to be converted from analog to digital and back. That means X.25 requires less overhead in the form of conversion. There is also less overhead per file. For dial-up, there can be as much as 40% overhead per file, but with X.25 overhead can be as little as 8%.

Discovering Other Protocols within the X.25 Suite

The following describes other protocols from the X.25 suite that you need to be familiar with:

➤ **X.28**. This protocol allows a dial-up asynchronous terminal or PC to connect to an X.25 PAD. An example of this is the X.25 PAD in NT Server and workstation under Remote Access Service.

➤ **X.29**.this protocol allows a PAD-to-host connection.

➤ **X.3**.This Protocol allows the PAD to connect to another PAD or DTE (Data Terminating Equipment) device.

➤ **X.75**.This protocol is use in internetworks. Creates a gateway between two different packet networks—for example, token ring and Ethernet, or IPX to IP. This is transparent to the user.

➤ **X.25**. The original X.25 protocol was a numbering system created by the CCITT and the ITU-TSS. The TSS (Telephony Standardization Sector) of the ITU works with the CCITT to ensure proper ratification of protocols like X.25. This particular protocol allowed every PAD in the U.S. to have a different number and thus differentiate from each other.

➤ **X.121**. The worldwide numbering plan for public X.25 networks and worldwide numbering.

Access http://www.google.com and query its Images page for the term "x.25 network diagram". Take a look at the images that come up. You will see diagrams for the national and international X.25 WAN technology.

Frame Relay, the Advancement of Packet Switching

Some key points about Frame Relay include the following:

➤ Frame Relay is a new form of packet switching that is designed for high speed.

➤ In Frame Relay, packets are referred to as *frames*. These are not to be confused with frames on the Data Link layer of the OSI.

➤ Like X.25, Frame Relay uses transmission links only when needed.

➤ Frame Relay also uses a virtual circuit, but one that is more advanced.

➤ Frame Relay created the virtual network, which resides in the cloud.

➤ Many customers use the same groups of wires or circuits, so they are thus known as *shared circuits*.

➤ Like private connections (true T-1, and so on) frame relay transmits very quickly.

➤ Unlike X.25, much less processing is needed with frame relay. Inside the switches or PSEs, much overhead is eliminated. The network only looks at the address in the frame.

➤ Unlike dedicated T-1 private connections, frame relay uses a public leased line.

➤ Frame relay was created to take advantage of the low-error, high-performance digital infrastructure now in place and to better service synchronous transmissions.

➤ Frame relay is a much simpler network compared to a private T-1 network.

Figure 2.65 depicts an example of a T-1 full mesh network. Connections are needed from each city and to each city.

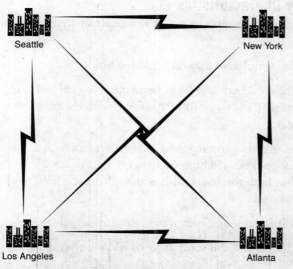

Seattle

New York

Los Angeles

Atlanta

Figure 2.65   Dedicated T-1 full mesh network.

Figure 2.66 shows an example of a Frame Relay WAN. It shows the contrast between a full T-1 dedicated network and a Frame Relay network. Only one connection is needed to the cloud per city.

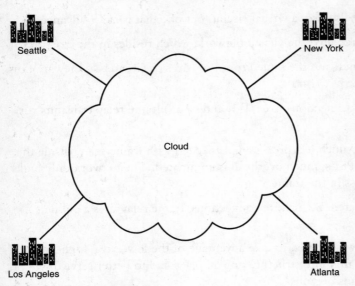

Figure 2.66   Frame Relay WAN.

Disadvantages of Frame Relay compared to a dedicated T-1 network are, of course, speed and privacy. Advantages of Frame Relay are significantly lower cost and less equipment.

Explore Frame Relay Characteristics

The following list highlights characteristics about Frame Relay that are critical to understand:

➤Multiple sessions can run simultaneously on the same link.

➤These connections to the cloud are known as permanent logical links or permanent virtual circuits (PVC—not to be confused with the plastic casing on a CAT5 cable).

➤The PVC links the sites together in the cloud. This is accomplished, once again, by the PSE (packet switching exchange). This is just like a private T-1 network, but here the bandwidth is shared at each PVC and with other customers as well.

➤Fewer routers, CSU/DSUs, and multiplexors are needed per site.

➤A PVC is always available, so the call setup time of X.25 is eliminated.

➤Constant fine tuning that is normally needed in mesh T-1 networks is not needed with frame relay.

➤Unlike a TDM (Time Division Multiplexed network), which waits on sessions, resulting in time lost, Frame Relay is dynamic. It sends information frame by frame regardless of session. This is more like the Stat-MUX (Statistical Time Division Multiplexing) style. A *multiplexor* (or MUX) is a device that takes raw data throughput and channelizes it for multiple users. More information about multiplexors can be found at http://www.technicalblog.com.

Purchasing Frame Relay

You must purchase Frame Relay service from an Internet services or Telco provider (Verizon, Sprint, or what have you).

With Frame Relay, you must commit to a certain amount of information over time. This is the *committed information rate* (CIR). The CIR is assigned to each PVC that services the company's account. Because this transmission is full duplex, there can be two CIRs for each PVC. The following are a few of the Frame Relay rates that are built into the service:

➤ **Br (burst rate).** This is LAN peak time. The network supplier will usually allow the burst rate to be twice that of the CIR. For example, if the CIR is 128Kbps, the Br will be 128Kbps beyond the CIR. If the entire infrastructure is not too busy, the customer could effectively burst more than this without extra cost. Unfortunately, the cloud is usually very busy.

➤**Be (burst excess rate).** This is 50% above the Br. For example, if the Br is 128Kbps beyond CIR, the Be will be 64Kbps beyond the Br.

NOTE

Burst rates are for two seconds max. The aggregate throughput in this example—where the CIR is 128Kbps, the Br 128Kbps beyond that, and the Be 64Kbps beyond the Br—is 320Kbps. If you purchase a 128Kbps frame relay leased line, then you get temporary 320Kbps. Obviously this is going to save you money; you get the bandwidth when we need it. The average price for 128Kbps of frame relay (with 320Kbps burst) is $275. Compare this to a fractional private T-1 line, which could be anywhere from $500 to $1,500 depending on the provider.

Identifying the Components of a Frame in Frame Relay

An example of the frame format can be found in Figure 2.67. This will show you the header, data section, and trailer components of the frame. The list that follows will give you further detail on these components seen in Figure 2.67.

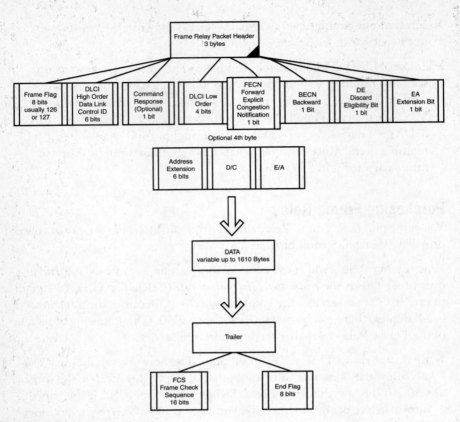

Figure 2.67 Frame relay format.

➤**Flag.** The flag is usually 126 or 127 (01111110 or 01111111 in binary). This marks the beginning and end of the frame.

➤**DLCI.** This is the Data Link Control ID. There are 1,024 LCNs (logical channel numbers) available maximum. These mark the PVC addressing scheme.

➤**FECN.** Forward Explicit Congestion Notification. The FECN is for notifying PADs of congested CIRs ahead of the router and of the order of priority.

➤**BECN.** Backward Explicit Congestion Notification. The BECN is for notifying PADs of congested CIRs behind the router and of the order of priority.

➤**CR.** Command Response rate. This is not usually used in Frame Relay.

➤**EA.** Extension bit. If this is 0, it extends the DLCI address to the address extension in the optional fourth byte.

➤**DE.** Discard Eligibility bit. This denotes whether a frame is eligible or if the CIRs are congested.

➤**2nd EA.** If this is 1, it ends the DLCI.

➤**FCS.** Frame Check Sequence. This is 2 bytes of error checking, very similar to the CRC.

Access http://www.google.com and query its Images page for the term "frame relay diagram". Look at the many images and diagrams associated with frame relay. You will see this technology in the field.

Explore other WAN Technologies

The following list highlights other WAN technologies you will need to understand:

➤**Circuit switching.** This is a WAN switching method in which a dedicated physical circuit through a carrier network is established, maintained, and terminated for each communication session. It is used extensively in telephone company networks and in PSTN, and operates much like a normal telephone call.

➤**Integrated Services Digital Network (ISDN).** This digital technology was developed to combat the limitations of PSTN. Users can send data, talk on the phone, and fax, all from one line. ISDN is broken down into the following:

> **Basic Rate ISDN (BRI).** A BRI circuit will have a data transfer rate of 128Kbps. This includes two equal B channels at 64Kbps each for data, and one 16Kbps D channel for timing.

> **Primary Rate ISDN (PRI).** A PRI Circuit will have a data transfer rate of 1.536Mbps. It runs on a T-1 circuit, and has 23 equal 64Kbps B channels for data, plus one 64 Kbps D channel for timing.

NOTE

Many companies still use ISDN for video conferencing or as a fault-tolerant second Internet access connection. Data commuters use this if DSL or cable is not available.

> **Fiber Distributed Data Interface (FDDI).** This standard is for transmitting data on optical fiber cables at a rate of around 100Mbps. It uses a ring topology.

▶ **Trunk carrier 1 (T-1).** This is an actual trunk carrier circuit that is brought into a company. It can run as a dedicated high-speed link or can have other shared technologies run on top of it, such as frame relay and ISDN. It is considered 1.544Mbps, but only 1.536Mbps of that is for data. The remaining 8Kbps is for T-1 trimming/overhead. The 1.536Mbps is broken into 24 equal 64Kbps channels and can be used with a multiplexor.

▶ **Trunk carrier 3 (T-3).** This is considered to be the equivalent of 28 T-1s. It boasts 44.736Mbps, using 672 64Kbps B channels. It comes to the company as roughly 224 wires and must be punched down to a DSX or like device.

▶ **OCx.** This is the standard for data throughput on SONET connections. SONET is the abbreviation for Synchronous Optical NETwork. The rates in Table 2.11 are known as synchronous transport signal rates.

OC Level	Transmission Rate
OC-1	51.84Mbps
OC-3	155.52Mbps
OC-12	622.08Mbps
OC-24	1.244Gbps
OC-48	2.488Gbps
OC-192	9.953Gbps

Table 2.11 Synchronous transport signal rates

▶**xDSL.** This is the standard for the various digital subscriber lines.

▶**Asymmetrical Digital Subscriber Lines (ADSL).** ADSL can run on your home telephone line so that you can talk on the phone and access the Internet at the same time. However, you are limited to 28,800bps upload speed, and the download is variable, spiking as high as 7Mbps. It is usually not as fast as cable Internet.

▶**Symmetrical Digital Subscriber Line (SDSL).** SDSL is installed (usually for companies) as a separate line, and is more expensive. SDSL data-transfer rates can be purchased at 384Kbps, 768Kbps, 1.1Mbps, and 1.5Mbps. The upload and download speed are the same, or symmetrical, hence the name.

▶**Broadband cable.** This is used for cable Internet and cable TV. It offers a higher speed than DSL; indeed, it can usually reach an average of 5–7Mbps, although the serial connection has the theoretical ability to go to 18Mbps. http://www.dslreports.com commonly shows people connecting with cable at speeds of 10Mbps.

➤ **Plain Old Telephone System (POTS)/Public Switched Telephone Network (PSTN).** This is used for regular phone lines, and has been around since the 1940s. These days it is digital at the switching office and some central offices, but there remain analog lines to the home.

➤ **Satellite.** This is another way of connecting to the Internet. It uses a parabolic antenna (satellite dish) to connect via line-of-sight data communications to a satellite, which is in geosynchronous orbit 22,000 miles above the earth. The dish connects to coax cable, which runs to a switching/channeling device for your computer. One of the issues with satellite is electrical and natural interference. Another problem is latency. Due to the distance (44,000 miles total) of the data transfer, there can be a delay of 0.5 to five seconds. In addition, you may need to install an analog line for uploads, limiting you to 28,800bps.

➤ **Wireless.** This RF-based service provides access to Internet e-mail and the World Wide Web. Radio waves are employed at places known as Wi-Fi hot spots. This is now being offered in some cities for a monthly charge by ISPs.

What Did I Just Learn?

In this lab you learned how to do the following:

➤ Identify, set up, purchase, and configure X.25 and frame relay.

➤ Define WAN technologies such as T-1, OCx, FDDI, and ISDN.

➤ Identify and define Internet access methods such as broadband cable, DSL, satellite, wireless, and PSTN.

Lab 10: Setting Up a VPN

Orientation

In this lab you will accomplish the following:

➤ Configure a VPN connection from client to server.

➤ Use encryption modes PPTP and L2TP.

➤ Discover the function of various remote access protocols.

➤ Prepare for the Network+ subdomains 2.16, 2.17, and 2.18.

Procedure

For some time, people have had the need to connect to the office LAN from remote locations—for example, home, on the road, and so on. The problem was always speed, security, and ease of use. Virtual private networking (VPN) combats all these issues. When you are at work, you log on to the LAN. The VPN connection makes it look exactly the same when you are outside the office—hence the "virtual" in its name. You can use a VPN connection over dial-up, cable, DSL, you name it! It is very flexible and uses the power of your ISP for its speed and direct connection via IP. In this lab you will set up a mock VPN connection from PC1 to PC2.

1. On the Windows 2000 domain controller do the following:

   a. Make sure that TCP/IP is the only protocol running on the domain controller.

   b. Disable RRAS if it is still running as a network router.

      i. In the RRAS console, right-click the server name and select Disable Routing and Remote Access.

   c. Open your MMC and add the RRAS (Routing and Remote Access) snap-in, or just access it from the administrative tools.

   d. Right-click Server Status and choose the This Computer option button. The server's name should appear with a red arrow pointing down. If it does not, click the + sign next to the server.

   e. Right-click the server's name and choose Configure and Enable Routing and Remote Access.

   f. Select the third option, VPN Server and click Next.

   g. Select the default protocol, which should be TCP/IP, and select the Yes, all of the available protocols are on this list option button. Then click Next.

   h. Because we are simulating this in a lab environment and there is no real multi-homed and routable connection as of yet, select the No Internet Connection option. Then click Next. In the real world, you would select the network card or device that connects directly to the Internet.

i. (Optional)Select the LAN card (10.x.x.x network) for VPN addressing *if it asks*.

j. In the IP address assignment screen, choose Have IP given to clients automatically and click Next.

k. In the next screen you will be asked about managing multiple remote access servers, Do not opt to use RADIUS, because you have only one RRAS server running currently. Instead, select the No I don't want to set up this server to use radius now option button.

l. The next screen is the Completion of the RRAS wizard screen. Click Finish to exit the setup.

2. Give rights to give end users in your domain the ability to dial in or VPN into the server. The administrator (on the domain) should automatically connect, but any other users you may have created will not have this right by default. You should check the administrator account just in case it has been modified in any way during the course these labs.

a. Open the MMC and select Active Directory Users and Computers. If this snap-in is not already there, add it or just connect to the console from the administrative tools.

b. Right-click the user who needs to VPN in and select Properties.

c. Select the Dial-in tab and click the Allow Access option button to select it, as shown in Figure 2.68. This user will now have the ability to remotely connect to the server by direct dial-in or VPN.

3. On the Windows 2000 Professional Clients, do the following:

a. Right-click My Network Places and choose Properties.

b. Double-click Make New Connection.

c. After the wizard starts, click the Connect to a private network through the Internet option button, as shown in Figure 2.69. Click Next.

d. Enter the IP address of your VPN server.

e. Select the For all users option button.

f. Name the VPN connection and click Finish.

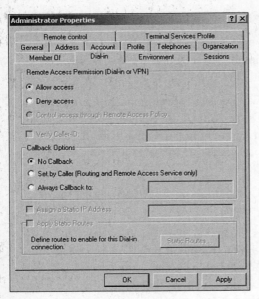

Figure 2.68 Applying remote access permissions to users.

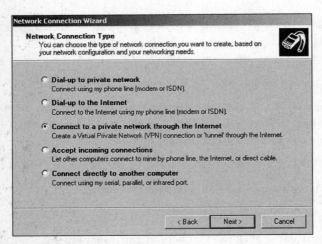

Figure 2.69 Adding a VPN adapter.

4. You should now see the login for the VPN connection. If not, double-click the VPN connection in the Network and Dial-Up Connections window.

5. Use your user name and password to access the VPN server and the domain.

6. Notice the additional network connection in your system tray on the bottom right. Now you can connect to the network just as if you were on the LAN. Go ahead and map drives and do whatever else you would normally do!

> If you get an error, such as error 691, check the user's VPN rights on the server. If you get other errors such as 721 or 768, it could be a protocol issue. Check to make sure you are entering the correct IP address. For information about an error, visit Microsoft's site and type in the error or run a search. An example of one of these search results is at the following URL: http://support.microsoft.com/default.aspx?scid=kb;en-us;318009.

Let's cover a few other remote access protocols:

- ➤ **Remote Access Service (RAS).** This service runs on a server, allowing people to connect remotely either by IP or by dialing in.

- ➤ **Point to Point Protocol (PPP).** This protocol is used for dial-up connections and for VPN connections. It allows multiple links and uses encrypted passwords.

- ➤ **Serial Line Internet Protocol (SLIP).** This mostly obsolete encapsulation of the Internet Protocol is designed to work over serial ports and modem connections.

- ➤ **Point-to-Point Protocol over Ethernet (PPPoE).** Used often with DSL, PPPoE is a specification for connecting multiple computer users on an Ethernet local area network to a remote site through common customer-premises equipment.

- ➤ **Point to Point Tunneling Protocol (PPTP).** This protocol creates the path (tunnels through the Internet) and encrypts the data in a VPN session.

- ➤ **Virtual Private Network (VPN).** This is a network that comprises the LAN and remote users who connect to the LAN via the Internet. It is secure and quick.

- ➤ **Remote Desktop Protocol (RDP).** The Remote Desktop Protocol (RDP 4.0) was introduced with Windows NT Server 4.0, Terminal Server Edition. Windows 2000 Terminal Services included enhanced RDP 5.0. It is assigned port 3389.

- ➤ **Internet Protocol Security (IPSec).** This is a set of protocols developed by the Internet Engineering Task Force (IETF) to support secure exchange of packets at the IPv6 layer. IT is also used in IPv4.

➤ **Layer 2 Tunneling Protocol (L2TP).** Developed by the IETF, this protocol is based on IPSec and combines Microsoft PPTP and Cisco Systems L2F tunneling protocols.

➤ **Secure Sockets Layer (SSL).** SSL uses port 443, and allows for secure 128-bit encrypted data session on the Web. It is commonly referred to as HTTPS.

➤ **Wired Equivalent Privacy (WEP).** WEP is a security system that uses a series of keys on both sides of a wireless transmission to encrypt data for secure transmission. An 802.11 security protocol for wireless networks, the WEP encryption method is designed to provide the equivalent security available in wire line networks.

➤ **Wi-Fi Protected Access (WPA).** WPA uses 802.11i, 802.1x, and EAP standards to enhance WEP, allowing for dynamic key assignment, stronger encryption, insurance that keys are not repeated, and the equivalent of a message hash to ensure data integrity.

➤ **Challenge Handshake Authentication Protocol (CHAP).** CHAP is an authentication system that uses an encryption scheme to secure authentication responses. CHAP is a commonly used protocol. As its full name suggests, anyone trying to connect is challenged for authentication information. When the correct information is supplied, the systems "shake hands," and the connection is established.

➤ **Microsoft Challenge Handshake Authentication Protocol (MS-CHAP).** Based on CHAP, MS-CHAP was developed to authenticate remote Windows-based workstations. There are two versions of MS-CHAP; the main difference between the two is that MS-CHAP version 2 offers mutual authentication. That means both the client and the server must prove their identities in the authentication process. Doing so ensures that the client is connecting to the expected server.

➤ **Password Authentication Protocol (PAP).** PAP is the least secure of the authentication methods because it uses unencrypted passwords. PAP is often not the first choice of protocols used; rather, it is used when more sophisticated types of authentication fail between a server and a workstation.

➤ **Extensible Authentication Protocol (EAP).** EAP is an extension for standard PPP, offering additional support for a variety of authentication schemes. It is often used with VPNs to add security against brute-force or dictionary attacks.

➤ **Shiva Password Authentication Protocol (SPAP).** SPAP is an encrypting authentication protocol used by Shiva remote access servers. SPAP offers a higher level of security than other authentication protocols such as PAP, but it is not as secure as CHAP.

Well, that pretty much does it for this lab, and for the chapter. Be sure to answer the practice questions at the end of the chapter before moving on.

What Did I Just Learn?

In this lab you learned how to create a functional VPN. You we also educated on the various remote access protocols, authentication methods, and encryption technologies. Specifically, you learned how to:

➤ Configure a VPN server with RRAS.

➤ Install a VPN adapter on the Windows 2000 platform.

➤ Connect to a working domain through VPN.

➤ Identify the most common encryption methods.

➤ Define the various authentication protocols.

➤ Prepare for the Network+ subdomains 2.16, 2.17, and 2.18.

Domain 2 Practice Questions

Lab 1: Upgrading to a Client/Server Domain

1. Which command allows you to promote a member server to a domain controller?
   - ❑ a. **ipconfig**
   - ❑ b. **ping**
   - ❑ c. **dcpromo**
   - ❑ d. **dcdemo**

2. In Windows 2000 Professional, what action would you take to access the DNS server setting?
   - ❑ a. Click the Start button, choose Run, type **CMD**, and then type **ipconfig** at the command line.
   - ❑ b. Right-click My Computer, choose Properties, and select Network Identification.
   - ❑ c. Right-click Internet Explorer and select Internet Protocol.
   - ❑ d. Right-click My Network Places, choose Properties, right-click the local area connection, choose Properties, and double-click Internet Protocol.

3. In Windows 2000 Professional, what action would you take to access the setting where you can change the network you log on to?
   - ❑ a. Right-click My Computer, choose Properties, and select Network Identification.
   - ❑ b. Right-click Internet Explorer and select Internet Protocol.
   - ❑ c. Right-click My Network Places, choose Properties, right-click the local area connection, choose Properties, and double-click Internet Protocol.
   - ❑ d. Click the Start button, choose Run, type **CMD**, and then type **ipconfig** at the command line.

4. In Windows 2000 Professional, when connecting to a domain, what setting do you have to configure prior to joining the domain?
   - ❑ a. ARP
   - ❑ b. WINS
   - ❑ c. Gateway
   - ❑ d. DNS

5. Which folder on the Windows 2000 CD holds all the network component information?
   - ❑ a. Bootdisk
   - ❑ b. Valueadd
   - ❑ c. I386
   - ❑ d. DOS

Objectives 2.1, 2.2, and 2.3

2.1 Identify a MAC (Media Access Control) address and its parts.

2.2 Identify the seven layers of the OSI (Open Systems Interconnect) model and their functions.

2.3 Identify the OSI (Open Systems Interconnect) layers at which the following network components operate: Hubs, Switches, Bridges, Routers, NICs (Network Interface Card), WAPs (Wireless Access Point).

1. Which command allows you to view your physical address?
   - ❏ a. **mac**
   - ❏ b. **ping**
   - ❏ c. **ipconfig**
   - ❏ d. **ipconfig/all**

2. The MAC sublayer is part of what OSI layer?
   - ❏ a. Network
   - ❏ b. Data link
   - ❏ c. Transport
   - ❏ d. Application

3. A bridge will operate at which layer of the OSI?
   - ❏ a. Network
   - ❏ b. Session
   - ❏ c. Transport
   - ❏ d. Data link

4. Which of these works on the Network layer?
   - ❏ a. TCP message
   - ❏ b. HTTP protocol
   - ❏ c. IP packet
   - ❏ d. Ethernet frame

5. A gateway resides on which layer of the OSI?
   - ❏ a. Application
   - ❏ b. Session
   - ❏ c. Presentation
   - ❏ d. Network

Objective 2.4

Differentiate between the following network protocols in terms of routing, addressing schemes, interoperability and naming conventions: IPX / SPX (Internetwork Packet Exchange / Sequence Packet Exchange), NetBEUI (Network Basic Input / Output System Extended User Interface), AppleTalk / AppleTalk over IP (Internet Protocol)and TCP / IP (Transmission Control Protocol / Internet Protocol).

1. On which layer of the OSI does FTP operate?
   - ❑ a. Application
   - ❑ b. Network
   - ❑ c. Transport
   - ❑ d. Data link

2. Which one of these protocols is not routable?
   - ❑ a. TCP/IP
   - ❑ b. IPX
   - ❑ c. NetBEUI
   - ❑ d. OSI

3. Where do you go to modify the binding order?
   - ❑ a. Control Panel
   - ❑ b. My Computer->System window
   - ❑ c. Advanced Settings in the Network window
   - ❑ d. Advanced Settings in Remote Assistance

4. On which layer does IPX reside?
   - ❑ a. Data link
   - ❑ b. Network
   - ❑ c. Physical
   - ❑ d. Application

5. On which layer of the OSI does HTTP operate?
   - ❑ a. Data Link
   - ❑ b. Network
   - ❑ c. Application
   - ❑ d. Transport

Objectives 2.5 and 2.6

2.5 Identify the components and structure of IP (Internet Protocol) addresses (IPv4, IPv6) and the required setting for connections across the Internet.

2.6 Identify classful IP (Internet Protocol) ranges and their subnet masks (For example: Class A, B and C).

1. What is the total number of hosts you can have on a Class C network?
   - ❑ a. 256
   - ❑ b. 65536
   - ❑ c. 254
   - ❑ d. 16,777,214

2. What is the structure of IPv6?
   - ❑ a. It's 32 bit.
   - ❑ b. It's 48 bit.
   - ❑ c. It's 256 bit.
   - ❑ d. It's 128 bit.

3. What is the binary equivalent of the Class B range?
   - ❑ a. 00000000–11111111
   - ❑ b. 10000000–10111111
   - ❑ c. 10101010–01010101
   - ❑ d. 10111111–10000000

4. Which of these is an example of a Class B network?
   - ❑ a. 172.16.0.0
   - ❑ b. 192.168.1.0
   - ❑ c. 10.0.0.0
   - ❑ d. 223.254.128.0

5. The network 65.0.0.0 is within which IP class?
   - ❑ a. Class C
   - ❑ b Class D
   - ❑ c. Class B
   - ❑ d. Class A

Objectives 2.7, 2.8, and 2.9

2.7 Identify the purpose of subnetting.

2.8 Identify the differences between private and public network addressing schemes.

2.9 Identify and differentiate between the following IP (Internet Protocol) addressing methods: Static, Dynamic, Self-assigned (APIPA (Automatic Private Internet Protocol Addressing)).

1. What is the Class A private network number?
   - ❏ a. 10
   - ❏ b. 15
   - ❏ c. 11
   - ❏ d. 169

2. What technology is functioning if you see an IP address on the 169.254 network?
   - ❏ a. Public networking
   - ❏ b. DHCP
   - ❏ c. Private networking
   - ❏ d. APIPA

3. Which of these are valid public IP addresses? (Select two.)
   - ❏ a. 65.88.154.25
   - ❏ b. 10.2.5.8
   - ❏ c. 207.128.210.255
   - ❏ d. 207.128.210.128

4. On the 255.255.255.240 subnet mask, how many hosts per subnetwork can you have?
   - ❏ a. 16
   - ❏ b. 14
   - ❏ c. 12
   - ❏ d. 240

5. Which of these is a valid private IP address?
   - ❏ a. 192.168.1.258
   - ❏ b. 207.325.111.022
   - ❏ c. 172.16.25.0
   - ❏ d. 192.168.1.25

Objectives 2.10, 2.11, and 2.12

2.10 Define the purpose, function and use of the following protocols used in the TCP / IP (Transmission Control Protocol / Internet Protocol) suite: TCP (Transmission Control Protocol), UDP (User Datagram Protocol), FTP (File Transfer Protocol), SFTP (Secure File Transfer Protocol), TFTP (Trivial File Transfer Protocol), SMTP (Simple Mail Transfer Protocol), HTTP (Hypertext Transfer Protocol), HTTPS (Hypertext Transfer Protocol Secure), POP3 / IMAP4 (Post Office Protocol version 3 / Internet Message Access Protocol version 4), Telnet, SSH (Secure Shell), ICMP (Internet Control Message Protocol), ARP / RARP (Address Resolution Protocol / Reverse Address Resolution Protocol), NTP (Network Time Protocol), NNTP (Network News Transport Protocol), SCP (Secure Copy Protocol), LDAP (Lightweight Directory Access Protocol), IGMP (Internet Group Multicast Protocol), LPR (Line Printer Remote).

2.11 Define the function of TCP / UDP (Transmission Control Protocol / User Datagram Protocol) ports.

2.12 Identify the well-known ports associated with the following commonly used services and protocols: 20 FTP (File Transfer Protocol), 21 FTP (File Transfer Protocol), 22 SSH (Secure Shell), 23 Telnet, 25 SMTP (Simple Mail Transfer Protocol), 53 DNS (Domain Name Service), 69 TFTP (Trivial File Transfer Protocol), 80 HTTP (Hypertext Transfer Protocol), 110 POP3 (Post Office Protocol version 3), 119 NNTP (Network News Transport Protocol), 123 NTP (Network Time Protocol), 143 IMAP4 (Internet Message Access Protocol version 4), 443 HTTPS (Hypertext Transfer Protocol Secure).

1. On which layer of the OSI does TCP reside?
   - ❏ a. Network
   - ❏ b. Transport
   - ❏ c. Application
   - ❏ d. Data link
2. Which port number does the Telnet service use?
   - ❏ a. 21
   - ❏ b. 32
   - ❏ c. 23
   - ❏ d. 25

3. Which syntax will synchronize network time to the computer named PC2?
   - ❑ a. Net time \\PC2
   - ❑ b. Net time /set \\PC2
   - ❑ c. Net time w32tm
   - ❑ d. Net time /Setsntp:PC2

4. On which layer of the OSI does POP3 reside?
   - ❑ a. Application
   - ❑ b. Network
   - ❑ c. Transport
   - ❑ d. Physical

5. Which commands will show the IP-to-MAC conversion? (Select two.)
   - ❑ a. **arp −a**
   - ❑ b. **arp −f**
   - ❑ c. **arp −g**
   - ❑ d. **arp −inet_addr**

Objective 2.13

2.13 Identify the purpose of network services and protocols (For example: DNS (Domain Name Service), NAT (Network Address Translation), ICS (Internet Connection Sharing), WINS (Windows Internet Name Service), SNMP (Simple Network Management Protocol), NFS (Network File System), Zeroconf (Zero configuration), SMB (Server Message Block), AFP (Apple File Protocol), LPD (Line Printer Daemon) and Samba).

1. What type of name is PC4.testlab.com?
   - ❑ a. A domain name
   - ❑ b. A hostname
   - ❑ c. An FQDN
   - ❑ d. A MAC address

2. Which service will convert between NetBIOS names and IP addresses?
   - ❑ a. DNS
   - ❑ b. WINS
   - ❑ c. ARP
   - ❑ d. Gateway

3. Which of these are normally examples of multi-homed computers? (Select two.)

- ❑ a. Router
- ❑ b. WINS server
- ❑ c. DNS server
- ❑ d. NAT/IP proxy server

4. What flat file did DNS replace?

- ❑ a. LMHOSTS.TXT
- ❑ b. HOSTS.TXT
- ❑ c. LManager.file
- ❑ d. ZeroConf

5. Which service allows you to share an Internet connection among multiple computers?

- ❑ a. DNS
- ❑ b. WINS
- ❑ c. ICS
- ❑ d. VPN

Objectives 2.14 and 2.15

2.14 Identify the basic characteristics (For example: speed, capacity and media) of the following WAN (Wide Area Networks) technologies: Packet switching, Circuit switching, ISDN (Integrated Services Digital Network), FDDI (Fiber Distributed Data Interface), T1 (T Carrier level 1) / E1 / J1, T3 (T Carrier level 3) / E3 / J3, OCx (optical carrier), X.25.

2.15 Identify the basic characteristics of the following internet access technologies: xDSL (digital subscriber line), broadband cable (cable modem), POTS / PSTN (Plain Old Telephone Service / Public Switched Telephone Network), satellite, wireless.

1. How many channels does a T-1 have?

- ❑ a. 24
- ❑ b. 28
- ❑ c. 128
- ❑ d. 64

2. What is the data throughput of a T-1 line?

- ❑ a. 1.536Kbps
- ❑ b. 128Kbps
- ❑ c. 1.536Mbps
- ❑ d. 45Mbps

3. Frame relay can reach what maximum speed to the consumer?
   - ❑ a. 622Mbps
   - ❑ b. 1.5Mbps
   - ❑ c. 1.2Mbps
   - ❑ d. 200Mbps

4. X.25 packets normally hold how much data?
   - ❑ a. 64 bytes
   - ❑ b. 1,024 bytes
   - ❑ c. 128MB
   - ❑ d. 128 bytes

5. OC-12 runs at what speed?
   - ❑ a. 622 Mbps
   - ❑ b. 155 Mbps
   - ❑ c. 1.536 Mbps
   - ❑ d. 3 Gbps

Objectives 2.16, 2.17, and 2.18

2.16 Define the function of the following remote access protocols and services: RAS (Remote Access Service), PPP (Point-to-Point Protocol), SLIP (Serial Line Internet Protocol), PPPoE (Point-to-Point Protocol over Ethernet), PPTP (Point-to-Point Tunneling Protocol), VPN (Virtual Private Network), RDP (Remote Desktop Protocol).

2.17 Identify the following security protocols and describe their purpose and function: IPSec (Internet Protocol Security), L2TP (Layer 2 Tunneling Protocol), SSL (Secure Sockets Layer), WEP (Wired Equivalent Privacy), WPA (Wi-Fi Protected Access), 802.1x.

2.18 Identify authentication protocols (For example: CHAP (Challenge Handshake Authentication Protocol), MS-CHAP (Microsoft Challenge Handshake Authentication Protocol), PAP (Password Authentication Protocol), RADIUS (Remote Authentication Dial-In User Service), Kerberos and EAP (Extensible Authentication Protocol)).

1. Which protocol will secure HTTP sessions with 128-bit encryption?
   - ❑ a. SSL
   - ❑ b. SSH
   - ❑ c. SCP
   - ❑ d. FTP

2. Port 3389 is used for sessions in programs like Remote Desktop in Windows XP. What is this protocol?

- ❑ a. PPTP
- ❑ b. VPN
- ❑ c. RDP
- ❑ d. PPP

3. Which console do you go to configure a VPN server?

- ❑ a. Active Directory Server
- ❑ b. Active Directory Users and Computers
- ❑ c. RAS
- ❑ d. RRAS

4. Which protocol is used by default when connecting to a VPN server?

- ❑ a. PPTP
- ❑ b. L2TP
- ❑ c. L2F
- ❑ d. IPSec

5. Which port is used by L2TP?

- ❑ a. 1723
- ❑ b. 1701
- ❑ c. 3389
- ❑ d. 4362

Answers and Explanations

Lab 1: Upgrading to a Client/Server Domain

1. Answer c is correct. dcpromo stands for Domain Controller Promotion. ipconfig shows your NIC card's IP settings, ping allows you to test your IP connection to other hosts, and dcdemo is not a command at all.

2. Answer d is correct. The Internet Protocol (TCP/IP) Properties dialog box is the final destination that you are looking for. This can only be accessed from the Local Area Connection Properties dialog box.

3. Answer a is correct. You need to access the Network Identification tab of the System Properties dialog box to modify what network you are connected to.

4. Answer d is correct. DNS is all-important when connecting to a domain because of the integration of Internet technologies to Windows 2000 Server domains. ARP is the Address Resolution Protocol, which resolves between MAC addresses and IP addresses. WINS deals with conversions between NetBIOS names and IP addresses. The gateway is the device that allows you access to the Internet or will convert between protocols and platforms. These other technologies will be covered later in this manual.

5. Answer c is correct. The i386 folder is where you go to add any networking components. Other folders like Bootdisk may have information for floppy disks, but they do not have networking information.

Objective 2.1, 2.2 and 2.3

1. Answer d is correct. ipconfig/all gives you detailed information about the NIC card. ipconfig only gives you the IP address, subnet mask, and gateway. ping tests connectivity to other computers, and MAC is the media access control sublayer of the DLL.

2. Answer b is correct. The Data Link layer is where the MAC and the LLC sublayers reside.

3. Answer d is correct. A bridge deals with MAC addresses and therefore belongs on the data link layer.

4. Answer c is correct. IP packets deal with logical network addressing and they are therefore on the network layer. TCP messages reside on

the transport layer, HTTP is on the application layer, and Ethernet frames reside on the data link layer.

5. Answer a is correct. Remember that a true gateway will convert between various platforms and/or protocols. This happens on the application layer because it requires the use of a computer with a logical operating system. Ignore the fact that many techs (and even OSes) refer to a router as a "gateway."

Objective 2.4

1. Answer a is correct. Because the FTP protocol is directly linked to the application known as FTP and works behind the scenes, it is an application layer protocol.

2. Answer c is correct. NetBEUI is not routable, whereas all other protocol suites are.

3. Answer c is correct. You need to access the Advanced Settings area in the Network and Dial-up Connections window to modify bindings.

4. Answer b is correct. IPX resides on the NETWORK (and Transport) layers. It is responsible for logical network addressing, which always happens on the Network layer.

5. Answer c is correct. HTTP, or HyperText Transfer Protocol, resides on the Application layer. All other answers are incorrect.

Objectives 2.5 and 2.6

1. Answer c is correct. Don't forget that you are not permitted to use the first and last IP addresses. 0 is reserved for the network number and 255 is reserved for broadcasting.

2. Answer d is correct. 32 bit is the structure of IP version 4, 48 bit is an older type of encryption structure, and 256 bit is used by very few technologies (PCI Express would be one).

3. Answer b is correct. The decimal range is 128–191. In binary, that would be `10000000–10111111`.

4. Answer a is correct. Remember that when referring to a network, you leave a zero(s) on the end where the host portion would normally go. 192 is Class C, 10 is Class A, and 223 would also be Class C.

5. Answer d is correct. The Class A range goes from 1 to 126, so the 65 network is going to be within that range. Remember that 127 is mathematically part of Class A but isn't really considered as part of Class A because it is reserved for local loopback testing.

Objectives 2.7, 2.8, and 2.9

1. Answer a is correct. 10 is the private Class A network assigned for your internal use.

2. Answer d is correct. Remember that APIPA (169.254) is not really DHCP. It self-assigns, but is not dynamic and does not invoke the DHCP protocol.

3. Answers a and d are correct. Answer b is private and answer c is not a valid IP address. The last octet cannot be 255, because that is the broadcast number for that Class C network.

4. Answer b is correct. Remember that you can't use the first and last, so instead of 16, it is 14.

5. Answer d is correct. 192.168.1.25 is a valid Class C private IP address.

Objectives 2.10, 2.11, and 2.12

1. Answer b is correct. TCP takes care of the transporting of data over the communications subnetwork. It also takes care of sequencing and guaranteeing delivery.

2. Answer c is correct. Port 23 is used by the Telnet service.

3. Answer b is correct. You need to type the command followed by the parameter /set and the UNC of the computer, in this case \\PC2.

4. Answer a is correct. POP3 is for receiving mail and works just behind the scenes of your e-mail client. Because of this, it is considered an application layer protocol.

5. Answers a and c are correct. -a and -g are the switches or parameters that you will use to show the recent sessions and their resolved IP-to-MAC entries.

Objective 2.13

1. Answer c is correct. An FQDN is a Fully Qualified Domain Name. This is the combination of a domain name like testlab.com and a host-name like PC4.

2. Answer b is correct. WINS converts between NetBIOS names and IP addresses. DNS resolved between host names and IP, ARP resolves between IP and MAC addresses, and the gateway allows the entire LAN access to the Internet.

3. Answers a and d are correct. A DNS server and a WINS server do not need more than one NIC in most instances because they are part of the LAN (or DMZ) only.

4. Answer b is correct. HOSTS.TXT was the flat file that had to be manually added to each machine and statically configured. DNS did away with this, and we are grateful! LMHOSTS.TXT was replaced by WINS.

5. Answer c is correct. ICS, or Internet Connection Sharing, allows you to share a NIC or modem so that multiple computers on your LAN can access the Internet without the need of a SOHO router.

Objectives 2.14 and 2.15

1. Answer a is correct. There are 24 channels in a T-1. Each are equal to 64 Kbps.

2. Answer c is correct. A T-1 line can carry 1.536 Mbps of data maximum.

3. Answer b is correct. Frame Relay to the consumer can be run at a maximum speed of 1.5Mbps. This means that you would need a T-1 to carry the technology.

4. Answer d is correct. Although there are versions of X.25 where you can have 512 bytes of data per packet, you will normally see 128 bytes of data.

5. Answer a is correct. OC-12 runs at 622Mbps and needs fiber to make the technology work.

Objectives 2.16, 2.17, and 2.18

1. Answer a is correct. Secure Sockets Layer will encrypt data sessions on the Web and show up as HTTPS. It uses port 443 and is a 128-bit encrypted technology.

2. Answer c is correct. RDP is the Remote Desktop Protocol and is used in Remote Desktop/Remote Assistance, Terminal Services and other remote-control programs.

3. Answer d is correct. RRAS, short for Routing and Remote Access, is the console window you need to access to set up VPN servers.

4. Answer a is correct. PPTP, short for Point to Point Tunneling Protocol, is what we use by default to connect to a VPN server or VPN concentrator. It uses port 1723.

5. Answer b is correct. L2TP uses port 1701. Port 1723 is used by PPTP, port 3389 is used by RDP, and port 4362 is used by the third-party instant messaging program known as ICQ.

Network Implementation

This chapter builds on your previous learning, and shows how to implement the network technologies and concepts from Chapter 1, "Media and Topologies," and Chapter 2, "Protocols and Standards." You will work with rights and permissions, physical layer implementations, TCP/IP configurations, operating system interoperability, firewalls and anti-virus software, fault tolerance, and backup. There are eight labs in total in this chapter, so let's get started.

Domain 3: Network Implementation

The following is a list of the exam objectives covered in this chapter:

➤ 3.1 Identify the basic capabilities (For example: client support, interoperability, authentication, file and print services, application support and security) of the following server operating systems to access network resources: UNIX / Linux / Mac OS X Server, Netware, Windows, Appleshare IP (Internet Protocol).

➤ 3.2 Identify the basic capabilities needed for client workstations to connect to and use network resources (For example: media, network protocols and peer and server services).

➤ 3.3 Identify the appropriate tool for a given wiring task (For example: wire crimper, media tester / certifier, punch down tool or tone generator).

➤ 3.4 Given a remote connectivity scenario comprised of a protocol, an authentication scheme, and physical connectivity, configure the connection. Includes connection to the following servers: UNIX / Linux / MAC OS X Server, Netware, Windows, Appleshare IP (Internet Protocol).

➤ 3.5 Identify the purpose, benefits and characteristics of using a firewall.

➤ 3.6 Identify the purpose, benefits and characteristics of using a proxy service.

➤ 3.7 Given a connectivity scenario, determine the impact on network functionality of a particular security implementation (For example: port blocking / filtering, authentication and encryption).

➤ 3.8 Identify the main characteristics of VLANs (Virtual Local Area Networks).

➤ 3.9 Identify the main characteristics and purpose of extranets and intranets.

➤ 3.10 Identify the purpose, benefits and characteristics of using antivirus software.

➤ 3.11 Identify the purpose and characteristics of fault tolerance: Power, Link redundancy, Storage, Services.

➤ 3.12 Identify the purpose and characteristics of disaster recovery: Backup / restore, Offsite storage, Hot and cold spares, Hot, warm and cold sites.

What You Will Need

The following is a list of the components and their minimum recommended requirements that you will need for the Chapter 3 labs.

➤ A PII 266MHz PC with 64MB RAM, 2GB HDD, CD-ROM, and network interface card (installed with Windows 2000 Professional). This will be known as PC1.

➤ A PII 266MHz PC with 128MB RAM, 2GB HDD, CD-ROM, and network interface card (installed with Windows 2000 Professional or Server). This will be known as PC2.

➤ A four-port wireless/wired router with built-in firewall.

➤ A Wireless NIC.

➤ Access to Windows 2000 Professional software.

➤ Access to Windows 2000 Server software.

➤ Access to the Internet.

➤ (Optional) A two- or four-port KVM switch.

For these labs, we will be referring to the following:

➤ Compaq Deskpro PIII 533MHz computers with 256MB RAM and 3Com 3C905 XL 10/100 PCI TX network interface cards. (These cards will automatically be recognized by Windows 2000 during the OS install.)

➤ Linksys wireless router model WRT54G.

➤ Linksys PCI Wireless NIC: model WMP54G.

➤ Belkin four-port KVM switch bundled with cables, PS/2, part #F1DJ104P.

➤ Cable Internet access.

Lab 1: Active Directory Structure and Permissions

Orientation

In this procedure you will accomplish the following:

➤ Add users and groups as well as organizational units.

➤ Assign permissions to user accounts.

➤ Identify basic client support and interoperability of different platforms.

➤ Prepare for the Network+ subdomain 3.1

Procedure

Now that you have a working domain and have practiced with some of the technologies inherent to client/server networks, it is now time to implement some of the user administration involved in today's Microsoft domains. In the following lab you will add a new administrator account on the domain controller, create additional users and groups, configure permissions, and compartmentalize the network's structure.

1. Create a second administrator account.

   a. Go to PC2 (Windows 2000 Server).

   b. Click the Start button, choose Programs, select Administrative Tools, and choose Active Directory Users and Computers to open the Active Directory Users and Computers console window.

   c. In the left pane, right-click the Users entry, select New, and then select User, as shown in Figure 3.1.

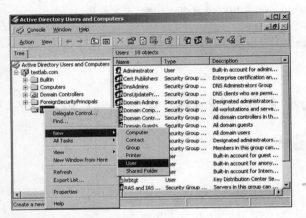

Figure 3.1 Creating a new user.

   d. In the New Object – User screen, type the following (see Figure 3.2):

     i. First name: John

     ii. Last name: Smith

     iii. Full name: John Smith (this should be entered automatically)

     iv. User logon name: john_smith Remember to put an underscore between john and smith, as illustrated in Figure 3.2.

   e. Click Next.

   f. Type a password that you will remember and then type it a second time to confirm it. Notice on this screen the additional options for passwords and the ability to disable the account as you see fit.

   g. Click Next.

   h. View the summarized information, and then click Finish. The new user should be listed at the bottom of your objects list, as shown in Figure 3.3.

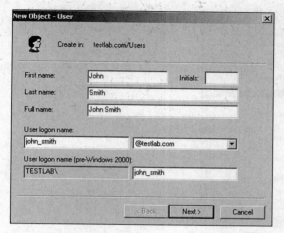

Figure 3.2 Details of the new user.

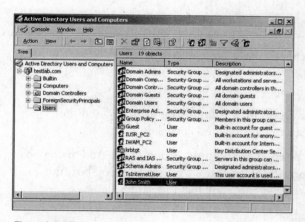

Figure 3.3 The new user.

2. By default, users are given restricted rights, and are only known as a *domain user*. To make this person an administrator, add him to the administrators group.

   a. Right-click the new user, John Smith.

   b. Select Properties.

   c. In John Smith's Properties dialog box, click the Member Of tab, as shown in Figure 3.4.

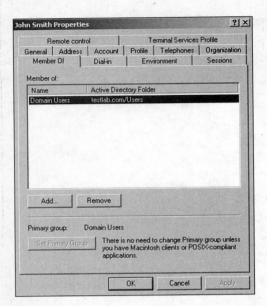

Figure 3.4 Member Of tab in the new user account's Properties dialog box.

d. Click the Add button.

e. In the new window select the Administrators group and the Domain Administrators group, and click Add.

f. Both groups are listed in the bottom section of the Add dialog box. Click OK to return to John Smith's Properties dialog box; the resulting information should look like Figure 3.5.

3. Set the primary group.

a. Click the Domain Admins entry and, in the bottom of the Properties dialog box, click the Set Primary Group button.

b. Click OK. You now have another account with which you can administer the domain.

c. Press Ctrl+Alt+Del.

4. Verify that you can log on as the new user, john_smith. Don't forget your new password for this account. When you're finished, log off the new account and log back on as administrator.

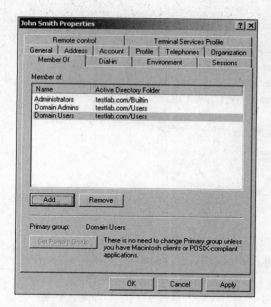

Figure 3.5   Member Of tab re-visited

 Normally, in the field, you would now rename the administrator account and give it a complex password. Then, you would use the new domain admin account only. The original administrator account would sit in the wings as a backup in the event your new account fails. The main reason you do this is for fault tolerance, but also because the administrator account has certain security flaws.

5. Create additional users and groups.

   a. Return to the Active Directory Users and Computers window.

   b. Using the same method as with the john_smith account, create a few more users for practice, calling them User1, User2, and User3. You do not need passwords for these accounts, nor do you need to change their group membership.

   c. Go to PC1 (Windows 2000 Professional).

   d. Boot the computer and log on as User1 to the testlab.com domain. (Remember to always select that network in the Log on To dropdown box.) You don't really need a password for the purposes of this lab, so click OK. Keep in mind, however, that you would normally want a password to protect your accounts.

   e. You are now logged on as a typical user with restricted rights. To prove it, right-click My Network Places and choose Properties.

f. Right-click the LAN card and select Properties.

g. Double-click Internet Protocol to open the Internet Protocol (TCP/IP) Properties dialog box. A pop-up window, shown in Figure 3.6, notifies you that you do not have sufficient privileges to access these configurations. Click OK.

Figure 3.6 Restricted user rights.

h. You may have noticed in the LAN Card's property box that the check boxes are grayed out, as are the buttons to install, uninstall, and so on. User1 doesn't have rights to configure anything on this system. User1 can save data, but that is about it. This is a security feature of Windows 2000/2003 domains.

You should know how to create users for the Network+ exam.

i. Return to PC2 and access Active Directory Users and Groups again.

j. After you have created users, you will usually want to group them. This time you will group your users together for purposes of assigning rights to multiple users at one time.

   i. Right-click Users, choose New, and select Group.

   ii. Type the name testgroup. It should look like Figure 3.7.

   iii. Click OK. If you scroll down, you should now see testgroup listed at the bottom. Notice that the icon has two heads instead of one; that signifies a group.

   iv. Add two of your test accounts to the group as members. To begin, double-click the testgroup group; the Testgroup Properties dialog box opens.

   v. Click the Members tab.

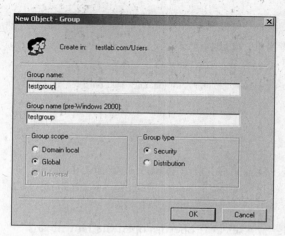

Figure 3.7   Creating a group.

    vi. Click Add.

    vii. Select User2 and User3 and click Add. The users you selected will appear in the bottom pane, as illustrated in Figure 3.8.

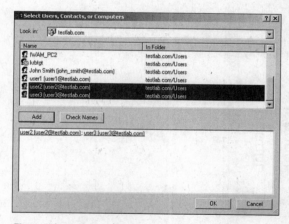

Figure 3.8   Adding members to a group.

    viii. Click OK. You will now see the users in the Members list.

    ix. Click OK to close the Testgroup Properties dialog box. You have made your group! You will apply rights to the group in just a little bit.

6. Configure permissions.

    a. Still on PC2, open Windows Explorer.

An easy way to open Windows Explorer is to right-click My Computer and select Explorer.

    b. Create a folder called Downloads and share it just as you did a while back on PC1. (Right-click it, select Sharing, select Share As in the pop-up window that appears, and click OK.)

    c. Right-click the folder and select Properties open the Downloads folder's Properties dialog box.

    d. Click the Security tab. The resulting dialog box should look like Figure 3.9.

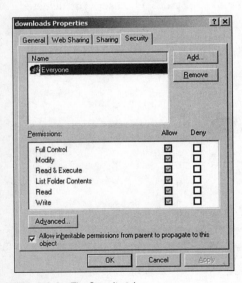

Figure 3.9 The Security tab.

    e. Click Add. The resulting dialog box contains a list of users and groups, which you can sort by their column header. For example, if you click Name, the objects will be sorted alphabetically or anti-alphabetically, depending on how many times you click.

    f. Scroll down until you find the Testgroup group. Click that group to select it and then click Add, as shown in Figure 3.10.

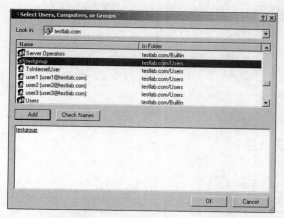

Figure 3.10   Adding a group to the permissions of Downloads.

g. Click OK. This returns you to the Security tab of the Downloads folder's Properties dialog box. Notice that the Testgroup is highlighted and that it shows a different set of permissions than the Everyone group. The Testgroup, which includes User2 and User3, has basic access to the Downloads folder, which you can customize at will.

h. Add one more set of permissions.

   i. Click Add.

   ii. Select Administrators from the list and click Add.

   iii. Click OK. The Administrators group should show up in the Security tab of the Downloads folder's Properties dialog box.

   iv. With the Administrators group selected in the top pane, click the Allow check box next to the Full Control entry in the bottom pane, as shown in Figure 3.11. Now the Administrators group has full control of the folder, and the Testgroup group has only limited control.

   v. Deselect the Allow inheritable permissions check box at the bottom of the window.

   vi. When the pop-up window appears, click Remove. This removes the Everyone group from the list.

   vii. Click OK.

   viii. Return to Windows Explorer, open the Downloads folder, and create a new text document inside it. Call the document Test.

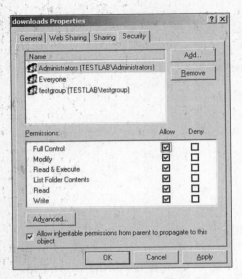

Figure 3.11 Giving full permissions to the administrators.

    ix. Switch to PC1.

    x. Log off and log back on as User2.

    xi. Access Windows Explorer.

    xii. Open Tools menu select Map Network Drive.

    xiii. In the window that appears, select drive letter F: and type the path \\192.168.1.200\downloads as shown in Figure 3.12. This will map the drive to the folder on PC2 that you just configured.

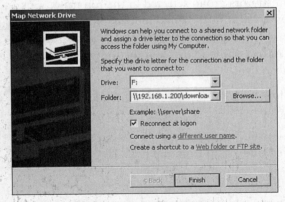

Figure 3.12 Mapping a drive to the Downloads share on PC2.

. . . .

xiv. Click Finish. This opens a new window for the mapped drive and shows the test file you created in the Downloads share.

7. Compartmentalize the network structure.

a. Return to PC2.

b. Open the Active Directory Users and Computers window.

c. In the left pane, right-click the name of your domain, `testlab.com`, select New, and select Organizational Unit, as shown in Figure 3.13.

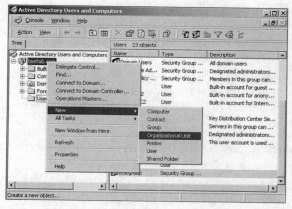

Figure 3.13 Creating an organizational unit.

d. Name the organizational unit `Marketing`.

e. Click OK. In the left pane, you should see the Marketing organizational unit listed. This entry is accompanied by the directory icon, which contains a folder with a book on it.

f. Right-click the Marketing organizational unit, select New, and select User.

g. Create a user named `User4`, just as you did before, and click OK. Notice that this user shows up in the Marketing organizational unit, as opposed to the main Users folder in the domain. This allows you to compartmentalize the user accounts, computer accounts, and groups. Normally an admin would do this by department—for example, creating organization units for customer service, accounting, marketing, and so on. You can also add policies for those specific objects in each organizational unit and have a different policy for each.

Working with Interoperability

Great work! That is some of the basic user administration you need to know for the field and for the Network+ exam. Now let's uncover a little bit on interoperability between the different platforms out there:

► **Client Services for NetWare (CSNW).** This is Microsoft software that can be installed to allow a Microsoft Windows client (for example, Windows 2000 Professional) to log in to a NetWare server, access NetWare resources and data, or both! It is installed from your NIC's Properties dialog box as an add-on component known as a client.

► **Gateway Services for NetWare (GSNW).** This is also Microsoft software, but it is an add-on to Windows 2000 Server. It allows an entire group of Windows 2000 Professional or other clients to access NetWare resources through one access point. That way, instead of the clients logging in to the Novell server, they can simply remain logged on to the Windows Server. Also, when GSNW is used, there is no need to load CSNW on every single individual client. You just load the GSNW service on the server.

► **Novell Client.** Novell makes software to allow Microsoft clients to connect to Novell NetWare resources. This software installs on the Windows client, and will automatically enable you to see any NetWare servers on the network upon login. It is free on Novell's website. Many administrators believe this to be better written software than the Microsoft client, but it will depend on your situation. The latest version is 4.91 and can be downloaded from http://download.novell.com. (You may have to search a little. If so, search for "Novell Client 4.91".) Alternatively, use the direct link at http://www.technicalblog.com in the Downloads section.

1. Connect Windows systems to Novell NetWare.

   a. Log off of PC1 and log back on as Administrator.

   b. Right-click My Network Places and select Properties.

   c. Right-click the LAN card and select Properties.

   d. Click the Install button.

   e. Choose Client, and click Add. The only client option that comes up is CSNW. We are not using this client right now so just cancel out of the windows for now.

f. On PC2, repeat steps a–c to access the LAN card's Properties dialog box.

g. Click the Install button.

h. Choose Client, and click Add.

i. You should see GSNW as the only option.

j. Cancel out of these windows.

2. Connect Windows systems to Linux. If you want Windows clients to access a Linux system, you must install Samba on the Linux system. This allows for the emulation of server message blocks, as with Microsoft systems. With this, Windows clients can map drives as they normally would. Linux uses the Line Printer Daemon for printing services. Of course, Windows clients can also connect via FTP, which is a common alternative without any other services needed.

3. Connect Windows systems to Apple and vice versa. Macintosh has developed a system known as Server Message Block/Common Internet File System (SMB/CIFS). This allows the clients on both platforms to access each other. AppleTalk Filing Protocol (AFP) can also be used on the Mac side for Mac clients to see the Windows Server resources. In addition, you can install File and Print services for Macintosh on the Windows 2000 Server.

   a. Go to PC2.

   b. Click the Start button, choose Settings, and select Control Panel.

   c. Double-click Add/Remove Programs.

   d. On the left side, click Add/Remove Windows Components.

   e. In the window that opens, scroll down to Other Network File and Print Services and click Details to view the File Services for Macintosh and Printer Services for Macintosh options.

4. Connect UNIX systems to Windows. Although both platforms are written in the C language, the two use different coding for TCP/IP and services. Therefore, you need to connect the two via a sort of gateway. You can allow clients on a UNIX network to access Windows systems by installing the proper component on the Windows Server.

   a. Go to PC2.

   b. Click the Start button, choose Settings, and select Control Panel.

   c. Double-click Add/Remove Programs.

d. On the left side, click Add/Remove Windows Components.

e. In the window that opens, scroll down to Other Network File and Print Services and click Details to view the Print Services for UNIX.

f. Cancel out of these windows for now.

For more information on interoperability of operating systems, see *Network+ Exam Cram 2, 2e.*

That's it for this lab. Let's go over what you covered.

What Did I Just Learn?

In this lab you learned how to add objects, set up permissions, create a network structure, and work with interoperability. Specifically, you learned how to do the following:

➤ Add users and groups.

➤ Create organizational units.

➤ Set permissions on resources.

➤ Configure Linux, UNIX, Apple, and Microsoft to talk to each other.

Lab 2: Services and nbtstat

Orientation

In this lab you will identify how clients connect to network resources and the main services that they use. You will cover the following:

➤ nbtstat

➤ The two main services in networking

➤ Prepare for the Network+ subdomain 3.2

Procedure

1. Identify services with nbtstat (NetBIOS over TCP/IP Statistics).

    a. Access PC1. Make sure you are logged on as Administrator to the domain. You can verify this quickly by pressing Ctrl+Alt+Del.

    b. Open the command prompt and type nbtstat /?. This should give you a list of options with the nbtstat command. These include -a for accessing by NetBIOS names and -A for accessing by IP address. Try to memorize these different switches.

    c. Type nbtstat -a pc1. This reveals information like that shown in Figure 3.14.

> You can also issue the **nbtstat –a** command for the other systems on your network including PC2. In fact, this command is usually used to diagnose remote machines on the network.

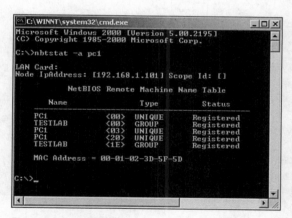

Figure 3.14   nbtstat in action.

    d. Notice the different line items. You have <00>, which is the hexadecimal ID for the Workstation service. You also have <03>, the ID for the Messenger service. Finally, you have the <20> ID for the Server service. These are the three basic services that all computers, servers and clients alike, use to transmit data across the network. There are others listed that deal with the domain. If one of the services is not listed, then you know that you will have to troubleshoot the system in question. It could have to do with what network the user logged in to, TCP/IP issues, or file corruption. Or it could be that the service is shut off. Let's take a look at the three main services from a graphical standpoint and show how they can be turned on and off.

e. Right-click My Computer and select Manage.

f. In the bottom-left area, click the plus (+) sign to expand the Services and Applications category.

g. Click the Services applet, as shown in Figure 3.15. Then select the Messenger service on the right side.

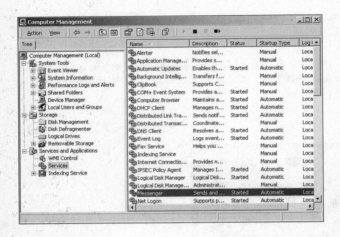

Figure 3.15 The Services window.

h. Although the Messenger service is very important to the system, it is not really considered one of the main services. This is because it is actually dependent on the Workstation service. Let's prove this now.

   i. Right-click the Messenger service and select Properties.

   ii. Click the Dependencies tab. You will see that the Messenger service is indeed dependent on the Workstation service.

   iii. Click the General tab. Notice that here you can start and stop the service as you see fit, as well as set how it will run at startup (or set it to not run at all).

   iv. Close the Properties dialog box, but leave the Computer Management window open.

i. There are several other ways to start and stop a service in the GUI and in the command prompt. For example, you can use the buttons at the top of the console window, as shown in Figure 3.16. You can also right-click the service and select Start/Stop, or you can use the net start and net stop commands in the command prompt.

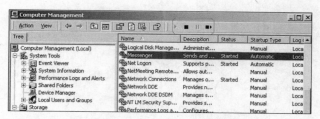

Figure 3.16   Start and stop buttons for services.

2. Identify the two main services, Server and Workstation. The Server service runs on every networked computer regardless of whether it is a client or a server. It allows the computer to share resources with other systems. The Workstation service also runs on both types of systems but does the converse, allowing your computer to access resources that have been shared on other systems.

a. You should still be in the Services section of the Computer Management console. Scroll down until you find the Server service.

b. Right-click the Server service and select Properties.

c. In the Server Properties dialog box, click the Dependencies tab, as shown in Figure 3.17. Notice that there are no services on which the Server service is dependent. That's because the Server service is considered a *foundation service*; everything else builds from it.

d. Let's take a look at the basis for this service, the srv.sys file.

i. Click the Start button, choose Search, and select Files or Folders.

ii. Search for srv.sys. Make sure to search your entire C drive. You should get results like the ones shown in Figure 3.18. That one system file is the basis for the Server service, and for all of the services that depend on it!

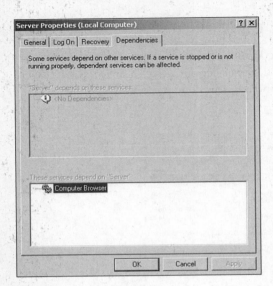

Figure 3.17 The Server service.

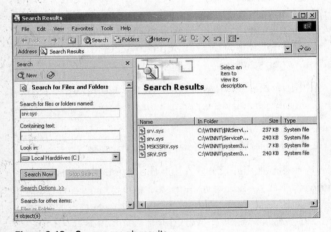

Figure 3.18 **Srv.sys** search results.

  e. Microsoft calls the other main service the Workstation service.
     This service allows your computer to connect to other systems'
     shares. However, most other platforms call it the Redirector. The
     system file that controls this service is known as nwrdr.sys. That
     stands for NetWare Redirector. Search a second time, this time for
     nwrdr.sys. You should get three results. One is the main service
     file, and the others are either backups or cache files.

  f. Return to the Computer Management window and scroll down to
     the Workstation service.

g. Right-click the Workstation service and select Properties.

h. Click the Dependencies tab. You should get results like those shown in Figure 3.19.

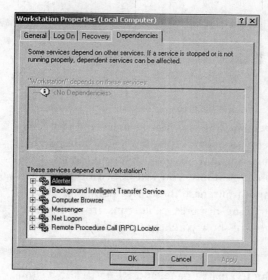

Figure 3.19 The Workstation service.

i. Notice that, like the Server service, the Workstation service is not dependent on any other services, yet many other services are dependent on it! This is often a trouble point for client computers because the Workstation service is a target of attack for malicious users, and is also easily corruptible. There are a few other reasons why this service might be stopped; what you must remember is how to check whether it's running. This is done remotely with the nbtstat command.

Services are the underlying building blocks of networking within the operating system, so you must be fluent with them. Be sure to know them for the Network+ exam.

What Did I Just Learn?

In this lab you identified how clients connect to network resources and the main services that they use. Specifically, you learned the following:

➤ How to correctly read a set of nbtstat results.

➤ The two main services in networking.

➤ How to troubleshoot services.

Lab 3: Wiring, Part II

Orientation

In Chapter 1, you examined layer 1 wiring and how to make and test a simple patch cable. I mentioned then that most of the time, you would purchase these patch cables, because doing so would save you time and money. What I did not mention was that more commonly, you will be wiring permanent layer 1 connections, and you cannot purchase these! By "permanent layer 1 connections," I am referring to long-distance cable runs from the patch panel to the RJ-45 jack. This lab will show you how to do the following:

➤ Use a punch down tool.

➤ Terminate Category 5e wiring to a patch panel and RJ-45 jack in a simulated environment.

➤ Test the connections with a continuity tester.

➤ Prepare for the Network+ subdomain 3.3.

Procedure

For this lab you will need the following additional tools:

➤ Punch down tool with 110 blade

➤ Category 5 or 5e patch panel

➤ RJ-45 jack

➤ 25 feet of Category 5 or 5e twisted pair cable

➤ Continuity tester

➤ Wire stripper

➤ Cutting tool

We are using the following:

➤ Paladin punch down tool with 110 IDC blade

➤ WiedMuller wire stripper

➤ Signamax 24 port patch panel

➤ Leviton 568B RJ-45 jack

➤ Testum continuity tester

1. Prepare your equipment.

   a. Lay your patch panel face down so you can see the colored 110 IDC clips where you will be punching down.

   b. Ready your RJ-45 jack. Have your tester at the ready as well.

   c. Cut a 6-foot length of Category 5e cable.

2. Punch down to the patch panel.

   a. Strip one of the ends with your wire stripper to expose the eight wires. Take off about two inches of the PVC jacket.

   b. Separate all eight wires as demonstrated in Chapter 1, but this time organize them in the original order, BOGB (blue pair, orange pair, green pair, brown pair). Always use the white with colored stripes first, and then the solid color for each pair. This is illustrated in Figure 3.20.

   c. Place each wire (pin) in its color-coded 110 connector. Normally you would start with white/blue and move on from there, but with the patch panel we are using, any color order will work. Temporarily place each wire with your fingers or a placing tool. Keep the PVC jacket as close to the connectors as possible. This is shown in Figure 3.21.

   d. Use the punch down tool to connect the wires. Make sure that the cut side of the tool (if you have one) is facing toward the end of the cable. If it is facing the wrong way, you will sever the connection before the terminating point. Double-punch each wire until all eight are done. (The cut side of the punch down tool should remove all the excess wiring beyond the 110 connector.) This is illustrated in Figure 3.22.

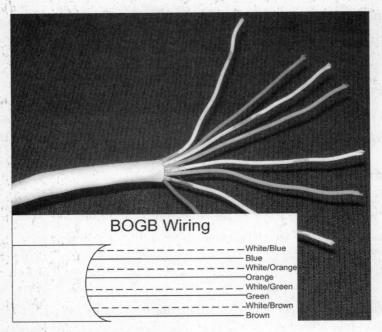

Figure 3.20 Category 5e cable in BOGB order.

Figure 3.21 Wiring the patch panel.

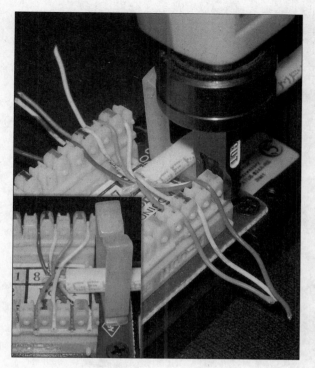

Figure 3.22 Punching down.

3. Punch down the other end to the RJ-45 jack.

   a. Strip the other end of the cable about two inches down.

   b. Separate the wires the same way you did before.

   c. Note the color-coded scheme on the jack. You can use the 568A or 568B standard. This all depends on what you want to use and what standard your patch panel is using. Most likely you are using the 568B standard, so wire the RJ-45 jack appropriately. Match the wires with the correct color.

   d. Place the wires in the colored connectors with your fingers or with a placing tool. Make sure that the PVC jacket runs as close to the edge of the jack as possible. This is shown in Figure 3.23.

   e. Punch down each wire. Make sure that the cut side of the tool is facing toward the outside of the jack. This will ensure that you do not sever the wires before the termination point, and that you remove the excess from the end of the wires. The finished product should look something like Figure 3.24.

Figure 3.23 Wiring the RJ-45 jack.

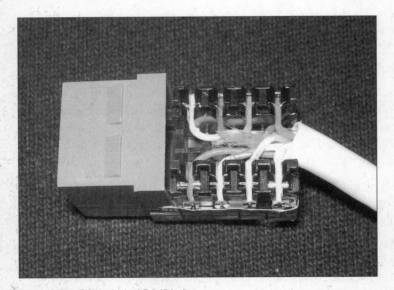

Figure 3.24 Finished wired RJ-45 jack.

4. Test the connection with a continuity tester.

  a. Connect your continuity tester to the jack using the supplied patch cable.

  b. Connect the supplied terminator to the patch panel. Use the port that you wired!

  c. Turn on the continuity tester and test. If all wires are correctly punched down on both ends, you should get a beep and/or a message that says "Pass." This is shown in Figure 3.25.

You will usually look for the test or pretest option. It may also be named 568B. It depends on the testing tool that you have purchased.

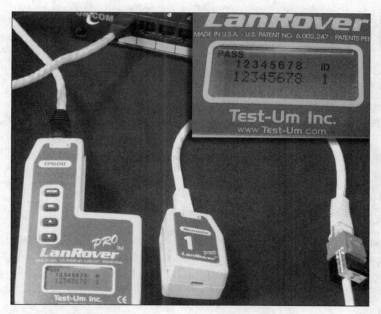

Figure 3.25 A tested cable run.

  d. It is possible that your test will not work the first time. With cabling, you have to remember that practice makes perfect! It may take you a few times to get it right. Check the pins (wires) carefully on each end. Make sure that you are wiring each one correctly. They are usually color-coded, so always check the colors. In addition, most testers will tell you what is wired incorrectly, so read the display carefully. An example of an incorrect wiring connection is shown in Figure 3.26.

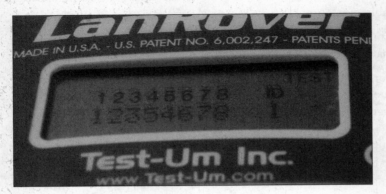

Figure 3.26 An incorrectly wired display.

Quite often, people who are new to cabling will reverse one of the pairs, or reverse two colors. Sometimes, you might wire the jack for 568A instead of 568B. Be alert for any potential wiring problems as they will most likely cause a connectivity failure.

And there you have it! In Chapter 1 you learned how to create temporary cables, whereas this chapter showed you how to wire the permanent connection. This is a necessary skill for all network administrators. You never know when you will need to add a cable run or re-wire a malfunctioning connection. Excellent work!

What Did I Just Learn?

In this lab you learned how to wire permanent physical connections to allow data transmissions over the physical layer. You used several tools to aid you in making proper network connectivity. In detail you learned how to do the following:

➤ Use a punch down tool and continuity tester.

➤ Wire a 568B cable connection.

➤ Terminate to a 568B patch panel and RJ-45 jack.

➤ Test your wiring connection.

Lab 4: VPN and Authentication Re-visited

Orientation

In this lab you will complete the following:

➤ Configure advanced protocols for your remote access connection.

➤ Learn of different ways to remotely connect to other platforms.

➤ Use third-party remote-control software.

➤ Prepare for the Network+ subdomain 3.4.

In Chapter 2, you configured VPN to connect a Windows 2000 Professional computer to a Windows 2000 Server. You used PPTP as your tunneling and encryption protocol. This is a fast and secure method of connecting remotely, but what if you want something more secure as far as the data and the authentication? Then you have to move into higher levels of VPN. And what if you want to connect to other platforms? Then you need other types of software to allow these secure VPNs.

Procedure

1. Configure MS-CHAP on the client.

   a. You should still have the VPN server running. Let's begin by configuring your client to connect to the VPN server using a more complex level of authentication (user name and password verification). This will be MS-CHAP II.

   b. Go to PC1.

   c. Right-click My Network Places and find your VPN adapter. If it is not there, create a new one. Refer to Chapter 2 for instructions on creating the VPN adapter.

   d. Right-click the VPN adapter and select Properties.

   e. Click the Security tab and select Advanced (Custom Settings).

   f. Click the Settings button. This opens the Advanced Security Settings dialog box.

g. Make sure that Require encryption is selected in the Data encryption drop-down list, and that the Microsoft CHAP (MS-CHAP) and Microsoft CHAP Version 2 (MS-CHAP v2) check boxes are selected, as shown in Figure 3.27. MS-CHAPII is already accepted by the server. MS CHAP will now be your challenge authentication scheme; it will work automatically.

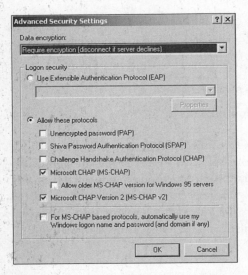

Figure 3.27   The Advanced Security Settings dialog box.

2. Configure L2TP and IPSec on the client. Connect through L2TP as opposed to PPTP. L2TP is a more secure way of connecting then PPTP when L2TP is used with IPSec.

a. Click OK to close the Advanced Security Settings dialog box.

b. In the VPN adapter Properties window, click the Networking tab.

c. Open the Type of VPN server that I am calling drop-down list and choose Layer 2 Tunneling Protocol (L2TP), as shown in Figure 3.28.

d. Click the Internet Protocol entry to select it and then click the Properties button.

e. Click the Advanced button.

f. Click the Options tab.

g. Click the Properties button to bring you to the IP Security (IPSec) window.

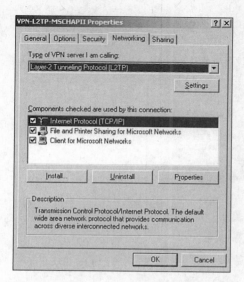

Figure 3.28 Modifying the tunneling settings.

    h. Click the Use this IP Security Policy option button and from the drop-down list, select Secure Server (Require Security). This enables the system to communicate normally with other systems unless it connects via VPN to the VPN server, at which point IPSec will take effect.

    i. Click OK in all four open dialog boxes to close them.

3. Install and configure a Certificate Authority on the server. Your client is set up, but if you were to try to connect to the VPN server you would get a 781 error because your client will now require an encryption certificate. The client must get that certificate from the server. Let's install and configure that now.

    a. Go to PC2.

    b. Click the Start button, choose Settings, and select Control Panel.

    c. Launch Add/Remove Programs.

    d. Select Windows Components.

    e. Click the Certificate Services check box to select it. A pop-up window opens; click Yes.

    f. Click Next.

g. When asked you what type of Certificate Authority you will be installing, choose the default option, Enterprise root CA, as shown in Figure 3.29. Then click Next.

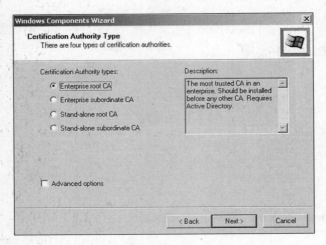

Figure 3.29 The Certificate Authority screen.

h. Name the CA test, and the organization testlab. Leave the rest of the information as is, and click Next.

 The certificate authority will last for two years by default.

i. Leave the Data Storage option as is and click Next.

j. A pop-up window asks you about IIS, which needs to be stopped during the installation of the CA. Click OK. The installation of the CA will begin.

k. If you are asked the CD, get the necessary information from D:\i386.

 You can copy the contents of the CD or at least the i386 folder to the HDD so that you don't have to access the CD all the time. For the purposes of this lab, do this now.

l. Click Finish. The Certificate Authority is now installed.

m. You are only half finished. Now you need to set up the CA to hand out certificates automatically and turn on the IP Security policy. First, though, set up an MMC if you have not already.

  i. Click the Start button, choose Run, and type MMC to open a new blank MMC.

  ii. Click Console and select Add/Remove Snap In (alternatively, press the Ctrl+M shortcut key). A second window opens.

  iii. Click Add. A third window called Add Standalone Snap-in appears, as shown in Figure 3.30.

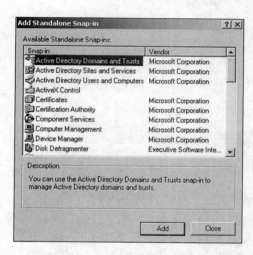

Figure 3.30 The Add Standalone Snap-in window.

  iv. To add a snap-in, select one from the list and click Add. You can add multiple snap-ins simultaneously from this window. For most of these, you will be selecting the Local Computer option. Add the following snap-ins:

  ➤ Active Directory Users and Computers

  ➤ Certificate Authority

  ➤ Routing and Remote Access

  ➤ Group Policy (click Browse, select Default Domain Policy, and click OK. Do not select the Local Computer option for this snap-in. Then click Finish.)

  v. Click the Close button to close the Add Standalone Snap In window.

vi. Click OK in the Add/Remove Snap-in window to return to your MMC. The MMC should look like Figure 3.31. Save the console; it will automatically be saved in your administrative tools.

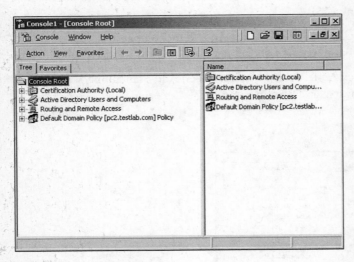

Figure 3.31 The finished MMC.

n. Set up the server to hand out certificates automatically.

i. In the MMC, click the Default Domain Policy entry, select Computer Configuration, choose Windows Settings, click Security Settings, select Public Key Policies, and choose Automatic Certificate Request Settings.

ii. Right-click the Automatic Certificate Request Settings entry, select New, and then select Automatic Certificate Request Settings.

iii. A wizard is launched. Click Next.

iv. When asked what type of auto certificate template you want to install, select Computer as shown in Figure 3.32. Then click Next.

v. In the Certification Authority screen, click Next.

vi. Click Finish. You should see a certificate template called Computer on the right side, as shown in Figure 3.33.

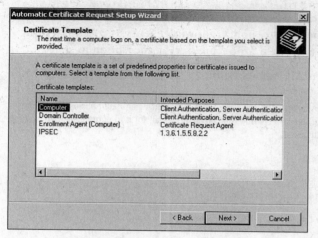

Figure 3.32   The Certificate Template screen.

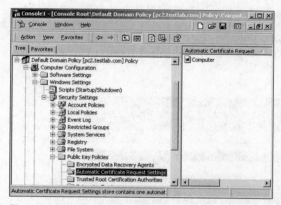

Figure 3.33   The finished certificate template.

   vii. Save the MMC.

   o. Turn on the IP security policy.

      i. Within the MMC, expand the following options in the left pane: Default Domain Policy, Computer Configuration, Windows Settings, Security Settings. Click IP Security Policies on Active Directory to select it.

      ii. This reveals three policies on the right side. None of these are yet assigned.

    iii. Right-click the Secure Server option and select Assign. This assigns the security policy, allowing clients to connect as long as they were set up for Secure Server encryption in step 2h.

    iv. Save the MMC and close it.

> You may have to restart the server and the client when new policies are assigned. When doing this, always boot the server first, wait for it to completely start up, and then boot the client.

4. Install a certificate on the client.

    a. Go to PC1.

    b. In many cases you will have to connect through a custom-made MMC, but in this case you will retain your certificate within the browser.

    c. Open Internet Explorer and, in the address bar, type http://pc2/certsrv. A Web page with the information you see in Figure 3.34 opens.

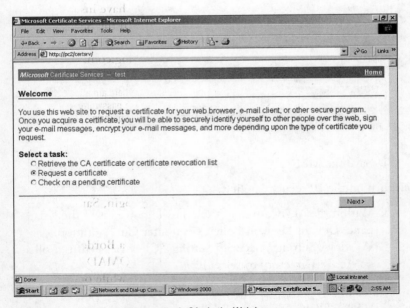

Figure 3.34 Connecting to the server's CA via the Web browser.

    d. Make sure the "Request a certificate" option button is selected and click Next.

e. The next screen talks about the type of request. Leave the default setting and click Next.

f. In the next screen, click Submit.

g. Click Yes in the pop-up window that appears.

h. The browser should talk to the server and retrieve a certificate. Choose to install it now.

i. Click Yes in the pop-up window that appears, and click Yes again in the next pop-up window to add the certificate to the store. You'll be informed that the certificate has been installed.

5. Now you can connect from your client to the server through the VPN connection. Connect through L2TP and MS-CHAP II.

a. On PC1, open the Network and Dial-up Connections window.

b. Double-click the VPN adapter and log on with the correct user name and password. You should now be able to get in! That does it for this portion of this lab. This is usually a tough one for my students, but I am sure that you can do it! If you get a 781 error (or any other errors), make sure that you have installed the automatic certificate correctly on the server and that you have installed a certificate on the client. Also, check if you assigned the Secure Server IP policy on the server. Of course, if there are more problems, feel free to post on my site: http://www.technicalblog.com.

 This may be the most in-depth lab so far, and as such, there are a lot of things that can go wrong. One of the most common problems is the password. Make sure that you are using the correct administrator password for the domain.

6. Connect remotely to different platforms.

a. To remotely connect to Linux, you can use Rlogin, Samba, SSH, FreeNX, and VNC.

b. To remotely connect to Novell, you can set up a Border Manager Authentication/RADIUS connection or use NOMAD (Novell Mobile Access Delivery). To remotely connect while on the LAN, you would use the Rconsole.

c. To remotely connect to Macintosh machines, you would need to use MACPPP connecting to a PPP server.

    d. To connect Macs to Microsoft, you would need to modify the RRAS setup.

        i. Install AppleTalk and/or Services for Macintosh.

        ii. Open RRAS.

        iii. Right-click the server and select Properties.

        iv. On the AppleTalk tab, configure remote access options as appropriate for the computer, and then click OK.

NOTE

We just listed some options here, because working with these technologies is outside the scope of the Network+ exam. That said, you should have at least one strategy to remotely connect to each of the types of platforms that are on your network.

7. Use other programs and hardware to connect and control remotely. These include the following:

➤ **Four-port SOHO routers.** Most of the 4 port routers like out Linksys WRT54H have the ability to connect to VPN servers. In the basic setup you can just change the Internet connection type from "Automatic Configuration- DHCP" to PPTP or L2TP. Then you can connect from the outside world. In addition, you can accept incoming remote access requests. Normally, you would open the port in question, for PPTP this would be 1723. And you would forward that port to the correct machine on your network (the VPN server) which in this case for you is PC2. An example of this is displayed in Figure 3.35. Now of course, you would have to know your router's WAN IP address, the one that was obtained automatically from the Internet. That would be what you would connect to with your Remote client (no matter where you are in the world!) Everything else remains the same as when you did the VPN lab.

➤ **Cisco.** Cisco makes a hardware device known as a VPN concentrator that can handle incoming VPN requests. You actually log on to the concentrator itself or you set the device to do port forwarding. Check out one of their latest devices, the VPN 3000, at the following URL: http://www.cisco.com/en/US/products/hw/vpndevc/ps2284/. There are plenty of other guys out there making VPN devices; run a couple Google searches for "VPN devices" and you should get a slew more information.

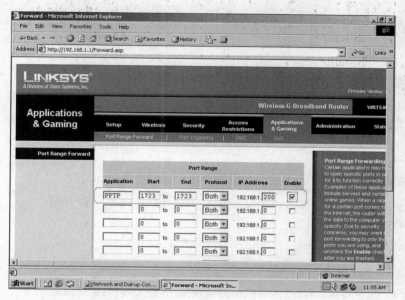

Figure 3.35   Port Redirection

> ➤ **Virtual Network Computing (VNC).** This is free software that will allow you to connect to other systems on the LAN or over the Internet. It has built-in encryption that you can turn on or off. This system allows you to not only connect remotely but to *control* remotely. Check out the free download at http://www.realvnc.com/download.html. Install it on both of your machines and remotely control the other!

> ➤ **Remote Assistance and Remote Desktop.** These are built-in remote connect/control programs in Windows XP. They can work over the Internet as well as on the LAN. We will show a little of this when you upgrade to XP in Chapter 4, "Network Support."

> ➤ **PC Anywhere.** This third-party program is a staple in the industry. It is one of the best for remote control over the Internet and is now Web based, meaning that you use your browser to connect. Check out version 11 at http://www.symantec.com/pcanywhere/.

There are many other programs for remotely connecting and controlling computers from Gotomypc, Laplink, LogMeIn, LanDesk, Dameware, Timbuktu, and so on. Run a Google search and check some of them out when you get a chance.

That pretty much does it for this lab. Great work! Let's go over what you covered.

What Did I Just Learn?

In this lab you learned how to connect via VPN but with a more secure connection and with more secure authentication. You also learned of some of the other remote access and remote control programs that are available to you. Specifically you learned how to:

➤ Use MS-CHAPII for more secure authentication of logon.

➤ Configure L2TP to be your tunneling protocol and IPSec as your encrypting protocol.

➤ Configure a Certificate Authority on your Windows 2000 Server.

➤ Install a certificate to the Windows 2000 client.

➤ Remotely access and remotely control other computers in additional ways.

Lab 5: Firewalls, Proxies, and Ports

Orientation

In this lab you will learn you how to do the following:

➤ Use a firewall to protect your PC or your network.

➤ Create an IP proxy.

➤ Configure ports to your best advantage.

➤ Work with a third-party free firewall.

➤ Identify VLANs, intranets, and extranets.

➤ Prepare for the Network+ subdomains 3.5–3.9.

When services are running, you have a security hole. It's that simple. If a service is started, the corresponding port is opened. Hackers have a point of entry to your system or network. *Firewalls* were developed to shield your network, so that your network's ports are considered closed or shielded, and so that your network's or computer's IP can't be seen by public users on the Internet. The problem is that you may want to run services, but not lose the firewall. This is where a DMZ comes in; firewalls can normally handle incorporating a DMZ. Your firewall will normally act as an IP proxy as well. This means that the device only displays one public IP address to the Internet, but it allows the entire private LAN to access the Internet though it. So it acts as a go-between or mediator or...proxy. In this lab, you are going to learn a little more about your Linksys firewall, and install a free firewall known as ZoneAlarm. Plus, you will learn how to configure your very own IP proxy and ICS device as well as how to best configure your ports.

Procedure

Revisit Your Linksys Firewall

You learned about port forwarding earlier. You can connect to the public IP address of the SOHO router with an application that uses a specific port—for example, PPTP, which uses 1723. The firewall forwards any packets sent on that port to whatever PC on your LAN you want. Take a look at Figure 3.36 for an example.

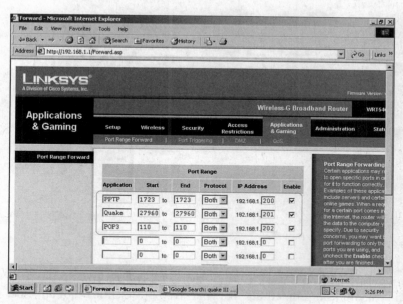

Figure 3.36 Forwarding applications via port number.

As you can see, you are running a POP3 mail server on 192.168.1.202, and a Quake III server on port 27960 as well as your VPN server on 1723. But for the client to access those servers, they must first get through the router, thus the need to forward those requests. The main thing here is to know which port is used by the application you want to serve. The big problem, though, is that you have just opened up those three ports to all of your computers! To combat this security breach, you can create a DMZ. When you do this on a SOHO router, however, all the ports become visible. You would then either have to get a second hardware firewall for those computers that you do not want visible from the Internet or load a software-based firewall on each of them. You also filter ports so that only certain ports are used, or so only certain ports are excluded. Most firewalls have this feature, normally referred to as *port filtering*.

If you are worried about specific applications not working because the outbound and inbound ports are different, you can use those outbound ports as a trigger to forward to the inbound ports for replies. For example, in Figure 3.37, we are using 6660–6670 as a trigger to forward to 113 for replies.

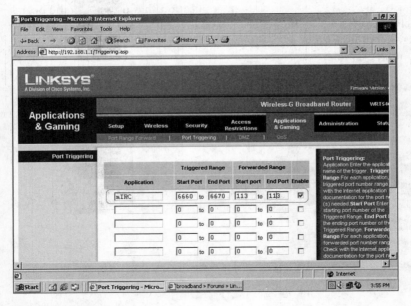

Figure 3.37 Port triggering.

Port triggering is mainly used for apps that send and receive on different ports. If you are using something like your Web browser, it is not an issue. But if you are using an IRC client or work with certain gaming servers, you may need to set this up on the SOHO router. In addition, port triggers work dynamically so that even if you have multiple PCs obtaining dynamic IPs through the router, port triggering will still work for them. Port triggering is not needed on software-based firewalls because the software interacts directly with the OS, therefore it knows what ports to keep open for applications that have varying inbound and outbound ports. Conversely, the hardware-based firewalls do not talk directly to your OS, so they don't really know if there is going to be a difference in port numbers for the request and the reply.

You can set up Quality of Service (QoS) to allow certain devices to get higher priority (and therefore faster access) to the Internet. This is shown in Figure 3.38. You can also set the QoS by the physical port.

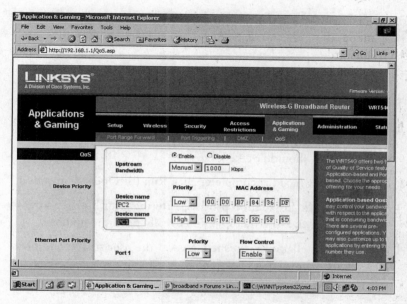

Figure 3.38 Quality of Service.

Try configuring on your router now for the following:

➤ Port forwarding

➤ DMZ

➤ Port triggering

➤ QOS

There is so much more to working with these SOHO routers. Feel free to ask additional questions on my website, http://www.technicalblog.com. Another good site for these types of questions is http://www.dslreports.com.

1. Install and test ZoneAlarm.

    a. Access PC1.

    b. Go to http://www.zonelabs.com.

    c. Click Download and Buy on the left side of the screen.

    d. On the top of the screen, click ZoneAlarm.

    e. Click the Free download link.

 NOTE   In case Zone Labs changes its site in the future, the idea here is to get the free version of ZoneAlarm firewall and download it.

    f. Click Download Free ZoneAlarm.

    g. Click Save in the pop-up window that appears and save the program in your Downloads folder. The program is about 6.5MB, so the download shouldn't take long.

    h. When the download is complete, click Run (or Open) to install it.

    i. Go through the installation process, entering your e-mail address when prompted. Note that you don't really need the updates.

    j. When the installation is finished, answer the user survey questions (see Figure 3.39). Then click Finish.

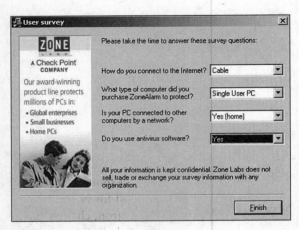

Figure 3.39 ZoneAlarm user survey.

k. A pop-up window will tell you that the installation is complete. Click Yes to start ZoneAlarm.

l. In the Zone Labs Security Options window, select the standard ZoneAlarm and click Next.

m. In the next window, click Finish.

n. Click Finish again in the next window unless you want to go through the tutorial.

o. Click Done in the Completion window.

p. Finally, Click OK to restart the computer.

q. When the tutorial comes back up, just exit out. You can read that at a later time if you wish. You should now be in the ZoneAlarm Overview screen.

r. Go to PC2.

s. Open the command prompt.

t. Type `ping pc1`. It shouldn't work. Instead of getting replies, you should get an "Unknown Host PC1" message.

u. Try browsing to the system. Again, you won't be able to get in.

v. Return to PC1.

w. Notice the ZoneAlarm icon in the system tray. Right-click it and choose Shutdown ZoneAlarm, as shown in Figure 3.40.

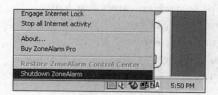

Figure 3.40 Shutting down ZoneAlarm.

x. Click Yes in the pop-up window that appears.

y. Return to PC2 and try pinging PC1 again. You should get replies because the firewall is off. Leave ZoneAlarm off for now. If you need it in the future, you can click the Start button, choose Programs, select Zone Labs, and choose Zone Labs Security to turn it back on. There you have it. ZoneAlarm, free, and it works. It's not the most comprehensive firewall out there, but if you are on a strict budget, it'll do the job. It also may help out if you have a four-port firewall like our Linksys and want a little added security on the local computer, but don't want the added cost or the extra burden on resources like other firewalls may trigger.

> There are other firewalls as well: Cisco PIX, CheckPoint Interspect, and software based firewalls like Microsoft ISA Server (which replaced Proxy Server). An ISA server introduction is available at the following link: http://www.microsoft.com/isaserver/downloads/2004/default.mspx. Scroll down to Demos and look for "Introduction to ISA Server 2004."

2. Configure ports to your best advantage. Whenever a computer starts a service, it opens a port on the network connection that corresponds to that particular service. The more services that are running, the more ports that are open—ergo more security risks! Your Windows 2000 Professional machine is probably pretty safe because it is not meant to serve data, but rather access other computers' data. Your Windows 2000 Server, however, is just that: a server. It runs lots of services. The first line of defense for a good network administrator is to shut down any unnecessary services.

   a. Go to PC1 (Windows 2000 Professional).

   b. Open the command prompt, type netstat -an, and press Enter. You should see a list of service ports that are open, but it will be pretty limited.

   c. Go to PC2 (Windows 2000 Server).

   d. Open the command prompt, type netstat -an, and press Enter. You should see a much larger list of service ports that are open; it should look something like Figure 3.41, although the list goes well beyond what's shown in the figure. Windows 2000 Server is chock full of open ports! Security is an issue.

Figure 3.41 Windows 2000 Server open ports.

e. Notice that ports 25 (SMTP), 80 (HTTP), and 443 (HTTPS/SSL) are open. You are not using a mail server or a Web server so these services can be shut off. You may ask, "Why were they open in the first place?" This is because Microsoft sets IIS to run by default upon installation of Windows 2000 Server. When IIS runs, it starts the HTTP, SMTP, and HTTPS services. Although HTTPS is great for securing Web transmissions, it uses a port nonetheless, so it creates a separate security concern. Let's turn all three of those off now.

   i. Right-click My Computer and select Manage to open the Computer Management window.

   ii. Click the Services and Applications entry in the left pane and then click the Services underneath.

   iii. Select the Simple Mail Transport Protocol entry in the right pane.

   iv. To stop the service, click the Stop button in the window's toolbar. This is circled in Figure 3.42. Alternatively, right-click the service and choose Stop from the menu that appears.

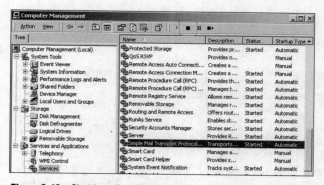

Figure 3.42 Shutting off the SMTP service.

   v. If you look at the service again, you will notice that its startup type is Automatic. That means when you restart the computer, the service will begin again! To change this to manual (thereby disabling it), double-click the SMTP service.

   vi. In the SMTP Properties dialog box, change the Startup type setting to Manual, as shown in Figure 3.43. Now you don't have to worry about the service starting back up next time you restart the server.

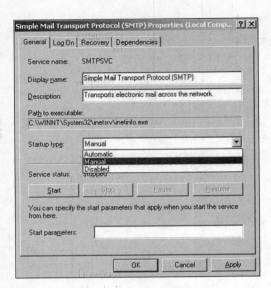

Figure 3.43 Setting the SMTP service to manual.

> **vii.** Repeat the process of stopping the service and setting it to manual for the following services:
>
> ➤ World Wide Web Publishing service
>
> ➤ IIS Admin service

Any changes you make to the IIS Admin service are propagated down to the WWW service, FTP, and NNTP, as well as HTTPS.

> **f.** Run netstat -an again. Ports 25, 80, and 443 should not come up. Great work! That is how you turn off services. This is very important. You should not rely on a firewall only. That is linear thinking. You must think three-dimensionally. Inside the network, outside the network, remote connections, intranets, and extranets must all be properly secured.

Be careful which ports you close. For example, port 88 is Kerberos, and is sorely needed by Windows 2000 domains. If you shut that guy off, you will have a tough time getting into the domain as Kerberos encryption is used by default on the Microsoft domain. Also, port 139 can't be closed without losing your network connection altogether! Port 53 is needed if you are running a DNS server, which you are. Port 42 is needed by domain controllers. In fact, there are a lot of ports that need to remain open on a Windows 2000 domain controller. Nevertheless, try to close the unnecessary ones. That said, ports 80 and 25 are common targets for hackers and the less of those open ports around your network, the better.

For more information on firewalls and ports , look for the *Network+ Exam Cram 2, 2e* by Drew Bird and Mike Harwood (ISBN: 0-7897-3254-8).

3. You learned how to check your local open service ports with `netstat -an`, and how to check your firewall's ports with www.grc.com's Shields Up. Now it's time to take it to the next level. What you need is a real port scanner. For this exercise you will use Advanced Administrative Tools to scan the server's ports.

   a. Go to PC1.

   b. Turn the ZoneAlarm firewall on. If you cannot access the Internet, restart the computer. If you still cannot, uninstall the ZoneAlarm program and restart the computer. If your computer reacts very slowly with ZoneAlarm running, uninstall it.

   c. Download and install an evaluation copy of WinZip if you have not already done so. You can get one from Download.com or from the following link: http://www.davidprowse.com/downloads/tech-tools/winzip70.exe.

   d. Download the AAtools program to your Downloads folder. You can get it from here: http://mirror1.glocksoft.com/aatools.zip.

   e. When the download is finished, click Open (or Run, depending on your OS). This will launch WinZip. Agree to the license for WinZip so that you can see the AAtools files.

   f. Double-click `aatools_setup.exe`. The installation will begin; it is extremely simple. Just click Next until you get to the last screen. Then click the check box to launch the program and click Finish. Click Close for the Live Update. The application should come up on your screen and look like Figure 3.44.

   g. Click the Port Scanner option button and click Start. The AAtools Port Scanner opens.

   h. In the Hosts to scan field, type `192.168.1.200`.

   i. In the Port set field, click the drop-down menu and select Everything.

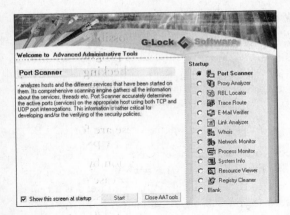

Figure 3.44 The main Advanced Administrative Tools screen.

j. Click the Start button (it's the green arrow toward the top of the window) to start the scan. (See Figure 3.45.) If you get a message from ZoneAlarm, just click Allow to let the Port Scanner program do its scan.

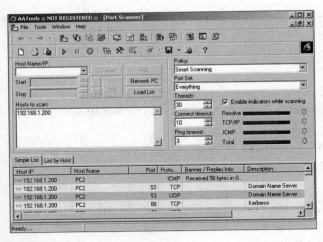

Figure 3.45 The Port Scanner window.

k. The first thing the application will do is ping the server. It sends ICMP echoes to verify that the IP address is valid. If it gets replies, it then scans all 65,536 ports. This may take a while, but after you get some results, you can click the red stop sign to abort the scan and view your results.

l. Notice that the program finds all open ports, but also gives you a description of them, as well as descriptions of possible attacks to those ports. This is the proper type of scanning program to use and you are using it in the proper way. When checking security vulnerabilities on a server, you want to scan it from another computer on the same LAN, and on the same IP network.

m. Notice that ports 1701 and 1723 are open. These are for L2TP and PPTP respectively. That is because you ran a VPN server previously. It secured your remote network connection by encrypting the data, either with PPTP or with IPSec (in the case of L2TP). Although this is an excellent way to protect your session to a VPN server, it does open up your VPN server to attack. Do you need that VPN server anymore? Not right now, so let's close those ports as well.

    i. Go to PC2.

    ii. Access your RRAS console.

    iii. Right-click the server name PC2 and choose Disable Routing and Remote Access. When you do this, you should see a downward-pointing red arrow, indicating that the service is off.

    iv. Return to PC1.

    v. Scan PC2 once again. Let the port scanner run for a while. (If you are wondering how to remove the data from the previous scan, just click one of the entries, press Ctrl+A to select all the entries, and press Del.)

    vi. Let the scan run until you see that it has scanned past port 2000. You can watch this in real time at the very bottom of the window. Then stop the scan.

    vii. Look for 1701 and 1723. They should not be there since you stopped the service.

    viii. Close all windows. Great work.

Another commonly used port scanner is NMAP, which is available at http://www.insecure.org.

4. Create an IP proxy. The type of IP proxy you will create will be based on Internet Connection Sharing (ICS). The whole idea of ICS is that you can use your computer to share the Internet connection instead of a four-port SOHO router like the Linksys you are using. You need two network connections on the computer, though. Luckily you have them! You have the LAN card and the Wireless LAN card. The basic premise here is to share the card that connects directly to the Internet. Then, connect the second card to a simple hub that offers connectivity for the rest of your systems. Sharing a card is a lot like sharing a folder or printer. It's just another resource.

a. Go to PC1.

b. Right-click My Network Places and select Properties.

c. Enable your wireless card (if it isn't already) by right-clicking it and selecting Enable. Tell ZoneAlarm to allow this setting.

d. Right-click the LAN card and select Properties.

e. In the Properties dialog box, you should notice a Sharing tab. This is not normally there, because most computers only have one NIC. Click the Sharing tab; it should look like Figure 3.46.

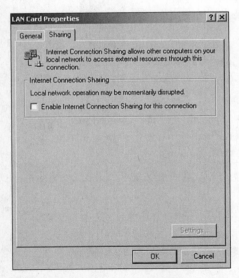

Figure 3.46 The Sharing tab of your NIC Properties dialog box.

f. Click the Enable Internet Connection Sharing check box to select it.

g. Click OK. A pop-up window tells you that your IP will now be changed to 192.168.0.1. Click Yes. Other computers on the network will now look to this system for their dynamic IP addresses, which, through ICS, your computer is now ready to offer.

h. Open the command prompt and run an ipconfig/all command. Note that it is actually the wireless card that was changed to 192.168.0.1. That is because your LAN card would now connect directly to the Internet, and because of that would need to get a public IP address. The other card (wireless) is automatically changed over because it will be on your private network. All other machines will be given numbers like 192.168.0.2, 192.168.0.3, and so on. Those IPs will come directly from your little old Windows 2000 Professional! This is the power of ICS. It is illustrated in Figure 3.47.

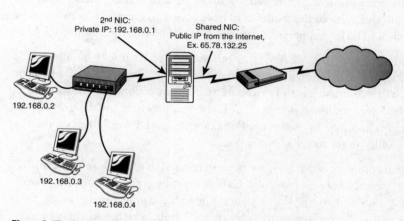

Figure 3.47   An illustration of ICS.

What you created is known as an *IP proxy*. A proxy is a go-between, a mediator of sorts. It allows all the computers on the LAN to access another network, usually the Internet. This way, many computers with many private IP addresses can access the Internet with just one WAN public IP address being displayed. To do this, the IP proxy must translate between the two NICs on the two different networks. It does this with Network Address Translation (NAT). Your SOHO router is an IP proxy because it displays only one address to the Internet, yet you can have many computers connected through that pipe.

A device with two or more network connections is known as a multi-homed machine.

VLANs

VLANs are the way of the present and the future. Short for virtual local area networks, VLANs can limit broadcasts and collisions, increase security, organize your network, and bring up performance. It is an alternative way of connecting or segmenting your network without the need for routers.

A scenario that could use VLANs would be the following: A school with three computer classrooms (20 computers each) and 10 computers for the office staff scattered around the building plus a library. You really wouldn't want the students from each classroom to be able to see each other, nor would you want any of the students to have access to the office network. The library should be kept separate as well. You could do this by creating VLANs.

The foundation of the VLAN rests on one device. It might be a switch, a Cisco PIX, a multi-homed server, or other device. Regardless of what you use, this device must have multiple network connections—in this scenario, five. What you could do is install a VLAN-ready switch and assign a different network number to each port. For example, port 1 would be 192.168.1.0, port 2 would be 192.168.2.0, and so on.

Then you connect a separate hub (or switch) to each of those ports. This will create a hierarchical star topology. Cables must be connected to their corresponding hub and room. For instance, the cable connections coming from classroom 1 will connect to the classroom 1 hub, which will then be connected to the 192.168.1.0 port on the VLAN switch. You get the idea.

In this way you can have total separation of your network without the use of a router! The ultimate beauty of this is that there may be staff connections all over the building that all lead to the same section of the VLAN. For example, admins have connections in a technical room, instructors need connections from every classroom, and other staff may be scattered around the office. The cables that come into the server room for each of these staff connections can be connected to the staff hub, which in turn connects to the staff port on the VLAN switch. This is known as a *port-based VLAN* and is illustrated further in Figure 3.48. Keep in mind that you can assign a VLAN to any port on the VLAN switch, but you should plan it first and make it organized!

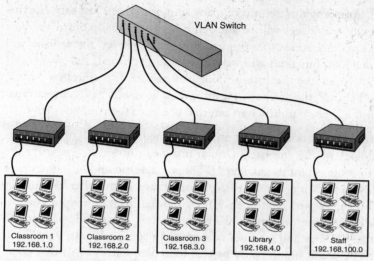

Figure 3.48   A port-based VLAN.

There are three main types of VLANs:

➤ **Protocol-based VLANs.** In this case, you would have a different protocol running on the various computers and/or ports that you wanted to
separate. It could be that you have a server with two NICs, each of
which runs a different protocol.

➤ **Port-based VLANs.** These are as explained previously, and are the
most common. If a computer needs to be moved to another area of the
office, then you would have to re-patch that system in the server room
to keep it on the same VLAN. This is not that time consuming and is
the default option for most administrators.

➤ **MAC address–based VLANs.** In this case, a switch will keep track of
all the MAC addresses on the entire network and you would have to
specify which belonged to each portion of the VLAN. This is time consuming but a benefit is that a computer can be moved anywhere in the
office without requiring anything to be reconfigured and the system will
still be on the same VLAN.

Intranets and Extranets

Intranets are networks that are privately owned by an organization or corporation. They use all the inherent technologies and offer all the inherent
capabilities of the Internet, but are restricted to employee use. For example,
you may have a set of Web servers in your company's office that are accessed

by the URL http://myintranet.mycompany.com or perhaps just http://myin-tranet, but only employees will be allowed to get in. Usually there will be a firewall used to deny access to unwanted visitors. However, the website will look the same, mail functions will work the same as normal, and so on. As I mentioned, it looks like the Internet but it is private. The intranet is nor-mally kept "behind" the firewall, meaning that it is not really an external presence on the Web, but rather an internal presence for your company.

Extranets are also networks that are privately owned and use all of the inher-ent technologies of the Internet. Unlike intranets, however, extranets are opened up to some extent to outsiders. These outsiders could be members of the company, worldwide employees, or sometimes even other companies that you do business with. Extranets go beyond the firewall in your compa-ny. Because of this, you will most likely need a user name and password to get into these websites and extranet resources. In some respects, your login to your bank or credit union could be considered an entryway to that com-pany's extranet, but normally an extranet is associated with employees of a company or sister company.

One of the big ideas behind intranets and extranets is that they enable users to connect using technologies they know and love—primarily, the Web browser. Everything is going Web browser–based because everyone has one, and almost everyone knows how to use one. You don't even need to be on your regular computer. This, of course, opens security concerns, but the pros have so far outweighed the cons.

What Did I Just Learn?

In this power-packed lab you learned how to install a free firewall, how to work with some advanced functions of a SOHO firewall, how to scan ports, and how to create an IP proxy. In particular, you learned how to do the fol-lowing:

➤ Install the ZoneAlarm firewall.

➤ Create an ICS device.

➤ Scan with `netstat -an` and Advanced Administrative Tools.

➤ Shut down services, including IIS, VPN, SMTP, and WWW.

➤ Configure application forwarding and port triggering.

➤ Prepare for the Network+ subdomains 3.5–3.9.

Lab 6: Anti-Virus Software

Orientation

In this lab you will learn how to do the following:

➤ Install a free anti-virus program.

➤ Identify the benefits and characteristics of AV software.

➤ Prepare for the Network+ subdomain 3.10.

Everyone needs to be protected from viruses, because there are millions of them out there. In fact, this is one of the big four when it comes to preventative maintenance for your computer. You really need to have a UPS, a firewall, software (and BIOS) updates, and rounding it out, anti-virus software. There are several to choose from. My personal choice is McAfee, but Norton is another big favorite. As long as you have one and, more importantly, as long as it is updated, that's what is important. For the purposes of this lab you will use a free service from Trend Micro to see if you have any viruses.

Procedure

1. Go to PC1.

2. Access www.trendmicro.com.

3. Click Products.

4. In the next screen, where it says House Call, click Scan Now.

5. In the next screen, click Scan Now, It's Free!

6. A pop-up window will ask you if you want to install and run Trend Micro. Click Yes.

7. The scanner will install. When the install is complete, you can use the program on the Web page. Click the My Computer check box and notice that everything beneath it also becomes checked, as shown in Figure 3.49.

8. Click the Scan button. The scan will begin.

9. If the House Call program finds a virus, it will tell you. You can instruct the program to remove the virus from your computer. Alternatively, you can select Auto Clean so that the program will remove viruses automatically.

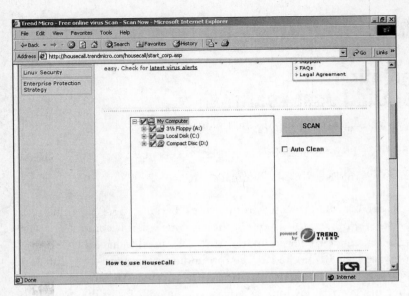

Figure 3.49 Trend Micro Web based virus scanner

Watch out, because sometimes these programs find legitimate .EXE files that they think they are viruses. If you do not select Auto Clean, you will be able to decide which files are to be removed and which are to stay.

For more information on viruses and other malicious attacks, see the *Network+ Exam Cram 2, 2e* by Drew Bird and Mike Harwood (ISBN: 0-7897-3254-8).

10. When the scan is complete, remove any found viruses from your machine and close the House Call program.

Trend Micro also has a pay service, of course. If you find viruses on its Web-based House Call program, then that means your virus protection software is not up to date. As long as you get one and keep it up to date, you should be in good shape. The following websites will help you find updates for anti-virus software:

➤ McAfee: http://www.mcafee.com/us/

Don't confuse McAfee with Macafee; they're not the same company!

➤ Norton: http://www.norton.com

➤ Trend Micro: http://www.trendmicro.com

What Did I Just Learn?

In this lab you learned how to do the following:

➤ Install a free anti-virus program.

➤ Identify the benefits and characteristics of AV software.

➤ Prepare for the Network+ subdomain 3.10.

Lab 7: Fault Tolerance

Orientation

In this lab you will accomplish the following:

➤ Set up a dynamic disk.

➤ Create strategies for redundant power, links, and for clustering.

➤ Prepare for the Network+ subdomain 3.11.

Procedure

1. Set up a dynamic disk.

   a. Go to PC1.

   b. Right-click My Computer and select Manage.

   c. In the Computer Management window, select Disk Management. You should see a screen like Figure 3.50.

   d. Right-click your main hard drive (it should be named Disk 0) and choose Upgrade to Dynamic Disk.

   e. In the next window, click OK.

   f. In the pop-up window that appears, click Upgrade.

   g. Click Yes in the next window to continue.

   h. Click OK to start the upgrade.

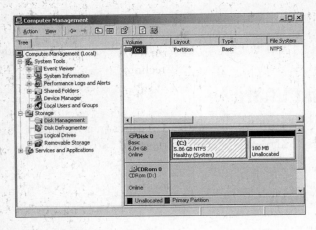

Figure 3.50 Disk management.

> **i.** You must reboot for the upgrade to complete. Restart and log back on.
>
> **j.** The system will have to restart again. Restart a second time and log back on.
>
> **k.** Open the Computer Management window and click Disk Management.
>
> **l.** Take note that the disk is not a basic disk anymore; it is a dynamic disk. Also notice that the partitions have now become *volumes*. This is shown in Figure 3.51.

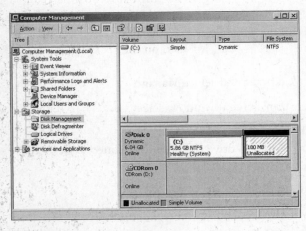

Figure 3.51 A dynamic volume.

The idea behind dynamic disk technology is that you can resize the volumes at will, thus the name *dynamic*. No longer are you stuck with static-sized partitions. In addition you can add disks to create spanned volumes, striped volumes, and RAID sets. The drawback is that this technology can cause errors and/or corruption to your operating system. Let's go over the differences between the various disk sets:

➤ **Spanned volume.** One drive letter (example C:) can span across multiple disks. When one disk fills up, the data starts getting stored on the next disk.

➤ **Striped volume.** One drive letter again deals with multiple disks, but when you write data, the files are dispersed among the drives one at a time, back and forth.

➤ **Redundant Array of Inexpensive Disks (RAID) 0.** This uses two disks minimum; it can be more. The data is striped across the disks. This is basically a striped volume.

So far the technologies we have mentioned are not fault tolerant. Let's talk about two that are:

➤ **RAID 1: Mirroring.** This uses two disks and two disks only to create a mirror. Data is written simultaneously to both disks so there is an entire copy of all information. If you lose one disk, the other takes over automatically! Writing is slower than conventional drive writing, but reading is the same because it only reads from the first disk in the mirror.

➤ **RAID 5: striping with parity.** Like RAID 0, the data is striped among multiple disks. The differences are that you need three disks minimum and that parity information is also striped across all disks. If one disk fails, it can be re-created from the parity data on the other remaining disks.

Clustering

There are two types of clustering, both of which normally need some kind of advanced server software. The following describe these two types:

➤ **Fail-over clustering.** This is when you have two like computers. The first takes care of all data transfers, but if it fails, all transmissions are sent over to the second computer until you can get the first back up and running.

➤ **True clustering.** This is when two or more computers (or server blades) work in unison. All processing, RAM, and HDD resources are used equally among the machines, thus making a type of super computer.

You want to have redundancy whenever possible. This means two power supplies, multiple processors, two NICs, and so on. Remember that the rule is hardware will fail—it's not a matter of if, it's a matter of *when*.

 For more information on fault tolerance, see the Que *Network+ Training Guide 2e.*

What Did I Just Learn?

In this lab you learned how to do the following:

➤ Set up a dynamic disk.

➤ Create strategies for redundant power, links, and for clustering.

➤ Prepared for the Network+ subdomain 3.11.

Lab 8: Disaster Recovery

Orientation

In this lab you will accomplish the following:

➤ Learn of the importance of making backups.

➤ Create a backup of the most important information on your computer.

➤ Utilize the built-in NTbackup program in Windows 2000.

Procedure

1. Go to PC1.

2. Click the Start button, choose Run, and type ntbackup. This opens the built-in backup program in Windows 2000 Professional.

3. Click the Backup tab, as shown in Figure 3.52. You can back up anything on your machine from here. Backup media include tape (the most common), floppy, HDD, and CD.

NOTE

Unfortunately, this program does not support backing up to DVD. You would need BackupMyPC, Nero, or a like program to accomplish that.

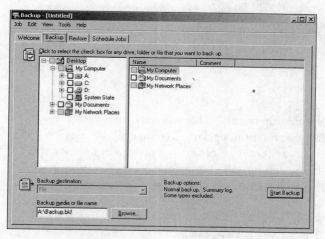

Figure 3.52   NTbackup.

4. Back up all the important information on your system, including all users, profiles, policies, drivers, the registry—everything that makes your system unique. This is known as the System State.

 a. Click the System State check box. Notice that doing so leaves a blue check mark. Also notice that if you open the C: drive and select a folder inside, that folder will become blue but the C: will get a grey check mark. Grey means that only certain components inside have been selected.

 b. Tell the system where you will place your backup file.

  i. Click the Browse button at the bottom of the window.

  ii. Navigate to your Downloads folder.

  iii. Name the backup backup1 and click Open. This brings you back to the main window.

c. Click Start Backup. You will see a window that looks like Figure 3.53.

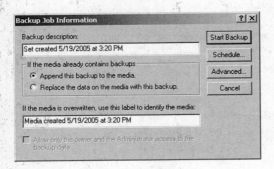

Figure 3.53 Starting the backup.

d. Click the Start Backup button. This will back up about 250–300MB of information, packing together all the files into one file known as `backup1.bkf`. You can use compression to make the file smaller, but watch out; the higher the compression ratio, the better the chance of corruption. I wouldn't recommend going past a 2:1 ratio. You can also set what type of backup you want to do, and schedule it to happen every day. There are a lot of options, so check them out when you get a chance.

For more on NTbackup and other disaster-recovery methods check out the Que *Network+ Exam Prep, 2e* and the Que *A+ Training Guide, 5e*.

e. When the backup is complete, check out the summary, (see Figure 3.54).

f. Close the report.

g. Close the Backup window.

5. Go to PC2 and run the same type of backup. This is going to be much larger, because it will back up all of what you just did plus the server components and Active Directory.

That's it! Great job on this chapter.

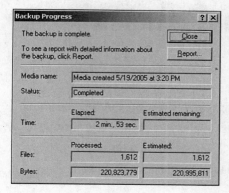

Figure 3.54   Backup completion and summary.

What Did I Just Learn?

In this lab you created a backup of the most important information on your computer. You also learned about the importance of the system state and how to use the NTbackup program.

That is all for Chapter 3. Excellent job! Make sure to go through the Domain 3 practice questions; they will aid you in your quest to pass the Network+ exam!

Domain 3 Practice Questions

Objective 3.1

3.1 Identify the basic capabilities (For example: client support, interoperability, authentication, file and print services, application support and security) of the following server operating systems to access network resources: UNIX / Linux / Mac OS X Server, Netware, Windows, Appleshare IP (Internet Protocol).

1. What service would you install to allow Microsoft clients access to Linux resources?
   - ❏ a. Samba
   - ❏ b. SMB
   - ❏ c. AFP
   - ❏ d. Printer Services for UNIX

2. Where would you go to add a user account in Windows 2000 Server?
   - ❏ a. Routing and Remote Access
   - ❏ b. Server Manager
   - ❏ c. User Manager for Domains
   - ❏ d. Active Directory Users and Computers

3. By default, what highest-level permission does the Everyone group have?
   - ❏ a. Read-only
   - ❏ b. Hidden
   - ❏ c. Full control
   - ❏ d. Encrypted

4. Which service would be the *best* solution if you needed to connect 500 Windows 2000 clients to a NetWare resource?
   - ❏ a. GSNW
   - ❏ b. Printer Services for Macintosh
   - ❏ c. Novell Client 4.91
   - ❏ d. CSNW

5. Which service would be the best solution to allow Novell clients access to Microsoft resources?
   - ❏ a. GSNW
   - ❏ b. FPNW
   - ❏ c. File and Printer Sharing
   - ❏ d. CSNW

Objective 3.2

3.2 Identify the basic capabilities needed for client workstations to connect to and use network resources (For example: media, network protocols and peer and server services).

1. What are the two main services in Windows 2000 Professional and Server? (Select two.)
   - ❏ a. Workstation
   - ❏ b. Messenger
   - ❏ c. Server
   - ❏ d. Redirector

2. What command will display the services that are running on a remote machine?
   - ❏ a. **netstat**
   - ❏ b. **ping**
   - ❏ c. **arp**
   - ❏ d. **nbtstat**

3. Which console window will give you information on all of the various services?
   - ❏ a. RRAS
   - ❏ b. Active Directory Users and Computers
   - ❏ c. Computer Management
   - ❏ d. Device Manager

4. Which option of nbtstat will show the remote computer's name table given its IP address?
   - ❏ a. **-a**
   - ❏ b. **-r**
   - ❏ c. **-R**
   - ❏ d. **-A**

5. Which hexadecimal number identifies the Server service?
   - ❏ a. <20>
   - ❏ b. <03>
   - ❏ c. <1f>
   - ❏ d. <00>

Objective 3.3

3.3 Identify the appropriate tool for a given wiring task (For example: wire crimper, media tester / certifier, punch down tool or tone generator).

1. What type of connector do you punch down to on a 568B patch panel?
   - ❏ a. 110 IDC
   - ❏ b. 66 connector
   - ❏ c. USB
   - ❏ d. Screw terminal

2. Which device will test a 568B twisted pair cable run from the patch panel to the RJ-45 jack? Select the best answer.
   - ❏ a. Patch tester
   - ❏ b. TDR
   - ❏ c. Continuity tester
   - ❏ d. Wire stripper

3. Which is the more common wiring standard?
   - ❏ a. 568A
   - ❏ b. 568B
   - ❏ c. 619A
   - ❏ d. 568C

4. Which device will aid you in connecting cables to a patch panel?
   - ❏ a. Crimper
   - ❏ b. RJ-45 patch tester
   - ❏ c. Punch down tool
   - ❏ d. TDR

5. What is a common mistake when wiring patch panels?
   - ❏ a. Reversed pair
   - ❏ b. RJ-45 plug is upside down
   - ❏ c. Punched down too many times
   - ❏ d. Crimped the plug too hard

Objective 3.4

3.4 Given a remote connectivity scenario comprised of a protocol, an authentication scheme, and physical connectivity, configure the connection. includes connection to the following servers: UNIX / Linux / MAC OS X Server, Netware, Windows, Appleshare IP (Internet Protocol).

1. Which would be considered a more secure VPN connection?
   - ❑ a. PPTP
   - ❑ b. L2TP
   - ❑ c. L2TP with IPSec
   - ❑ d. IPSec

2. What port would you open on your SOHO router if you wanted to connect to your home network remotely?
   - ❑ a. 3389
   - ❑ b. 1723
   - ❑ c. 80
   - ❑ d. 23

3. What path would you type in the browser's address bar if you wanted to request a secure certificate from the server on your LAN?
   - ❑ a. http://www.verisign.com
   - ❑ b. https://servername
   - ❑ c. http://certificateserver
   - ❑ d. http://servername/certsrv

4. L2TP works on which layer of the OSI model?
   - ❑ a. Network
   - ❑ b. Application
   - ❑ c. Data link
   - ❑ d. Session

5. What do you need to turn on the server to allow L2TP to function properly?
   - ❑ a. IP security policy
   - ❑ b. Auditing
   - ❑ c. NTFS permissions
   - ❑ d. IPSec

Objectives 3.5–3.9

3.5 Identify the purpose, benefits and characteristics of using a firewall.

3.6 Identify the purpose, benefits and characteristics of using a proxy service.

3.7 Given a connectivity scenario, determine the impact on network functionality of a particular security implementation (For example: port blocking / filtering, authentication and encryption).

3.8 Identify the main characteristics of VLANs (Virtual Local Area Networks).

3.9 Identify the main characteristics and purpose of extranets and intranets.

1. If you wanted to close port 25, which service would you shut off?
   - ❑ a. NNTP
   - ❑ b. SMTP
   - ❑ c. SNMP
   - ❑ d. SMB
2. Which port number is used by L2TP?
   - ❑ a. 1723
   - ❑ b. 1724
   - ❑ c. 1700
   - ❑ d. 1701
3. Which of these devices would be known as multi-homed machines? (Select two.)
   - ❑ a. Router
   - ❑ b. IP proxy
   - ❑ c. Domain controller
   - ❑ d. WINS Server
4. If you were staying at a hotel and wanted to VPN to your home network, which of the following would you have to enable on your SOHO router?
   - ❑ a. Port triggering
   - ❑ b. DMZ
   - ❑ c. Port forwarding
   - ❑ d. Port replication
5. Which of these is the most common type of VLAN?
   - ❑ a. Router based
   - ❑ b. Port based
   - ❑ c. MAC based
   - ❑ d. Protocol based

Objectives 3.10–3.12

3.10 Identify the purpose, benefits and characteristics of using antivirus software.

3.11 Identify the purpose and characteristics of fault tolerance: Power, Link redundancy, Storage, Services.

3.12 Identify the purpose and characteristics of disaster recovery: Backup / restore, Offsite storage, Hot and cold spares, Hot, warm and cold sites.

1. Which fault tolerant method uses two disks only?
   - ❑   a. RAID 0
   - ❑   b. RAID 1
   - ❑   c. RAID 5
   - ❑   d. Striped volumes

2. Which of the following will protect you against viruses?
   - ❑   a. Firewall
   - ❑   b. UPS
   - ❑   c. Line conditioner
   - ❑   d. AV software

3. Which of these disperses resource usage among multiple computers?
   - ❑   a. Fail-over clustering
   - ❑   b. RAID 5
   - ❑   c. True clustering
   - ❑   d. RAID 1

4. Which program allows you to back up the system state?
   - ❑   a. RAID 1
   - ❑   b. RRAS
   - ❑   c. **nbtstat –a**
   - ❑   d. ntbackup

5. Which fault-tolerant method stripes data *and* parity across multiple disks?
   - ❑   a. RAID 0
   - ❑   b. RAID 1
   - ❑   c. Disk duplexing
   - ❑   d. RAID 5

Answers and Explanations

Objective 3.1

1. Answer a is correct. Samba allows Microsoft clients to connect to Linux systems. SMB and AFP are something that you could possibly load on a Macintosh system. Printer Services for UNIX allows UNIX systems to access printers connected to a Windows 2000 Server.

2. Answer d is correct. Active Directory Users and Computers is used to add accounts, groups, and organizational units. Routing and Remote Access (RRAS) has nothing to do with accounts; instead, it allows you to transform your server into a VPN server, network router, and so on. User Manager for Domains and Server Manager are the Windows NT 4.0 Server applications for adding users and computers respectively.

3. Answer c is correct. The Everyone group has the full control permission by default. Encrypted and hidden are considered attributes of a file. Read-only can be both a permission and an attribute, but the Everyone group has much more than that by default.

4. Answer a is correct. GSNW (Gateway Services for NetWare) would be the best answer. If you have many clients, it would be very time consuming to load CSNW or the Novell Client 4.91 on every one. Instead, the clients could log on to the Microsoft server, and that machine would act as the gateway for all the clients out to the Novell resources.

5. Answer b is correct. FPNW (File and Print services for NetWare) is what you would use to connect Novell clients to Microsoft resources. GSNW and CSNW are for connecting Microsoft clients to NetWare resources, and File and Print Sharing is a built in service for Microsoft operating systems.

Objective 3.2

1. Answers a and c are correct. Messenger is an important service but not considered one of the main services, and Redirector is what Novell calls the service that allows computers to access remote resources.

2. Answer d is correct. netstat shows connections or sessions to other machines, ping verifies connections between two computers, and arp resolves between IP and MAC addresses.

3. Answer c is correct. Computer Management has, among other things, the Services and Applications Applet, which allows you to view the services that are running and work on various other apps. RRAS is for turning your server into a network router or a VPN device. Active Directory Users and Computers is for working within the structure of the network and configuring objects and organizational units. Device Manager (which is within Computer Management, by the way) is for viewing, troubleshooting, and configuring your hardware devices.

4. Answer d is correct. -A is for use with IP addresses, and -a is for use with host names. -r lists names resolved by broadcast. -R purges and reloads the remote cache name table.

5. Answer a is correct. <20> identifies the Server service. <00> is for the Workstation service, <03> is for the Messenger service, and <1f> deals with domains.

Objective 3.3

1. Answer a is correct. The 110 IDC connector is the correct one for punching down. 66 connectors will be found primarily on 66 telephone blocks and are for POTS. USB is the universal serial bus connection, which is for peripheral devices; and screw terminals are normally found on NIDs (network interface devices) for telephone. They are also found on older RJ-11 jacks.

2. Answer c is correct. A continuity tester will test the connection between an RJ-45 jack and the patch panel. A patch tester will only test a patch cable, where both ends are present in the same area. A TDR is a time domain reflectometer, which normally finds the break in a cable if you are troubleshooting. It may have built-in continuity-testing functionality, but it is still not the best answer. A wire stripper is used for removing the PVC (plastic) jacket from the cable to expose the wires.

3. Answer a is correct. 568B is the most common wiring standard today. 568A is the older version. 568c and 619 are not actual data communications wiring standards.

4. Answer c is correct. You would use a punch down tool to connect wires to a patch panel.

5. Answer a is correct. Often, you will find miswiring in the form of reversed wires and pairs.

Objective 3.4

1. Answer c is correct. L2TP has the capability to be more secure than PPTP but it needs IPSec in this regard to encrypt the data. IPSec alone would not be enough as it does not tunnel to create a VPN.

2. Answer b is correct. Normally you would open 1723 (PPTP) to allow incoming remote access connections. Keep in mind that this creates a minor security issue because that port is now visible on your system. 3389 is for RDP (Remote Desktop Protocol), 80 is for HTTP, and 23 is for Telnet. By the way, L2TP uses 1701 if you decide to go that route.

3. Answer d is correct. All other URLs are incorrect. Although Verisign is a huge player in the security field, the question was asking about a server on your LAN.

4. Answer c is correct. As the name implies, L2TP (Layer 2 Tunneling Protocol) is on the data link layer.

5. Answer a is correct. You need to create an MMC, and navigate through the Default Domain Policy down to the IP Security Policies. Then you need to assign the policy that you wish to use.

Objectives 3.5–3.9

1. Answer b is correct. SMTP stands for Simple Mail Transport Protocol and is known as Send Mail To People. (See the word association?) It uses port 25 to transmit mail to an SMTP server. NNTP is the Network News Transfer Protocol and uses port 119, and SNMP is the Simple Network Management Protocol and uses port 161. Finally, SMB is the Server Message Block protocol that allows Windows computers to share data.

2. Answer d is correct. L2TP is the Layer 2 Tunneling Protocol and uses port 1701. 1723 is used by its cousin, PPTP, and the other two ports are not commonly used.

3. Answers a and b are correct. A router and an IP proxy will both have multiple connections, thus making them multi-homed machines. A domain controller and a WINS server need only one network connection because they only need to connect to the LAN.

4. Answer c is correct. Port forwarding allows your VPN requests on port 1723 or 1701 to be forwarded to the VPN server (RRAS device).

5. Answer b is correct. Port-based VLANs are by far the most common. They are easy to set up, they are logical, and simple patching can move computers wherever you would like them to go while retaining their VLAN membership.

Objectives 3.10–3.12

1. Answer b is correct. RAID 1 Mirroring can use only two disks—no more and no less.

2. Answer d is correct. Anti-virus software will protect you against viruses. Just make sure that the software engine and the definitions are updated!

3. Answer c is correct. True clustering will spread resource usage across multiple computers.

4. Answer d is correct. ntbackup allows you to back up any data on your system as well as the system state set of data that Windows 2000 has compiled for you.

5. Answer d is correct. RAID 5 is striping with parity. This stripes the data and the parity across a minimum of three disks and a maximum of 32. RAID 0 is striping only and is not fault tolerant. RAID 1 is mirroring and while it is fault tolerant, it does not use parity. Disk duplexing is used in RAID 1 configurations and provides a secondary controller.

4

Network Support

Welcome to the final chapter in the Network+ Lab Manual. The fourth domain deals with network support—specifically troubleshooting, analysis, and diagnosis. It is extremely important for the test (and most important for the field) that you can show the ability to work with TCP/IP utilities and troubleshoot connectivity problems. In this chapter you will troubleshoot with TCP/IP, configure DHCP, diagnose connectivity issues, and learn a troubleshooting methodology that you can rely on both during the exam and in the field.

In this chapter there are five labs, plus one optional lab. Although this is fewer than in the two previous chapters, do not underestimate the importance of this domain. It accounts for 35% of the Network+ exam, so you need to really delve into the troubleshooting methodology...starting now!

Domain 4: Network Support

The following is a list of objectives covered in this chapter:

➤ 4.1 Given a troubleshooting scenario, select the appropriate network utility from the following: Tracert / traceroute, ping, arp, netstat, nbt-stat, ipconfig / ifconfig, winipcfg, nslookup / dig.

➤ 4.2 Given output from a network diagnostic utility (For example: those utilities listed in objective 4.1), identify the utility and interpret the output.

➤ 4.3 Given a network scenario, interpret visual indicators (For example: link LEDs (Light Emitting Diode) and collision LEDs (Light Emitting Diode)) to determine the nature of a stated problem.

➤ 4.4 Given a troubleshooting scenario involving a client accessing remote network services, identify the cause of the problem (For example: file services, print services, authentication failure, protocol configuration, physical connectivity and SOHO (Small Office / Home Office) router).

➤ 4.5 Given a troubleshooting scenario between a client and the following server environments, identify the cause of a stated problem: UNIX / Linux / Mac OS X Server, Netware, Windows, Appleshare IP (Internet Protocol).

➤ 4.6 Given a scenario, determine the impact of modifying, adding or removing network services (For example: DHCP (Dynamic Host Configuration Protocol), DNS (Domain Name Service) and WINS (Windows Internet Name Service)) for network resources and users.

➤ 4.7 Given a troubleshooting scenario involving a network with a particular physical topology (For example: bus, star, mesh or ring) and including a network diagram, identify the network area affected and the cause of the stated failure.

➤ 4.8 Given a network troubleshooting scenario involving an infrastructure (For example: wired or wireless) problem, identify the cause of a stated problem (For example: bad media, interference, network hardware or environment).

➤ 4.9 Given a network problem scenario, select an appropriate course of action based on a logical troubleshooting strategy.

What You will Need

The following is a list of the components and their minimum recommended requirements that you will need for the Chapter 4 labs:

➤ A PII 266MHz PC with 64MB RAM, 2GB HDD, CD-ROM, and network interface card (installed with Windows 2000 Professional). This will be known as PC1.

➤ A PII 266MHz PC with 128MB RAM, 2GB HDD, CD-ROM, and network interface card (installed with Windows 2000 Professional or Server). This will be known as PC2.

➤ A four-port wireless/wired router with built-in firewall

➤ A wireless NIC

➤ Access to Windows 2000 Professional software

➤ Access to Windows 2000 Server software

➤ Access to the Internet

➤ (Optional) a two- or four-port KVM switch

For these labs you will be referring to the following:

➤ Compaq Deskpro PIII 533MHz computers with 256MB RAM and 3Com 3C905 XL 10/100 PCI TX network interface cards. (These cards will automatically be recognized by Windows 2000 during the OS install.)

➤ Linksys wireless router: Model WRT54G

➤ Linksys PCI wireless NIC: Model WMP54G

➤ Belkin four-Port KVM switch bundled with cables, PS/2, part #F1DJ104P

➤ Cable Internet access

Lab 1: Troubleshooting with TCP/IP Utilities

Orientation

In this procedure you will accomplish the following:

➤ Test connectivity problems with ping and tracert.

➤ Learn the order of networking events with arp, ping, and ipconfig.

➤ Troubleshoot with netstat and nbtstat.

➤ Identify name-resolution problems with nslookup.

➤ Customize the Windows 2000 command prompt.

➤ Prepare for the Network+ sub domains 4.1 and 4.2.

The TCP/IP suite of protocols is vast. Because of this, many utilities have been developed to aid in the identification of problems and the resolution of those issues. These utilities are normally accessed via the command prompt. In Windows environments, CMD.exe is the preferred option, but in many cases command.com can also be used. The problem with command.com is that it does not offer full access to all the TCP/IP utilities. So we will be using CMD.exe throughout this chapter.

I estimate that about 80% of client-connectivity problems can be diagnosed and troubleshoot through the use of the command prompt. Although there are many other tools out there, the command prompt will quite often be your best friend. Let's cover seven of these command-prompt utilities now.

Procedure

1. Modify the look of the command prompt.

   a. Turn on PC1

   b. Log on to the domain.

   c. Open the command prompt by clicking the Start button, choosing Run, and typing cmd.exe.

   d. Right-click the Command Prompt window's title bar and select Properties to open the Properties dialog box, shown in Figure 4.1.

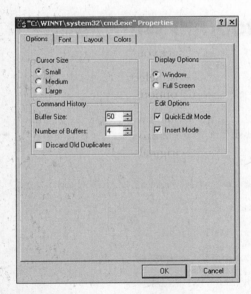

Figure 4.1   The Command Prompt Properties dialog box.

The title bar is always the colored bar at the top of a window. In the Command Prompt window, the title bar has an icon of a command prompt followed by the path **c:\winnt\system32\cmd.exe**.

e. Click the Font tab.

f. Select the 12×16 Font size.

g. Click the Layout tab.

h. Deselect the Let System Position Window check box at the bottom of the options so the system will not position the window for you.

i. In the Window Position area, change both the Left and Top options to 0.

j. In the Window Size area, change the Width to 60 and the Height to 30.

k. Click the Colors tab.

l. The Screen Background option button is selected by default. Change the screen background color to white by clicking the white block underneath the Screen Background option button.

m. Click the Screen Text option button. Then change the screen text color to black by clicking on the black block underneath the Screen Text option button.

n. The selected screen colors should reflect your changes. Click OK.

o. The Apply Properties dialog box opens. Select the Save Properties for Future Windows with Same Title option.

p. Click OK. Your command prompt should now morph to the new settings. You can double-click the title bar to maximize it, and double-click again to restore it to its original size.

Keeping the background of your command prompt white can really save on ink costs when printing!

2. Copy and paste command-prompt text.

a. Shut down ZoneAlarm by right-clicking the icon in the System Tray and choosing Shut Down.

If you ever have to restart the computer, ZoneAlarm will start up as well. In the future, this application will check all of your TCP/IP utilities, so you will have to either allow the utility to get past the firewall or shut the firewall down entirely. Remember this for future labs.

b. Click once in the Command Prompt window to make it the active working window.

c. Press the Alt+Enter shortcut key to open a full-screen version of the Command Prompt window.

d. Type `ipconfig` to view the IP information for your cards.

e. Press the Print Screen key on your keyboard to take a snapshot of the current screen, also called a *screen shot*.

You will find the Print Screen key near the Scroll Lock and Pause keys, in the upper-right part of your keyboard.

f. Press Alt+Enter again to return to the regular command prompt.

g. Click the Start button, choose Programs, select Accessories, and choose WordPad to open the WordPad program.

h. Press the Ctrl+V shortcut key to paste the text from the command prompt into WordPad.

i. Scroll up in the WordPad document to see the text, as shown in Figure 4.2. Notice that instead of pasting the entire window, it only pasted the text—a great ink saver.

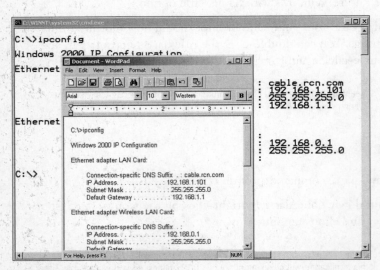

Figure 4.2 Pasted text in WordPad.

In some operating systems, you can simply click and drag to highlight text in the Command Prompt window, press the Ctrl+C shortcut key, and then press the Ctrl+V shortcut key to paste the text into WordPad to get the same text-only results. It all depends on the version you are running.

3. Copy and paste help files into WordPad.

   a. Press Alt+Tab to switch back to the Command Prompt window. Leave WordPad open.

   b. Press Alt+Enter to switch the command prompt to full-screen mode.

   c. Type `ipconfig/?` and press Enter to open the `ipconfig` help file.

   d. As before, press the Print Screen key to take a screen shot, and press Ctrl+V to paste the text into WordPad.

   e. Repeat steps c and d for the following commands:

   ➤ ping/?

   ➤ arp/?

   ➤ tracert (no /? is needed for this command)

   ➤ netstat/?

   ➤ nbtstat/?

   f. When you have all the help files pasted into your WordPad document, press Ctrl+S to save it. Use this document to help you study all the different options (switches) of the various TCP/IP commands. Print it out and bring it with you for those times when you want to squeeze in some extra study when you are away from home.

More information on the TCP/IP utilities can be found in the *Exam Cram2 Network+ 2e*.

4. Diagnose issues with `ipconfig`.

   a. Return to the command prompt.

   b. Type `ipconfig`. Examine the results. You should see the following:

       ➤ The IP address

       ➤ The subnet mask

       ➤ The gateway address

   c. Although these results can help you to troubleshoot many problems, it usually preferable to first type `ipconfig/all` so that you can have detailed information from the start. Type `ipconfig/all` now.

   d. Notice a few issues with your network connections. On our test connections, we sure do have a couple, as shown in Figure 4.3:

       ➤ We never disabled ICS, so our second NIC is still using the IP address `192.168.0.1`.

       ➤ That NIC is not using a gateway or DNS address, so it has no hopes of connecting to the Internet.

       ➤ Our primary NIC has a DNS setting that shows a public IP. This means that it is using the ISP's DNS server only and not our domain controller. Optimally, we would like it to use both.

That's just a few of the common problems you will find with `ipconfig/all`. Let's go ahead and fix the three issues mentioned.

   e. Jot down the DNS server addresses listed on your computer. (Yours will obviously be different from ours.) Once again, this is shown in Figure 4.3.

   f. Turn off ICS.

      i. Right-click My Network Places and select Properties.

      ii. Right-click the LAN card and choose Properties.

      iii. Click the Sharing tab.

      iv. Deselect the Enable Internet Connection Sharing check box.

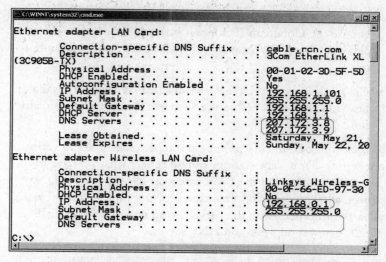

```
C:\WINNT\system32\cmd.exe                                              _ □ ×

Ethernet adapter LAN Card:

        Connection-specific DNS Suffix  . : cable.rcn.com
        Description . . . . . . . . . . . : 3Com EtherLink XL
(3C905B-TX)
        Physical Address. . . . . . . . . : 00-01-02-3D-5F-5D
        DHCP Enabled. . . . . . . . . . . : Yes
        Autoconfiguration Enabled . . . . : No
        IP Address. . . . . . . . . . . . : 192.168.1.101
        Subnet Mask . . . . . . . . . . . : 255.255.255.0
        Default Gateway . . . . . . . . . : 192.168.1.1
        DHCP Server . . . . . . . . . . . : 192.168.1.1
        DNS Servers . . . . . . . . . . . : 207.172.3.8
                                            207.172.3.9
        Lease Obtained. . . . . . . . . . : Saturday, May 21,
        Lease Expires . . . . . . . . . . : Sunday, May 22, 20
Ethernet adapter Wireless LAN Card:

        Connection-specific DNS Suffix  . :
        Description . . . . . . . . . . . : Linksys Wireless-G
        Physical Address. . . . . . . . . : 00-0F-66-ED-97-30
        DHCP Enabled. . . . . . . . . . . : No
        IP Address. . . . . . . . . . . . : 192.168.0.1
        Subnet Mask . . . . . . . . . . . : 255.255.255.0
        Default Gateway . . . . . . . . . :
        DNS Servers . . . . . . . . . . . :

C:\>
```

Figure 4.3 Diagnosing with ipconfig/all.

g. Modify the DNS settings.

  i. Click the General tab in the LAN Card Properties dialog box.

  ii. Double-click Internet Protocol.

  iii. In the DNS Server section, select the Use the following DNS Server address option button.

  iv. Make the preferred DNS server 192.168.1.200 or whatever IP you are using for your LAN DNS server. This should be PC2's IP address.

  v. Make the alternate DNS server the IP you jotted down before.

  vi. Click OK in the Internet Protocol (TCP/IP) Properties dialog box.

  vii. Click OK in the LAN Card Properties dialog box.

h. Apply a working IP to the wireless card.

  i. In the Network and Dial-up Connections window, right-click the wireless card and select Properties.

  ii. In the NIC Properties dialog box, double-click Internet Protocol.

    iii. In the Internet Protocol (TCP/IP) Properties dialog box choose the Obtain an IP address automatically option button and the Obtain DNS server address automatically option button.

    iv. Click OK in the Internet Protocol (TCP/IP) Properties dialog box, and then click OK in the Wireless Card Properties dialog box.

  i. Go back to the command prompt and type `ipconfig/all` to verify your settings. Your new settings should reflect what we have in Figure 4.4. Notice that the LAN card now has the correct DNS settings, allowing it to communicate properly on the domain *as well as* the Internet. Also, the wireless card now has a proper IP address, gateway address, and DNS server.

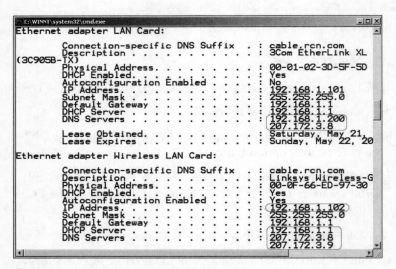

Figure 4.4 Verifying changes with ipconfig/all.

5. When you set your NIC to obtain the IP address automatically, it usually receives that address from a DHCP server. In this case, our LAN card and wireless card are getting the address automatically from the router, and the router is getting its external IP address from the ISP. Sometimes, however, there are issues with DHCP servers, or they are reset or reconfigured. This can lead to issues with your computer, such as the need for a new IP address or the need to reset the current one. The following steps show you how to combat these issues.

a. Type `ipconfig/release` to release the IP addresses for both NICs one at a time.

b. Type `ipconfig/all` to display both cards, each void of an IP address (it will actually show `0.0.0.0`). This is shown in Figure 4.5.

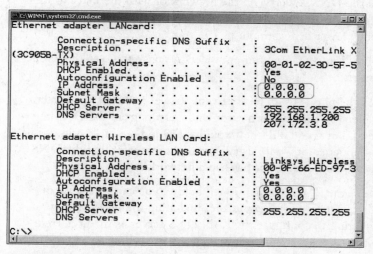

Figure 4.5   Released network adapters.

c. Type `ipconfig/renew` to allow your cards to broadcast out to the network and obtain a new IP, or to renew the same IP address.

d. Type `ipconfig/all`. You should see the old IP addresses back in style! This is a common troubleshooting technique when dealing with DHCP servers and ISPs.

> You can release/renew one of your adapters at a time. The syntax would be **ipconfig/release *lancard***. Notice the name of the card, though. You cannot have a space in the name for this to work. If you wanted to do this, you would need to rename your NIC. In fact, omitting spaces is the proper way to name your NICs, as well as just about everything else in networking.

6. Use `ipconfig` to troubleshoot DNS issues. Sometimes you will need to clear out the DNS cache on the local machine. There may be issues surrounding a DNS server that is no longer on the network, or a DNS server that has been reconfigured. If your system is not up-to-date on all the latest resolutions, and if your client has not reported to a new DNS server, you may have to do the following syntax.

a. Type `ipconfig/flushdns`. Although you don't see anything happen, this command clears out the resolver cache, allowing your computer to start anew so to speak.

b. Type `ipconfig/registerdns`. This will re-register your computer with the DNS server(s) on the network or with the ISP. Notice that you get a message stating that errors will show up in the Event Viewer in 15 minutes.

c. Right-click My Computer and select Manage to go to the Event Viewer.

d. Click the plus (+) sign in the Event Viewer and click the System log file. You should not have any new errors from the DNS registration, but if you did, they would show up here in 15 minutes. If this happened, it would usually be due to the fact that the DNS server is non-existent or has had a network failure.

e. Type `ipconfig/all`. As mentioned before, you can view a lot of information from this command, including the DNS setting. Forgetting to configure the LAN DNS server as the preferred DNS server is a common mistake for new technicians. Quite often, users and techs are only interested in connecting to the Internet, so new technicians input only the ISP DNS server. If you do not have the LAN (domain) DNS server configured, you could have all kinds of problems logging on, connecting to the network, browsing, and so on. This is because everything in today's Windows networks is DNS based. Don't fall into this trap.

7. Test connectivity problems with `ping` and `tracert`. Probably half of all connectivity problems can be troubleshot with the `ping` command. It is simple, but yields a lot of information. That said, although `ping` works well on your network, `tracert` will be needed to effectively test beyond your network. The basic idea you need to keep in mind is when testing, start locally and then branch out step by step. Imagine, for example, that you cannot connect to the Internet. You have already typed `ipconfig/all`, and everything seems to be in place, including your IP address, subnet mask, gateway, and DNS server addresses. Start by troubleshooting with yourself first and then expanding step-by-step through the network and the Internet. Then I will show how to shorten the troubleshooting phase into fewer steps.

a. Type `ping 127.0.0.1`. This pings the local host, you. Because this test does not generate network traffic, it will work without a network cable connected as long as TCP/IP is installed and configured properly. You can also use `ping localhost` or `ping loopback`, but notice the difference between the two in Figure 4.6. One tries to resolve names while the other does not. Because of this host-name resolution (which can be time consuming), you will often want to stick with the syntax `ping 127.0.0.1`.

```
C:\WINNT\system32\cmd.exe                                    _□×
C:\>ping 127.0.0.1

Pinging 127.0.0.1 with 32 bytes of data:

Reply from 127.0.0.1: bytes=32 time<10ms TTL=128
Reply from 127.0.0.1: bytes=32 time<10ms TTL=128
Reply from 127.0.0.1: bytes=32 time<10ms TTL=128
Reply from 127.0.0.1: bytes=32 time<10ms TTL=128

Ping statistics for 127.0.0.1:
    Packets: Sent = 4, Received = 4, Lost = 0 (0% loss),
Approximate round trip times in milli-seconds:
    Minimum = 0ms, Maximum =  0ms, Average =  0ms

C:\>ping localhost

Pinging pc1.testlab.com [127.0.0.1] with 32 bytes of data:

Reply from 127.0.0.1: bytes=32 time<10ms TTL=128
Reply from 127.0.0.1: bytes=32 time<10ms TTL=128
Reply from 127.0.0.1: bytes=32 time<10ms TTL=128
Reply from 127.0.0.1: bytes=32 time<10ms TTL=128

Ping statistics for 127.0.0.1:
    Packets: Sent = 4, Received = 4, Lost = 0 (0% loss),
Approximate round trip times in milli-seconds:
    Minimum = 0ms, Maximum =  0ms, Average =  0ms

C:\>_
```

Figure 4.6 Two types of local-host pings.

To find out your computer name real quick in the command prompt, just type **hostname**.

b. Ping your actual IP address. Type `ping` and the actual IP address of the same computer. An example for us would be the computer we are sitting at right now: 192.168.1.101. On most of today's operating systems, this will not create network traffic, but some other operating systems may actually broadcast over the 192.168.1.0 network when you ping yourself. Because of this varying factor, it is again more suitable to use 127.0.0.1 to ping your localhost. If you do not receive replies from yourself, it is usually a bad sign. TCP/IP is either not installed or is not correctly configured—or worse yet, is corrupted. You may also have an issue with a socket file like `wsock32.dll`. These things would need to be checked before moving on. If you do receive replies, however, then you know that TCP/IP is installed correctly, so you can move on to the next step.

c. Ping another computer on the `192.168.1.0` network, preferably a known good, like the server. For us, the syntax is `ping` `192.168.1.200`. Once again, if you get replies, then you know you can connect to other computers on the network. If you cannot connect, you should try pinging other machines on the network or try the next step.

d. Type `ping 192.168.1.1`. (This may be different depending on which router you are using.) That should ping the gateway address, which is the most reliable of any devices on the network as it is usually not hard-drive based and is always on. If you can connect to the gateway address, then you should be able to connect to other networks, assuming routes are set up properly. You should also be able to connect to the Internet if your DNS information is set up right.

e. Type `ping novell.com`. This should travel past the gateway and, if everything is set up correctly, you should get replies from `novell.com`. If you have trouble receiving replies from novell.com, then it is time to check settings like DNS with the `ipconfig/all` command, and make sure the DNS server is functioning with the `nslookup` command (which we will go over later). Also, make sure the router is functioning properly and that other routers are working between you and your destination. This can be done with the `tracert` command.

f. Type `tracert novell.com` and press Enter. You should get a whole list of information. It should show the routers that are being crossed between you and the final destination of `novell.com`. Each entry is a *hop* or router that is being crossed. As you can see, your system hits each hop with three pings. The routers may be computers or black boxes and may have FQDNs, IP addresses, or both in the listing. The final destination should be `novell.com`: `130.57.4.70`. Figure 4.7 illustrates all the `ping` steps and `tracert` testing we just talked about. The `tracert` has been shortened in the figure, omitting hops 4–15.

Your computer might take a long time to resolve names to IP and vice versa when running the **tracert** command. If this is the case, try using the **tracert –d** switch. This parameter bypasses name resolution and only displays IP addresses. You'll be amazed at the difference in speed!

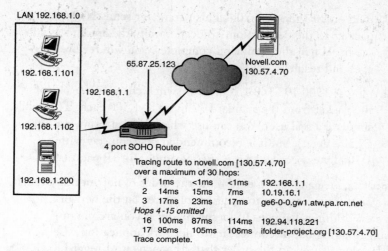

Figure 4.7　Map of network illustrating testing.

g. If you cannot connect to novell.com and have ruled out any local TCP/IP problems, gateway, or DNS problems, use `tracert` to determine which router between you and your destination is malfunctioning. This will show up as a set of asterisks at the bad router. You will see connections to each router along the way, but the first break in the link will be displayed by `tracert`. You then know what router to troubleshoot.

Although this list of steps is very good for the learner, you will find that shortcuts will save you time as you ascend the ranks of computer geekdom. For example, if you work for a company that has a history of problems with its Internet connection, you will probably not bother pinging **127.0.0.1**. Instead, you might jump right to pinging the gateway or a Web site. If a company has a history of router issues in an internetwork or WAN, you might bypass **ping** altogether and just run tracert. You get the feel for this with the network that you are servicing as time goes by. Overall though, it is a good idea to run the preceding steps in order, especially the first time, when troubleshooting a network that is new to you. It will give a lot of insight as to how the network functions.

h. Sometimes you will need a little bit more substance out of your `ping` results. When testing for intermittent problems or trying to create a baseline, you will need to use one of the following switches. Try them now to see the differences:

　i. ping –t 192.168.1.200. This sends an endless ping to the server. Press Ctrl+C to break out of the loop.

    ii. ping –n 20 192.168.1.200. This parameter sends 20 ICMP packets to the destination. You can modify the amount as you see fit. When the command completes, you will receive averages and results.

    iii. ping –l 1500 192.168.1.200. This switch changes the size of the packet from the standard 32 bytes to 1,500 each. This will simulate a real user. You can use whatever size you want (up to 65,500 bytes), but it is recommended that you stay within 1,500 bytes because that is the maximum for IP packets.

8. Use ipconfig, ping and arp to determine the order of networking events. When you want to connect to another computer on the network, a whole slew of things happen. It doesn't matter if you are pinging, browsing, logging on, or connecting to network applications. Let's show the ping process in the order that it happens with regard to IP, ARP, and ICMP.

    a. IP (Internet Protocol) is responsible for giving applying the IP address to you machine, it also takes care of applying an IP address to any other machine on the network. It also calculates the math involved with IP addressing, subnetting, and CIDR. The command ipconfig shows what the IP protocol has done for you. Type ipconfig now. It should show you your IP address, subnet mast, and default gateway address. IP takes care of configuring the math behind your IP address, and converts it to binary for proper transmission over the network.

    b. ARP (Address Resolution Protocol) is the protocol that takes care of converting IP addresses on the Network layer to MAC addresses on the Data Link layer. Type arp -a. You should see at least one line item. Your logon to your domain controller provides you with a permanent connection that should show in the arp table. If it does not show an entry, then type ping 192.168.1.200 and then run arp -a one more time. Our arp table shows the domain controller's IP (192.168.1.200) and its corresponding MAC address.

    arp –g will have the same results as **arp –a**.

    c. Type ping 192.168.1.1 (or whatever your SOHO router's IP is) and press Enter.

d. Type arp -a again. You should now see two entries—one for the IP-to-MAC resolution of the domain controller, and one for the router. This is displayed in Figure 4.8. Notice that the SOHO router gets a MAC address as well, just like any other device on the network. Also notice the Dynamic entry. This means that these particular entries are dynamic in nature. They will disappear from the table in a few minutes. Run arp -a again in about five minutes and you will see what I mean.

```
C:\WINNT\system32\cmd.exe                                    _|□|×|
Interface: 192.168.1.101 on Interface 0x1000003
  Internet Address      Physical Address      Type
  192.168.1.1           00-13-10-2d-2e-ed     dynamic
  192.168.1.200         00-d0-b7-84-36-df     dynamic
C:\>_
```

Figure 4.8 Example of an arp table.

e. Type ping 192.168.1.1 one more time. The ping command sends ICMP (Internet Control Message Protocol) echoes across the network and back. This command really makes use of IP, ARP, and ICMP. First, the IP protocol uses your IP address and later embeds it into the IP packet. IP also works on the destination host and calculates the math across the board. Your computer then performs ARP to resolve from IP address to MAC address as the data moves down the OSI model to the Data Link layer. ARP sees your local MAC address, and then broadcasts across the Ethernet network to find the destination MAC. It then resolves between the two types of addresses on both computers. Finally, the ICMP packet is generated and encapsulated inside an IP packet. This is sent across the network to the receiving computer and is echoed back in the form of replies.

9. Troubleshoot with netstat and nbtstat.

a. Go to PC2.

b. Open the command prompt.

c. Type netstat and study the results. You should see all the outbound ports that are open on the Windows 2000 Server, as shown in Figure 4.9. Although this gives you insight as to what other destinations your server is connecting to, it doesn't reveal the inbound open ports.

Figure 4.9   **netstat** results.

d. Type netstat -an. This will show the inbound TCP and UDP ports that are open as well as some (if not all) of the outbound ports. Notice that ports 53 and 88 are open in Figure 4.10. Also notice that ports 80, 21, and 25 are closed (not shown), because you shut down their corresponding services in a previous lab. Netstat -an is extremely useful when you suspect that there are problems with services or that there are services that need to be shut off. You do not need to download, install, and configure a port scanner to check this on the local machine.

Figure 4.10   **netstat –an** results.

e. Type netstat -e. This will show you the Ethernet statistics of your NIC. It is kind of like double-clicking on your NIC icon in the system tray; the only difference is netstat -e is not dynamic.

f. Type netstat -r. This will show you the routing table for your machine, which allows you to see what connections you have to other networks. It also shows the path or gateway you take to get there, as illustrated in Figure 4.11.

Figure 4.11 The routing table.

g. Type nbtstat -a pc1. This shows the name table for PC1 (the Windows 2000 Professional client). It should look something like Figure 4.12. Notice that the three services—workstation, messenger, and server—are up and running. Also notice that the computer is logged in to a domain named testlab as the administrator. This command is great because you can determine whether any services are not functioning. Let's show that now.

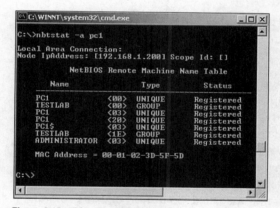

Figure 4.12 PC1 remote name table.

h. Go to PC1 and shut off the ZoneAlarm firewall.

i. Right-click My Computer and select Properties to open the Computer Management console.

j. Expand the Services and Applications category.

k. Click the Services applet.

l. Scroll down on the right side until you get to the Workstation service.

m. Right-click the Workstation service and select Stop. It may tell you that other services are dependent on this service, and that they must be stopped as well. Agree to that in the pop-up dialog box if you see it. It may take a few seconds for the Workstation service to stop; be sure it does before you proceed.

Another way to stop this service is by accessing the command prompt and typing **net stop workstation**.

n. Return to PC2 and type nbtstat -a pc1 in the command prompt. You will notice that the host cannot be found, as shown in Figure 4.13.

Figure 4.13   nbstat –a results.

o. Type nbtstat -A *IPaddress*, where *IPaddress* is the IP of PC1. For us, it is 192.168.1.101, so our syntax is nbtstat -A 192.168.1.101. Your IP may be different. Also, notice the capital A in this command. The results should look like Figure 4.14. Notice that you can see PC1 this time; also, you can tell that only the server service ID <20> is running. Because the workstation service has been stopped, name resolution has failed. So instead of connecting by name, we connected by IP, thus avoiding name resolution altogether. You see that name resolution, messaging, and replies will be stopped when the workstation service is stopped. This is a common problem caused by conflicts within TCP/IP or applications. The workstation service is also a big target for hackers. Now that you know the problem, you can go ahead and repair it.

p. Go to PC1 and access the command prompt.

q. Type net start workstation. Your past few responses should look like Figure 4.15.

Figure 4.14 nbtstat –A results.

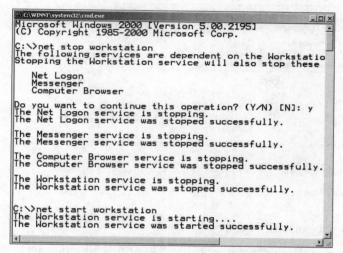

Figure 4.15 The **net start** command.

r. Although this restarts the workstation service, you still have the other dependent services to deal with. They do not start up automatically when workstation is restarted. You can either restart the computer or restart the other individual services in the reverse order of how they were stopped. Return to the Computer Management console and restart these services in order: Computer Browser, Messenger, and Net Logon.

s. Switch to PC2.

t. Type nbtstat -a pc1. Your response should be back to normal! All services are running on PC1 and you can see the whole name table as it originally was except for who is logged in at the current time. To see this, the person at PC1 would either have to restart the computer or log off and log back on. Great work! You can see that nbtstat can be a very helpful tool to you in troubleshooting. The greatest thing is that it is built in and right at your fingertips. Although nbtstat -a and -A are used normally to see remote machines, you can also see the complete list of names for the local machine by using nbtstat-n and nbtstat -r. You can also use nbtstat -R for purging and reloading the name cache. An example of -r and -R is shown in Figure 4.16.

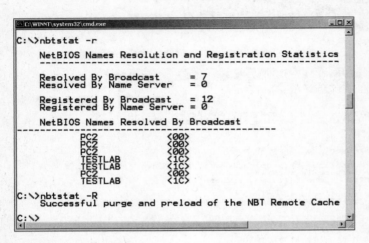

Figure 4.16 nbtstat variations.

10. Use nslookup to resolve DNS issues.

   a. Type nslookup. Notice that it probably did not find your domain controller as the DNS server, and instead only found the ISP DNS server. You should have a valid connection to the LAN DNS server, so you always want to make sure that it is functioning properly. Check the NIC and its DNS setting, then the binding order of the NICs, and finally make sure the firewall is not preventing you from talking to the DNS server. Sometimes, nslookup does not work properly with the Microsoft DNS server, so another way to check whether you are resolving correctly is to type ping pc2. If you get the FQDN as the response (pc2.testlab.com), then you know that DNS is working on your LAN. Also, notice that nslookup drops you into another shell with a different prompt. The prompt does not have the C:\ that you have seen in this lab to this point. Instead you only have the greater than sign. This is the nslookup program.

   b. While still in nslookup type novell.com. You should get the resolved IP address 130.57.4.70. You can find out any IP address or domain name using this nslookup utility. There is much more, however, to this utility. With additional commands, you can find out about servers, debug DNS computers, and use the Finger command to find out more about users. For now we will use nslookup for resolving names to IP only. Try typing the following domain names and check out the results:

    i. Microsoft.com

    ii. Cnn.com

    iii. Davidprowse.com

c. Type ? to see all of the possible options.

d. When you are finished, type exit to return to the regular command prompt and out of the nslookup window.

For more information on TCP/IP utilities like **nslookup** as well as utilities like **dig** and **winipcfg**, reference the *Exam Cram2 Network+ 2e*.

What Did I Just Learn?

In this lab you learned how to work with the various TCP/IP utilities. You took advantage of their commands using syntax in the command prompt. Specifically you learned how to do the following:

➤ Troubleshoot issues with ipconfig.

➤ Use Ping and tracert to overcome networking problems.

➤ Identify the usefulness of netstat and nbtstat.

➤ Utilize nslookup to verify DNS connections.

➤ Modify the command prompt to your liking.

➤ View the network process of IP, ARP, and ICMP.

➤ Prepare for the Network+ sub domains 4.1 and 4.2.

Lab 2: Troubleshooting Physical Links

Orientation

In this procedure you will identify the different link light options on a NIC and a SOHO router. A *link light* is a simple LED (light emitting diode) that resides on the back of your NIC and on hubs and switches. These lights tell you whether you have a physical link to the network and if there is activity on the network connection. You will also learn how to troubleshoot the different light sequences that you see. This applies to the Network+ sub domain 4.3.

Procedure

1. Uninstall ZoneAlarm.

   a. Go to PC1.

   b. Click the Start button, choose Programs, select ZoneLabs, and choose Uninstall ZoneLabs Security.

   c. Click Uninstall.

   d. Click OK when the uninstall finishes.

   e. Click OK to restart the computer.

2. Change NIC and DNS settings.

   a. Right-click My Network Places and select Properties.

   b. Right-click the wireless card and select Enable.

   c. Right-click the LAN card and select Properties.

   d. Double-click Internet Protocol to bring up the Internet Protocol (TCP/IP) Properties dialog box.

   e. Select the Obtain DNS server address automatically option button.

   f. Click OK.

   g. Click OK in the LAN Card Properties dialog box.

   h. Restart PC1.

   i. Log back on to the domain.

3. View link lights and their different modes.

    a. Look at the back of PC1; you should have a couple options for link speed lights. If you are connected as Fast Ethernet, then the 100Mbps light should be on and should be solid. If you are connected as regular Ethernet, you should see the 10Mbps light. You want to connect as fast as possible, and if you have the same Linksys router as I do, it should be at 100Mbps. If this light is not on, then you need to troubleshoot. When the link light is not lit, it means that there is no physical connection. In this case you would do the following:

 Sometimes you will see a yellow or green light. Generally yellow means 10Mbps, and green means 100Mbps. In some cases, with some high-speed cards, you may even see 1,000Mbps showing up as red.

      i. Check the patch cable.

      ii. Check the patch panel port if you have one.

      iii. Check the port on the hub or SOHO router.

      iv. Make sure that the router is plugged in.

    b. Disconnect the patch cable. Notice that the link light turns off immediately.

    c. Reconnect the patch cable and verify that the link light comes back on.

 Some technicians will incorrectly diagnose a missing link light as a TCP/IP problem. It is not. Link lights deal with the Physical layer only. The operating system is not involved. Even if you disable the card, the link light will remain.

    d. Take a look at Figure 4.17 and notice the different NIC link lights.

    e. Look at the back of PC1; there should be a second light on the NIC that blinks on and off intermittently. This is the activity light. Whenever it is blinking, it is sending data across the network. Even if you are not actively transmitting data, the light will blink every one or two seconds. This is a standard broadcast and you should not be alarmed by it.

    f. Go to PC1 and open the command prompt.

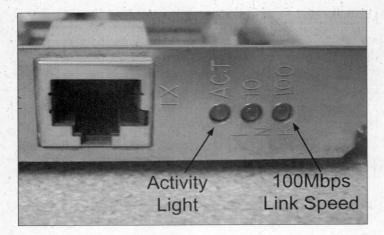

Figure 4.17 NIC link lights.

g. Type `ping -t -l 65000 192.168.1.1`. This will start a very large and endless ping. Leave it running and take note of the activity light on the NIC.

h. Look at the link lights on the front of your SOHO router. Our Linksys has a traffic link for WLAN and link lights for all the physical connections. It also has a link showing that we are connected to the Internet. The power link light is on and the DMZ link light is off. This is shown in Figure 4.18.

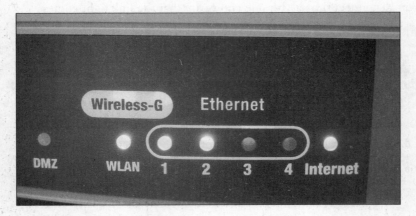

Figure 4.18 SOHO router link lights.

i. Notice that the WLAN link light is steadily getting hit with traffic. That is from your `ping`.

j. Go to PC1 and stop the ping by pressing Ctrl+C.

k. The WLAN link light should now be relatively calm.

l. On PC1, run the same command by pressing the up arrow. You will notice the WLAN light and perhaps the other link lights for the ports showing some life.

m. Leave that running, open a new command prompt, and run the command again, thus doubling the transfer.

n. Go to PC2 and open a command prompt and run the same command.

o. Look at the SOHO router once again. Notice that the WLAN link light is much busier. Also notice that the pings are around 20–50ms instead of less than 10ms. You could keep this up until the router becomes flooded and the network becomes unusable. If this were to happen, you would see the light blinking so fast that it would almost look solid. You can perpetuate this on any port or any computer, and that specific link light would then blink faster and faster as you add traffic. This is the idea behind a Ping of Death. The PoD attack is a huge packet, 1,000,000 bytes. It is designed to take down a server or a router, but today's firewalls can block such attacks easily. In addition, unless you hack the Registry, Windows will limit your packet size to 65,500 bytes.

NOTE The more data transmissions you have, the more collisions you will have. This is a fact of Ethernet networks. For this reason, some devices will have a collision light. This LED light may be red or it may share with the link light. Always check your manufacturer's documentation to see how they offer the collision light. For example, older versions of the Linksys SOHO router that you are using had a separate link light for collisions, but now the light has been removed and it only shows the link/activity light.

p. Press Ctrl+C for all running pings on PC2. Close those command prompts.

q. Press Ctrl+C for all running pings on PC1. Close those command prompts.

To sum up what you have covered, see Table 4.1, which outlines what link lights may show.

Table 4.1	The various link lights notifications.		
Link Speed Light	**Notification/Fix**	**Link Activity Light**	**Notification/Fix**
Solid yellow	Working at 10Mbps. No light	No light	No data is being transmitted. Could indicate a bad connection. Check all links.
Solid green	Working at 100Mbps.	Solid light	Bad connection or flooded with data transmissions. End sessions and/or check links.
No light	Not connected. Check all physical connections. Make sure router and computer are turned on.	Randomly blinking light	Normal transmission
Fast blinking light	Bad connection. Check patch cables, patch panel port, RJ-45 jack, and NIC.	Patterned blinking (for example, every two or three seconds)	Regular broadcast
		Fast patterned blinking (for example, four times every second)	Bad connection. Check all physical links.

NOTE

Here's an example of a common 3Com switch and a summary of its functions as well as the port indicators: http://support.3com.com/infodeli/tools/switches/ss3/3300/3c16986a/chap1.htm.

What Have I Just Learned?

You just prepared for the Network+ sub domain 4.3. You have learned that link lights can tell you a whole lot about the physical connectivity of your network including the following:

➤ Link speed at 10 or 100Mbps

➤ Different types of activity

➤ Whether or not there is a connection

➤ If you have current data transfer

Lab 3: Setting Up Terminal Services and Troubleshooting Operating-System Connectivity Issues

Orientation

In this lab you will set up Terminal Services so that you can control your server remotely from your client. Then you will identify several common problems, their causes, and the solutions to those issues. This will include scenarios where users are not able to connect to the following:

➤ File services

➤ Print services

➤ VPN server

➤ Windows 2000 domain controller

This lab will also help prepare you for the Network+ sub domains 4.4 and 4.5.

Procedure

1. Install Windows 2000 Terminal Services to the Windows 2000 domain controller.

   a. Go to PC2.

   b. Click the Start button, choose Settings, select Control Panel, and choose Add/Remove Programs.

   c. Choose Add/Remove Windows Components.

d. Scroll down and select the Terminal Services and Terminal Services Licensing check boxes. Click Next.

e. In the Terminal Services Setup screen, leave the default option of Remote administration mode and click Next.

f. In the screen that shows the Terminal Services licensing setup, leave the defaults and click Next.

g. If the OS asks you for the Windows 2000 Server CD, insert it now, and install from the i386 folder. The path should be d:\i386. If you have already copied the I386 folder to the HDD, then the path will be c:\I386.

h. When it is complete, click Finish.

i. If you haven't done so already, copy the Windows 2000 Server I386 folder from the CD to the server's hard drive.

j. Share the following path for later mapping:
`C:\winnt\system32\clients\`
`tsclient\win32\disks.`

k. Share it as `tsdisks`.

2. Install the Windows 2000 Terminal Client to the Windows 2000 Professional machine.

   a. On PC1, map a drive to `\\servername\tsdisks` where *servername* is the name of the server (for example, `\\PC2\tsdisks`) or `\\serverip\tsdisks` where *serverip* is the server's IP address (for example, `\\192.168.1.200\tsdisks`).

   b. Double-click Disk1.

   c. Run `setup.exe` and complete the installation on the client side.

3. Run Terminal Services.

   a. Click the Start button, choose Programs, select Terminal Services Client, and choose Terminal Services Client again.

   b. Type the IP of the server you would like to control remotely (for example, `192.168.1.200`).

   c. Log in to the server as you normally would. You can now use this service to remotely control the server. It will show up on your client as just another window!

You have multiple options for ending a remote-control session when you are finished. The first is to click the Start button, select Shutdown, and choose logoff. This closes all applications that you had open on the server, ends the session, and logs you out. The other option is to disconnect, which is also in the Shutdown window. This ends your remote session but not the actual logon. That means that if you had applications open, they will stay open. If you were to reconnect via Terminal Services and log on you, would see the applications just as they were. This can be very helpful when running longer installs or batch files. Another way to disconnect is to close the Terminal Services window by clicking the × in the upper-right corner, but the session will still be running on the local domain controller. Keep that in mind as the number of concurrent sessions you can have to the DC are limited.

If you are working on a Windows XP machine, you may also use Remote Desktop to connect to Terminal Services on a Windows 2000 Server.

    d. If you have trouble connecting via Terminal Services, make sure of the following:

       ➤ You are using the correct name, or better yet, IP address of the server you want to remotely control.

       ➤ The server is available.

       ➤ You have not reached the maximum sessions allotted.

       ➤ Other admins are logging off when finished with a session as opposed to disconnecting only.

       ➤ Terminal Services is running on the server in question.

4. Identify issues when users are trying to map a network drive. If a user calls you and says he or she is having trouble mapping a network drive within the command prompt, do the following:

    a. Find out what he or she is trying to map to.

    b. Find out whether he or she has permissions to this share.

    c. Find out whether he or she has ever been able to connect to this share before.

    d. Verify the path to the share.

    e. Verify that the user is typing the syntax as follows: `net use x: \\computername\sharename`.

    f. Verify that there is a space between `net` and `use` as well as between the drive letter and the path.

g. Verify the computer name (or IP address) and the name of the share (which may be different from the name of the folder).

h. If the user still cannot make the connection, skip to step 6, "Verify TCP/IP settings, logon information, and connections."

5. Identify issues when users are trying to connect to printing resources. If a user cannot print, there can be a myriad of reasons. Check the following:

   a. Does the user have rights to the printer?

   b. Did the printer ever work before?

   c. Is the local job halted for any reason?

   d. Is the printer online?

   e. Is the printer over queued?

   f. Has anyone paused the print job or the printer? (See Figure 4.19).

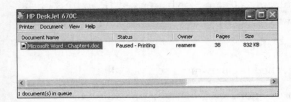

Figure 4.19 A paused print job.

g. Does the printer work for you when you print from your machine?

h. Does the printer have paper, ink, and so on?

i. If the user still cannot make the connection, proceed to step 6, "Verify TCP/IP settings, logon information, and connections."

6. Verify TCP/IP settings, logon information, and connections.

   a. Make sure the user is logged in correctly. Have him or her press Ctrl+Alt+Del to see what network he or she is logged onto and who he or she is logged on as. For example, you are logged onto the domain testlab.com as administrator. This is shown in your Security dialog box as `testlab\administrator`.

   b. Verify that the user has a solid link light on his or her NIC and a working activity light. If there is no link, you will have to physically fix the problem. Refer to Chapter 1, "Media and Topologies," and Chapter 3, "Network Implementation," for information about the various wiring problems that can occur and what tools to use to fix them.

c. Have the user type `ipconfig/all`.

d. Verify that the user is on a valid network with the correct subnet mask.

e. Make sure that the user has the proper gateway and DNS addresses configured.

f. Have the user ping the gateway to verify that he or she can connect on the network.

7. Identify issues when connecting to a VPN server.

a. Find out what error number is being received by the user—for example, 721, 781, and so on.

b. Collect information about the VPN logon and validate its correctitude. This includes but is not limited to the following:

➤ IP address

➤ User name and password

➤ Type of authentication

➤ Type of tunneling

c. Verify that the user has a working Internet connection.

d. Have the user connect again and give the exact error.

e. If you have not seen the problem before, visit http://support.microsoft.com and query `"Error 721"`, `"Error 792"`, or whatever the error might be.

f. Verify that the user has the dial-in permission enabled in his or her User Account Properties on the Windows 2000 Server.

8. Identify issues when clients cannot connect to the domain controller.

a. Verify the user's user name and password, and check to make sure the Caps Lock is not on!

b. Verify that the user is logging on to the domain and not the local machine. This option is found in the drop-down menu in the Ctrl+Alt+Del logon dialog box.

    c. Make sure that the user has the correct IP settings, especially the DNS server. Refer to step 6, "Verify TCP/IP settings, logon information, and connections," for more on this.

    d. Verify that the user is actually a member of the domain. This can be done by right-clicking on My Computer, selecting Properties, and then selecting Network ID.

    e. Make sure the user has rights or permissions to the specific part of the domain he or she wants to access.

You have many other resources at your disposal when troubleshooting. First and foremost, these include the techs around you and the other members of your team. Chances are they have seen a particular problem before. Other resources include the following:

➤ Manufacturers' Web sites

➤ Help files, READMEs, and CD-ROM manuals

➤ Online manuals

➤ Message-board systems

➤ Resource kits

➤ Tech-support hotlines

 People are usually your best bet because they are probably close by, and are likely to have seen the exact problem in the past.

What Did I Just Learn?

In this section you found that troubleshooting is a big part of networking. You also learned how to install Terminal Services, which can be instrumental in aiding you to troubleshoot server issues remotely on the LAN. In the lab you learned how to identify and diagnose some basic issues concerning the following:

➤ Logging on

➤ Connecting to the domain

➤ Mapping to shared resources

➤ Print jobs

➤ Remote sessions

Lab 4: Installation of DHCP and Comprehension of Service Issues

Orientation

In this lab you will install the DHCP service. Installing DHCP will allow your client machines to obtain IP addresses automatically. You will also discover some troubleshooting techniques for common problems with a client/server DHCP environment. This lab will also prepare you for the Network+ sub domain 4.6.

DHCP (Dynamic Host Configuration Protocol) was created to ease administration on network administrators. It automatically assigns IP address and advanced IP information to clients. It eliminates the chance of IP conflicts and a host of other problems. Like any other client/server application, however, it requires more design and configuration in order for it to work properly. That said, a little bit of time preparing a DHCP server can save you that time tenfold when it comes to the client side. Let's go ahead and set up DHCP on the server and then on the client.

Procedure

1. Install the DHCP Service on the Windows 2000 domain controllers.

    a. Click the Start button, choose Settings, select Control Panel, and choose Add/Remove Programs.

    b. Choose Add/Remove Windows Components.

    c. Scroll down and click Networking Services, and then click Details.

| Make sure not to remove the check mark, just click the words "Networking Services."

    d. Select the DHCP check box and install the service from the I386 folder. This is illustrated in Figure 4.20.

2. Create a new scope for DHCP.

    a. Open your saved MMC.

    b. Insert a new snap-in, the DHCP console.

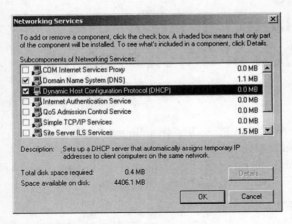

Figure 4.20 DHCP installation.

    c. Right-click DHCP and choose Add Server.

    d. Add your domain controller (PC2) as a DHCP server if it is not there already. You will see that the server has a red arrow pointing down. This means that the DHCP server service has not been started yet.

    e. Right-click the server and choose New Scope.

    f. Name the scope and click Next.

    g. Create a range of IP addresses that will be used—for example, 192.168.1.150–192.168.1.199, as shown in Figure 4.21.

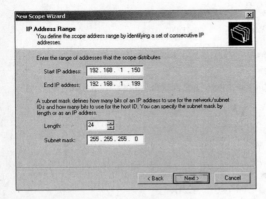

Figure 4.21 A new DHCP scope.

    h. Your subnet mask will be 255.255.255.0. Click Next.

i. You do not need exclusions or reservations at this time. Click Next.

j. Choose the default lease time. Click Next.

3. Configure advanced options.

a. Select the Yes, I want to configure these options now option button and click Next.

b. Establish the router as being at the following IP address: 192.168.1.1. This may also be referred to as the *gateway*.

c. The DNS server is your domain controller and should be 192.168.1.200, as shown in Figure 4.22. (If you chose a different IP for your DNS server, enter that now.)

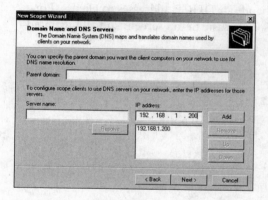

Figure 4.22   DNS server advanced option.

d. Do not configure WINS.

e. In the next window, select Activate the scope.

4. Set the server in motion.

If you haven't done so already, you can make the scope active by right-clicking on it in the MMC and selecting Activate.

a. Right-click the server (PC2) and choose Authorize Server. When you do this, the server should get a green arrow pointing up. If you don't, try the following:

    i Collapse the − sign to a plus sign and then expand it.

    ii. Save the MMC, close it, and then re-open it.

    iii. Collapse and expand the DHCP service once again.

This is a glitch in Windows 2000 Server when utilizing the MMC. It might take you a few attempts, but keep at it until you get the green arrow pointing up. When you see the green arrow, you know that the DHCP service is running. Another service that can get in the way of DHCP is RRAS. If you are still running a network router or VPN server within RRAS, try shutting it down and restarting the server. Then see if DHCP works.

5. Turn off DHCP on the SOHO router.

    a. Log in to your router.

    b. Turn off the ability to hand out DHCP addresses to clients. For our Linksys, this is in Setup>Basic Setup screen, and is illustrated in Figure 4.23.

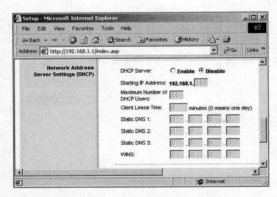

Figure 4.23   Turning off the router's DHCP function.

Make sure to turn off the DHCP feature, the ability for the router to *hand out* DHCP addresses. Do *not* turn off the feature allowing the SOHO router to *receive* an IP address automatically from the ISP.

6. Configure the clients to obtain IP addresses automatically from the server.

    a. Go to the Internet Protocol (TCP/IP) Properties dialog box for your client (PC1).

    b. Select the Obtain an IP address automatically option button.

c. Do the same for DNS.

> If you have more than one DHCP server, you may notice that *all* clients get their IP from the same DHCP server. This is because all servers are connected to the same switch on the same network. When this is the case (and this is rare in a company), the first DHCP server to come up is the one to lease the addresses!

    d. You may also need to run an `ipconfig/release` to release the IP from the NIC. Then run `ipconfig/renew` to find a new IP, which should come from the DHCP server.

7. Test the clients.

    a. Run an `ipconfig/all` and view your information. Verify that you are getting your IP from the DHCP server, `192.168.1.200`.

    b. Ping a known good address. Try `ping 192.168.1.1`. You should get replies.

8. Return everything back to normal.

    a. Go back to the server and stop the DHCP service. You can do this from the DHCP section in your MMC by de-activating the scope and unauthorizing the server or turning off the service in Services and Applications. If you prefer the former, simply right-click the scope and select Deactivate, and then right-click the server and choose Unauthorize.

    b. Turn DHCP on within your SOHO router.

    c. Go to PC1 and open the command prompt.

    d. Type ipconfig/release and then ipconfig/renew.

Some Common DNS and WINS Issues

DNS (Domain Naming System) can have several problems. These are usually due to incorrect setup. The following is a list of a few of these and their proper solution:

➤ **Clients are not resolving properly.** If you want to verify whether clients are resolving correctly to a Microsoft DNS server, you can go to a client command prompt and type `ping pc2`. You can also ping another client or server on the network. When we do that here, we want the correct response `pinging pc2.testlab.com`. That is a Fully Qualified Domain Name (FQDN). If the response said only `pc2`, then you would know that DNS is not resolving properly. Most likely you would modify the DNS IP setting within the client's Internet Protocol (TCP/IP) Properties dialog box. Next, you would make sure that the DNS server is functional.

➤ **Wrong type of zone.** There are many reasons why this could have occurred, but if you are running a Windows 2000 domain with a Windows 2000 Server taking care of your DNS resolution, then you normally want an Active Directory Integrated Zone for client resolution. If you instead see a primary or secondary zone, you will want to install an ADIZ, and then run an `ipconfig/flushdns` and `ipconfig/registerdns` on each of the clients. You would most likely batch this out in one shot.

➤ **The domain is looking to the incorrect DNS server.** Some technicians love to have every computer access the Internet. Unfortunately for them, if a Windows 2000 Server is set to access the Internet with the ISP's DNS server in the Internet Protocol (TCP/IP) Properties dialog box, it will cause all kinds of grief when promoting that server to a domain controller. Instead of looking to a LAN DNS server for resolutions of everything within Active Directory, it will be looking to the Internet DNS server. This server will just bounce all the requests back, and it will knock out a little bit of data throughput on the Internet connection. To fix this, you would need to reconfigure the Active Directory and reconfigure the DNS server and its Active Directory Integrated Zone (if it has one). In reality, you want to prevent this from happening at all costs. Whenever promoting a server to a domain controller, make sure to check all TCP/IP settings, especially the DNS server IP address. Also, use `nbtstat -A 192.168.1.200` (or whatever IP your server is) to make sure the three big services are running.

WINS (Windows Internet Naming Service) is really only used if you have legacy Windows 95/98/Me systems on the network. This is because the Windows 9x clients don't work well (if at all) with DNS. They need to use NetBIOS name-to–IP address resolution instead of host name–to–IP address resolution. Even though WINS is automated and creates and maintains the `WINS.mdb` for you automatically, you may still encounter a few of the following problems:

➤ **Windows 9x clients are not resolving to Windows NT/2000 clients properly.** If you have a hybrid network (for example, one with Windows 98 and Windows 2000), you will need to set up the WINS server IP in the Internet Protocol (TCP/IP) Properties dialog box of all clients, Windows 98 and Windows 2000 alike. Even though Windows 2000 clients normally use DNS, the Windows 9x clients cannot. So the WINS server will need a list of *all* clients on the network that the Windows 9x clients may need to talk to.

➤ **The WINS service is stopped.** Services can be stopped for a plethora of reasons. To restart the WINS service on the server, go to Computer Management, choose Services and Applications, select Services, choose WINS, and choose Start.

➤ **Clients are using the wrong broadcast method.** Windows 9*x* clients have several options when it comes to broadcasting their NETBIOS names. 0X8 hybrid mode is usually the choice of admins. Make sure that all clients are set the same way, and that the WINS server is accepting that type of broadcast transmission.

For more information on WINS, DHCP and other client/server services, reference the *Network+ Exam Prep, 2e.*

What Did I Just Learn?

In this lab you learned how to set up a working DHCP environment. You also learned how to enable and disable DHCP on the server and the router. Specifically, you learned how to do the following:

➤ Set up the DHCP service in Windows 2000 Server.

➤ Create an IP scope in DHCP.

➤ Activate and Authorize the DHCP server.

➤ Enable and disable DHCP on the SOHO router.

➤ Obtain IP on the clients from your server.

➤ Troubleshoot common DHCP problems.

➤ Troubleshoot common WINS and DNS problems.

Lab 5: Novell Server and Client Install (Optional)

Orientation

For this lab you will need a Novell Server (Products) version 5.0 CD. An evaluation copy of this is available at http://www.novell.com. You will also need to download the latest free client version 4.91 from http://www.novell.com.

You have three choices when booting up a Novell Server install. The first is to boot off of CD. Unfortunately, this will only be possible if your BIOS is El Torito 2.0–compliant. This is usually only available on servers. The other two options are to boot off of a Netware boot floppy or a Windows 95 CDRSD (CD-ROM Setup Disk). The NetWare boot floppy can be created from the Novell CD and the Windows 95 CDRSD can be downloaded from http://www.bootdisk.com. I recommend skipping to step 2 and booting from the Windows 95 CDRSD.

Procedure

Installing Novell Products 5.0

1. Boot NetWare 5.0 Products (Server) DOS from the NetWare boot floppy.

   a. Make sure the BIOS is configured to boot to removable devices (floppy) first.

   b. Boot the machine with the boot disk. Run the FDISK program and notice the differences from MS FDISK. Remove all partitions.

 If you have a CD-ROM driver that is NetWare-compatible, then you should have no problem using this boot disk in conjunction with the CD. But because the CD-ROM drivers have only Microsoft drivers available, we are going to use the DOS disk 1 as a boot disk. Again, it is possible to boot off of the NetWare CD-ROM itself but only if your system BIOS is El Torito 2.0–compliant.

or

2. Install NetWare 5.0 by booting off of Windows 95 CDRSD.

   a. Boot to the Windows 95 CDRSD. Run FDISK and wipe out all partitions.

   b. Restart the computer with a Ctrl+Alt+Del.

   c. Create a primary partition for the Novell DOS partition as C: and make it 2,047MB.

   d. Set the primary partition as Active.

   e. Restart the system, booting to the floppy.

f. Format the C: drive using the `format c: /s` command (if you were using the Novell boot disk, you would need to type `format c:/s/x` where *x* is a fixed disk.)

g. Copy the `mscdex.exe` file from the Windows 95 CDRSD to C: using the following command: `copy a:\mscdex.exe c:.`

h. After the system is transferred, reboot the machine into C:.

  i. Load the CD-ROM driver and reboot. For this you can use any standard CD-ROM driver floppy. You can download this from any major CD-ROM manufacturer's Web site or from http://www.bootdisk.com.

3. Install from the CD.

  a. Insert the Novell Products 5.0 CD and look at the D: drive. Run the `install.bat` program off the root directory in the CD.

  b. Continue through the Novell installation in the text mode using the tab-delimited format.

Choose SVGA or Standard VGA Mode. For many video cards, you must choose Standard mode, even though it may be an SVGA card.

  c. Install the proper NIC.

  d. At the Volume SYS portion, choose 5,000MB for the partition.

  e. Continue with the GUI portion of the installation:

    i. Tree: testlabtree

    ii. Context: testlabcontext

    iii. User name: Admin

    iv. Password: password. We are using the word `password`. Although you can use whatever you want, I recommend that you stick to `password` for now.

    v. IP address: `192.168.1.201`

    vi. Subnet mask: `255.255.255.0`

    vii. Components: Agree to the default components only.

viii. Path: If at any time the install asks for a path and shows `:Netware.` or something similar, just change the path to D:.

f. The file copy may take some time, so you can skip to the "Installing the Novell Client" exercise that follows while the installation is completing.

g. Check the configuration.

h. Reboot the Novell servers to check the installation.

i. Go to the System Console (press Ctrl+Esc for the menu). Then choose number 1 for System Console.

j. Run `tping 192.168.1.1` to make sure that your server can connect on the network.

k. Press Ctrl+Esc and return to the GUI.

l. When you are finished working with Novell Server, press Ctrl+Esc, then select the System Console. Then type `down`, which will down the server to DOS mode. After that, you can just power down the machine.

Installing the Novell Client

The Novell Client is freeware, and can be installed on any Microsoft Windows platform.

1. Install the Novell Client 4.91 (you can also use 4.9 or 4.83).

a. Download the new client from http://`www.novell.com`, under "Downloads."

b. Unzip if necessary, and Install it to the Windows 2000 Professional computer.

c. Restart the Windows 2000 Professional computer.

d. Log in to the network as admin with the password you selected previously. This will most likely be `password`. Select the tree, context, and server by browsing.

For more information about Novell, or if you have any questions about this lab, visit http://www.technicalblog.com.

Lab 6: Physical Layer Troubleshooting and Methodology

Orientation

In this lab you will cover the standard CompTIA troubleshooting methodology, and apply it to a couple of different concepts:

➤ Star topology network connectivity issues

➤ Interference issues

The CompTIA Network+ Troubleshooting Methodology

CompTIA's troubleshooting methodology is a set of eight steps that help you identify, diagnose, and fix network problems. You can use this methodology to help organize your thought process. Whenever you encounter a problem, try to break it down according to these steps:

1. Identify the symptoms and potential causes.

2. Identify the affected area.

3. Establish what has changed.

4. Select the most probable cause.

5. Implement an action plan and solution including potential effects.

6. Test the result.

7. Identify the results and effects of the solution.

8. Document the solution and process.

Star Topology Network Connectivity Issues

One of the biggest problems on the network is an incorrectly configured physical connection. Because the star topology is the most commonly used, let's go over a scenario and troubleshoot it step by step.

Scenario: You are the administrator for an Ethernet network with 40 computers, two servers, a router, and two cascaded switches to which all the hosts connect. You get a call from a user (Sally) stating that she cannot connect to the network. You have already narrowed it down to a Physical layer problem. You note that the link light on the switch for that person's computer is not lit. Troubleshoot!

Procedure

1. Identify the symptoms and potential causes.

   a. Symptom: User cannot get on the network.

   b. Symptom: The user's link light is not lit.

   c. Possible causes: Bad port on the switch, bad patch cable to the switch, incorrectly terminated patch panel or RJ-45 jack, faulty patch cable to the computer, faulty NIC, computer is not on.

2. Identify the affected area.

   a. All other link lights are solid and working, so you know the affected area is one computer only.

3. Establish what has changed.

   a. The user tells you that she had access yesterday, but when she came in this morning, she could not connect when booting up normally. Sally mentions that the cleaning people came last night and were vacuuming around her desk. She was aggravated because they vacuumed right over some designs that she had rolled up on the floor next to and in front of her desk.

4. Select the most probable cause.

   a. Most likely the patch cable at Sally's computer is causing the problem, as shown in Figure 4.24. It has either been disconnected, damaged by the vacuum, or vacuumed away! This is common. Assume the worst, that the cable has been damaged.

5. Implement an action plan and solution including potential effects.

   a. Request a new patch cable from supply and bring it to Sally's desk.

   b. Turn off Sally's computer.

   c. Replace the faulty patch cable with the new one. Make sure that the speed of the patch cable is correct to allow for maximum data transmission.

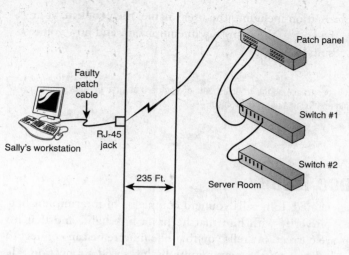

Figure 4.24 Star topology diagram showing faulty area.

6. Test the result.

  a. Boot Sally's computer.

  b. Look for a link light.

  c. Test to see if you can ping, connect to mapped drives, connect to the Internet, and so on.

  d. Make sure there are no sporadic link light changes, and run a `ping -t -l 1500 192.168.1.1` to get a good idea of whether the cable will be okay.

  e. Restart the computer one more time and test once more.

7. Identify the results and effects of the solution.

  a. The results show that the patch cable was indeed faulty. Place the old patch cable in the garbage or recycling as per company policy.

  b. Note that patch cables should either be mounted better, or that a memo should be sent to the cleaning team!

8. Document the solution and process.

  a. Documentation should actually have started in the beginning. In most companies, you will have some kind of ticketing system, whether on paper or online. When a user first contacts you, you must open up a trouble ticket and document everything that you do as it happens.

b. Enter information including the user's name, the problem, your solution, the cost to the company in equipment, and how you tested your results.

Remember to use all the troubleshooting resources at your disposal when diagnosing and fixing a network problem.

Interference Issue

Scenario: A user named Tom calls you and complains of intermittent network problems. You verify with him that he has a link light, and that his TCP/IP settings are correct. He tells you that one minute he can connect to a mapped network drive and the next minute he loses said connection. He also tells you that the fluorescent light above him starts buzzing louder than usual at times, and at those times, he loses the network connection to his mapped network drive. You note that there are no defective link lights and that all link status looks normal.

Procedure

1. Identify the symptoms and potential causes.

   a. Symptom: Intermittent connections to mapped network drives.

   b. Symptom: Buzzing from light happens concurrently with network loss.

   c. Possible cause: Light fixture is too close in proximity to network cabling causing EMI (electromagnetic interference).

   d. Possible cause: Faulty patch cable.

   e. Possible cause: Intermittently faulty punch down.

2. Identify the affected area.

   a. Only the user, Tom.

3. Establish what has changed.

   a. Over the past couple days, Tom has noticed the buzzing of the fluorescent light.

4. Select the most probable cause.

   a. Light fixture. Fluorescent lights can put out enough EMI to make a network connection intermittently weak or to force network loss altogether.

5. Implement an action plan and solution including potential effects.

   a. Make a service call to Tom's desk. Inspect above the drop ceiling and locate the network cable with a Fox and Hound testing kit (tone Generator and inductive amplifier). Secure the cable to the deck (ceiling above the drop ceiling), and make sure that it is far from the fluorescent-light fixture.

   b. Have someone in maintenance replace the ballast in the light fixture to reduce audible noise.

6. Test the result.

   a. Return to Tom's computer and connect to the mapped network drive. Reconnect a few more times and tell Tom to watch the results over the next day or so.

7. Identify the results and effects of the solution.

   a. If after a day passes you have not heard from Tom, give him a call to find out whether the problem has occurred again. If not, then you can identify that the light fixture was the culprit and that your solution was viable.

8. Document the solution and process.

   a. Document the entire process in your trouble ticketing system and have Tom sign off if necessary.

There are several different troubleshooting processes out there, but one of the keys to remember is to *stay calm*. Before you start *doing* anything, you really want to analyze the situation. Identify what is happening so that you don't rush any unnecessary or even dangerous configurations. Don't let the stress of the workplace get in your way. Just step back and look at the situation as if you were a computer yourself! Think like Spock from *Star Trek*, and all should be fine.

Another thing to remember is to prioritize when troubleshooting. For example, your boss's printer is going to be more important than an accountant's CD-ROM drive. This is not only because of the chain of command but also because of the severity of the problem.

For more information on troubleshooting, check out Que's *Network+ Exam Cram 2, 2e.*

Well, that wraps it up for this lab, and for this chapter. Let's review what you have covered.

What Did I Just Learn?

In this section you learned the value of proper troubleshooting. You also worked through a couple of scenarios and how the troubleshooting process applies to them. In this lab you learned how to do the following:

➤ Identify the eight CompTIA troubleshooting steps.

➤ Troubleshoot connectivity problems.

➤ Diagnose and fix interference issues.

➤ Recognize the value of prioritization and patience.

Farewell

This is the end of the fourth and final chapter. If you have made it this far, I commend you! Hopefully you have gained from what I have had to share. It has been my pleasure to bring this lab manual to you. Don't forget to go through the exam questions and the appendix information and to contact me at my Web site if you have any questions! These resources will help you greatly. Until next time, take good care of yourself.

Sincerely,

David L. Prowse

http://www.technicalblog.com

Domain 4 Practice Questions

Objectives 4.1 and 4.2

4.1 Given a troubleshooting scenario, select the appropriate network utility from the following: Tracert / traceroute, ping, arp, netstat, nbtstat, ipconfig / ifconfig, winipcfg, nslookup / dig.

4.2 Given output from a network diagnostic utility (For example: those utilities listed in objective 4.1), identify the utility and interpret the output.

1. Which command would you use if you wanted to verify a router's existence that is three hops away?
   - ❑ a. **tracert**
   - ❑ b. **arp**
   - ❑ c. **nbtstat**
   - ❑ d. **netstat**

2. Which command will send ICMP echoes that have been increased to 1,500 bytes each?
   - ❑ a. **arp -1500**
   - ❑ b. **ping −n 1500**
   - ❑ c. **ping −l 1500**
   - ❑ d. **ping −t 1500**

3. Which command will resolve domain names to IP addresses for you?
   - ❑ a. **arp**
   - ❑ b. **netstat**
   - ❑ c. **nbtstat**
   - ❑ d. **nslookup**

4. What command will turn off a service?
   - ❑ a. **net send**
   - ❑ b. **net share**
   - ❑ c. **net stop**
   - ❑ d. **net start**

5. Which utility command will show all open inbound ports?
   - ❑ a. **nbtstat −r**
   - ❑ b. **netstat −an**
   - ❑ c. **netstat**
   - ❑ d. **nbtstat**

Objective 4.3

4.3 Given a network scenario, interpret visual indicators (For example: link LEDs (Light Emitting Diode) and collision LEDs (Light Emitting Diode)) to determine the nature of a stated problem.

1. Which light on a NIC will show if you have a good physical connection?
   - ❑ a. LED light
   - ❑ b. Link light
   - ❑ c. Activity light
   - ❑ d. Normal light

2. What color is normally associated with 100Mbps?
   - ❑ a. Yellow
   - ❑ b. Red
   - ❑ c. Green
   - ❑ d. Purple

3. If your link light is blinking, what should you check?
   - ❑ a. Patch cables
   - ❑ b. Activity light
   - ❑ c. NIC driver
   - ❑ d. TCP/IP settings

4. Which type of networking technology sends broadcasts?
   - ❑ a. Ethernet
   - ❑ b. Token Ring
   - ❑ c. Token passing
   - ❑ d. 10BASET

5. Which of the following best describe a collision?
   - ❑ a. Two tokens sharing the same bandwidth
   - ❑ b. Two frames of data hitting each other, rendering both unusable
   - ❑ c. One token crashing into another
   - ❑ d. Two packets going in opposite directions

Objectives 4.4 and 4.5

4.4 Given a troubleshooting scenario involving a client accessing remote network services, identify the cause of the problem (For example: file services, print services, authentication failure, protocol configuration, physical connectivity and SOHO (Small Office / Home Office) router).

4.5 Given a troubleshooting scenario between a client and the following server environments, identify the cause of a stated problem: UNIX / Linux / Mac OS X Server, Netware, Windows, Appleshare IP (Internet Protocol).

1. Terminal Services allow you to do which of the following?
   - ❏ a. Remotely connect to a VPN server
   - ❏ b. Remotely control a Windows XP computer
   - ❏ c. Remotely control a Windows 2000 Server
   - ❏ d. Remotely connect to a Cisco router

2. If a user cannot log on to the domain, what should you check first? (Select two.)
   - ❏ a. Caps Lock
   - ❏ b. User name and password
   - ❏ c. IP address
   - ❏ d. Subnet mask

3. If only one user out of 10 cannot connect via VPN to the corporate network, what should you check? (Select two.)
   - ❏ a. IP address of the VPN server
   - ❏ b. Name of the server
   - ❏ c. Dial-in permissions
   - ❏ d. The corporate firewall

4. If a user cannot map a network drive, what should you check first?
   - ❏ a. Whether the server is functional
   - ❏ b. Whether the user is logged on to the domain
   - ❏ c. Dial-in permissions
   - ❏ d. Whether the syntax correct

5. If a print job is too large for a printer and is being held in status, and you can't get it passed the print queue, what should you do?
   - ❏ a. Pause the print job
   - ❏ b. Delete the print job
   - ❏ c. Uninstall the printer
   - ❏ d. Reinstall the print driver

Objective 4.6

4.6 Given a scenario, determine the impact of modifying, adding or removing network services (For example: DHCP (Dynamic Host Configuration Protocol), DNS (Domain Name Service) and WINS (Windows Internet Name Service)) for network resources and users.

1. What type of name resolution do Windows 98 computers use?
   - ❑ a. DNS
   - ❑ b. ARP
   - ❑ c. DDNS
   - ❑ d. WINS

2. What is the default lease time for a DHCP address?
   - ❑ a. Eight days
   - ❑ b. One month
   - ❑ c. Eight months
   - ❑ d. One year

3. You ping a Windows 2000 Professional client from your Windows XP computer, Yet your result is the name PC1 instead of the FQDN PC1.TESTLAB.COM. What is the most likely reason?
   - ❑ a. The DNS server is down
   - ❑ b. The WINS server is down
   - ❑ c. The DNS server IP address is incorrectly configured
   - ❑ d. The WINS Server IP address is incorrectly configured

4. How do you make a DHCP scope ready to hand out IP addresses?
   - ❑ a. Authorize it
   - ❑ b. Activate it
   - ❑ c. Trigger it
   - ❑ d. Initiate it

5. You have a network with two subnets. There is a DHCP server on subnet A that is configured to hand out IP addresses to all computers. If you have a router separating subnet A and subnet B and you need to hand out DHCP addresses to computers on the subnet B, what should you install?
   - ❑ a. A second DHCP server
   - ❑ b. A DNS server
   - ❑ c. A WINS server
   - ❑ d. A DHCP Relay Agent

Objectives 4.7–4.9

4.7 Given a troubleshooting scenario involving a network with a particular physical topology (For example: bus, star, mesh or ring) and including a network diagram, identify the network area affected and the cause of the stated failure.

4.8 Given a network troubleshooting scenario involving an infrastructure (For example: wired or wireless) problem, identify the cause of a stated problem (For example: bad media, interference, network hardware or environment).

4.9 Given a network problem scenario, select an appropriate course of action based on a logical troubleshooting strategy.

1. Which of the following steps should you do first when troubleshooting?
   - ❑ a. Identify symptoms
   - ❑ b. Identify the affected area
   - ❑ c. Panic
   - ❑ d. Test the result

2. What is the last step in the troubleshooting process?
   - ❑ a. Select the most probable cause
   - ❑ b. Identify symptoms
   - ❑ c. Document the solution
   - ❑ d. Establish what has changed

3. If you do not see a link light on the NIC, what is the most probable cause?
   - ❑ a. The hub is broken
   - ❑ b. A patch cable is faulty
   - ❑ c. TCP/IP is incorrectly configured
   - ❑ d. There are collisions on the network

4. Which of the following could cause EMI (electromagnetic interference)? (Select two.)
   - ❑ a. Junction box
   - ❑ b. Plenum
   - ❑ c. Radio waves
   - ❑ d. Fluorescent light fixture

5. Which of the following could cause RFI?
   - ❑ a. Junction box
   - ❑ b. Plenum
   - ❑ c. Wireless access point
   - ❑ d. Category 5e UTP

Answers and Explanations

Objectives 4.1 and 4.2

1. Answer a is correct. `tracert` will check each step along the way to the final destination, whatever it might be. `arp` resolves between IP addresses and MAC addresses. `nbtstat` will show you the remote (or local) name table and services that are running. `netstat` shows the local sessions.

2. Answer c is correct. `-l` is the switch that increases the buffer size for the ping packets. ICMP is the echo packet that is sent when you ping another host on the network. Answers a and d are incorrect syntax. Answer b would send 1,500 packets but won't change the size of the packets.

3. Answer d is correct. `nslookup` is a command and a mini program that will resolve domain names to IP and vice versa.

4. Answer c is correct. `net stop` will turn off a service in the command prompt. An example would be `net stop messenger`. `net start` will allow a service to start up, `net share` will share a folder or printer, and `net send` allows you to send text messages across the network.

5. Answer b is correct. `netstat -an` will show all inbound ports as well as many outbound ports. `netstat` by itself will show only a few (if any) of the inbound ports, yet it shows all the TCP outbound ports. `nbtstat` by itself will bring up the help file and `nbtstat -r` will show the name resolution and registration statistics.

Objective 4.3

1. Answer b is correct. The link light shows if you have a good physical link to the network. The activity light shows when data is being transmitted by the card. They are all considered LED lights and there is no normal light.

2. Answer c is correct. Green is normally associated with 100Mbps, yellow with 10Mbps, red sometimes means 1000Mbps or 1Gbps, and to my knowledge there is no purple light!

3. Answer a is correct. In fact, if your link light is blinking, then something is wrong with your physical connection and you should check all physical links. The activity light will not give you any more information if the link light is not properly solid. If you ever have problems

with a link light, you need to fix the physical problem first. TCP/IP does not cause link light errors, nor does software.

4. Answer a is correct. Ethernet uses broadcasts as its transmission standard. Token Ring and token passing use one token in most cases, which jumps from computer to computer.

5. Answer b is correct. When two frames collide, the data is unusable and must be resent by the transmitting computer.

Objectives 4.4 and 4.5

1. Answer c is correct. You can use Terminal Services to remotely control a Windows 2000 Server. This is a great feature because the server room is usually far away, and could very well have less-than-hospitable environmental conditions! To remotely control a Windows XP computer, you would use Remote Desktop. To remotely connect to a Cisco router, you would use Telnet, and to remotely connect to a VPN server you would use a simple VPN adapter or VPN client.

2. Answers a and b are correct. The Caps Lock and the user name/password combination are the most likely culprits when users have problems logging on. There may be a TCP/IP issue, but that is not nearly as likely.

3. Answers a and c are correct. The IP address of the VPN server and dial-in permissions are the most important. You would also want to check if the user is using the correct user name and password.

4. Answer d is correct. Always check that the path (syntax) is being typed properly. Later, you can check IP settings and whether the user is logged on to the domain. The server should always be up, but in some cases, it might not be. Either way, that would be farther down the list. Dial-in permissions would only be checked if this was a remote user.

5. Answer b is correct. Delete the print job so that others will be able to print. You will then need to troubleshoot why the print job was held up. Check the amount of RAM on the printer, and then make sure that printing is set up to spool to the hard drive.

Objective 4.6

1. Answer d is correct. WINS is what the Windows 95, 98, and Me computers use for name resolution. DNS is used by UNIX, Linux, and

Windows NT/2000/2003/XP. ARP is not name resolution at all; it resolves between IP addresses and MAC addresses.

2. Answer a is correct. Eight days is the default, Although some companies will use one month, it is not recommended. Some ISPs renew IPs as often as every day to avoid some common malicious attacks.

3. Answer c is correct. The most common problem on networks is that admins and users alike forget to enter the correct DNS server address. Servers are not supposed to go down, and if they do, it should not be often! WINS is not involved because the two systems were NT based, which utilizes DNS instead of WINS.

4. Answer b is correct. Activation is needed before an IP scope will work. After that, you need to authorize the server (which starts the DHCP service). The other two answers are not valid options.

5. Answer d is correct. By default, DHCP packets cannot cross a router. There are two possible solutions to this: installing the BootP protocol on the router or installing a DHCP relay agent on the other subnet. The relay agent will talk directly through the router to the DHCP server and allow the packets to cross to the other network. This way, you do not need a second DHCP server.

Objectives 4.7–4.9

1. Answer a is correct. Identify symptoms before you actually do anything. Never panic. Then you would identify the area affected, and much later, test the result.

2. Answer c is correct. Documenting the solution is last on the list. Although it is last, it is a very important step, because you or others may need to refer to this solution one, two, or six months from now.

3. Answer b is correct. The patch cable is the most likely answer. Remember that if you do not have a link light, it is going to be a Physical layer problem. So TCP/IP is not possible because it is logical and part of the operating system. If there were collisions on the network, you would still have some sort of link, whether blinking or solid, but it wouldn't be unlit. Finally, it is possible that the hub could fail, but it is far more likely that a patch cable is faulty.

4. Answers a and d are correct. An electrical junction box (even if fully grounded) will cause EMI as will almost all electrical devices to some extent. Radio waves cause RFI (Radio Frequency Interference) and a

plenum is really just an airway, although most techs will refer to a plenum as the area above the drop ceiling where all the duct work is. Remember to keep your network cables secured to the top ceiling or to an I-beam and to keep them away from any electrical devices.

5. Answer c is correct. A WAP (wireless access point) can create RFI (radio frequency interference). A junction box could create EMI, but a plenum and Category 5 cable would not create any type of interference by themselves. Cat 5 cable could, however, have crosstalk.

Classroom Setup

This manual works just as well in the classroom as it does in the home lab. Just remember to substitute IP configurations and computer names with the information that follows.

10.0.0.0 Network Documentation

Table A.1	Instructor PC Cluster Setup	
Type	**Computer Name**	**IP Address**
Windows XP Professional, Main Instructor System	**Instructor1**	**10.10.2.199**
Windows 2000 domain controller (**teacher.com**)	**Instructor2**	**10.10.2.198**
Windows 2000 Professional (duplicate of student machines)	**Instructor3**	**10.10.2.197**
Windows 2000 Server with ISA (optional)	**Instructor4**	**10.10.2.196**
Windows 98 (optional)	**Instructor5**	**10.10.2.195**
Windows NT Server (PDC) (optional)	**Instructor6**	**10.10.2.194**

Table A.2 Student Setup (Windows 2000 Professional Clients, 16 Max.)

Computer Name	IP address	Domain
WS1	10.10.2.1	Newyork.com
WS2	10.10.2.2	Newyork.com
WS3	10.10.2.3	Newyork.com
WS4	10.10.2.4	Newyork.com
WS5	10.10.2.5	Australia.com
WS6	10.10.2.6	Australia.com
WS7	10.10.2.7	Australia.com
WS8	10.10.2.8	Australia.com
WS9	10.10.2.9	Japan.com
WS10	10.10.2.10	Japan.com
WS11	10.10.2.11	Japan.com
WS12	10.10.2.12	Japan.com
WS13	10.10.2.13	England.com
WS14	10.10.2.14	England.com
WS15	10.10.2.15	England.com
WS16	10.10.2.16	England.com

Table A.3 Server Setup (For Windows 2000 Server and Novell 5.0)

Server Name	IP Address	Domain	Novell Tree Name	Novell Context Name	2nd NIC IP Address
Nycserver	10.10.2.21	Newyork.com	Newyorktree	Newyorkobject	65.43.18.1
Sydneyserver	10.10.2.22	Australia.com	Australiatree	Australiaobject	65.43.18.2
Tokyoserver	10.10.2.23	Japan.com	Japantree	Japanobject	68.21.152.1
Londonserver	10.10.2.24	England.com	Englandtree	Englandobject	68.21.152.2

Table A.4 Other networking configurations for the 10.0.0.0 network

Switch	10.10.2.100
Gateway (router)	10.10.2.200
Subnet Mask	255.0.0.0

NOTE

This network can also be considered classless if the instructor wishes it so. To do this, the network number would be **10.10.2.0** and the default subnet mask would be changed to **255.255.255.0**. This isn't really recommended but will work if the instructor wishes to show CIDR (Classless Internet Domain Routing) or super-netting.

Additional Configurations

➤ All Windows 2000 Professional computers must be minimum PII 266MHz with 64MB RAM.

➤ All Windows 2000 Servers must be minimum PII 266MHz with 128MB RAM.

➤ All computers should be connected to a configurable switch.

➤ The four city servers should be in a separate area of the classroom. It is recommended that they connect to a separate switch to be cascaded to the main switch.

➤ All Windows 2000 and XP client systems should be oriented so that they can access the Internet when needed.

➤ All computers should be updated with the latest service packs and drivers after operating-system installation is complete.

➤ All *server* systems should be multi-homed with two network adapters.

➤ Be sure to set the DNS IP in the Internet Protocol (TCP/IP) Properties dialog box of the domain controllers to their own IP address. Very important!

Important Information

Table B. 1	BOGB standard	
Pair #	**Pin #/Color**	**Pin #/Color**
Pair 1	Pin 1: white/blue	Pin 2: Blue
Pair 2	Pin 3: white/orange	Pin 4: Orange
Pair 3	Pin 5: white/green	Pin 6: Green
Pair 4	Pin 7: white/brown	Pin 8: Brown

Table B.2	EIA/TIA wiring standards
EIA/TIA 568B	**EIA/TIA 568A**
White/orange	White/green
Orange	Green
White/green	White/orange
Blue	Blue
White/blue	White/blue
Green	Orange
White/brown	White/brown
Brown	Brown

Table B.3	TCP/IP Classes		
Class	Decimal Range	Binary Range	ID
Class A	1–126	00000001–01111110	Net.Node.Node.Node
Class B	128–191	10000000–10111111	Net.Net.Node.Node
Class C	192–223	11000000–11011111	Net.Net.Net.Node
Class D	224–239	11100000–11101111	Testing
Class E	240–255	11110000–11111111	Future Use

127.0.0.1 is reserved for loopback (localhost) testing.

Table B.4	TCP/IP Viewing
Platform	Command
Windows 95/98	**winipcfg**
Windows NT/2000	**ipconfig or ipconfig/all**
Novell	**inetcfg**
Linux	**ifconfig**

Table B.5	OSI Layers		
Layer Number/Name	Data Unit	Protocols	Devices
Layer 7/Application		FTP, Telnet, SMTP	Gateways
Layer 6/Presentation		Encryption, etc.	
Layer 5/Session		Logon	
Layer 4/Transport	Messages	TCP, UDP	
Layer 3/Network*	Packets	IP, ARP, ICMP	Routers
Layer 2/Data Link*	Frames	Ethernet, Token Ring	Bridges
Sub-layers			
Logical Link Control (LLC)			
Media Access Control (MAC)			
Layer 1/Physical*	Bits	Hubs, cables, etc.	Cables

*Part of the communications sub-network that is managed by the Transport layer

Table B.6 Assigned ports*	
Port Number	**Service**
20	**FTP**
21	**FTP**
22	**SSH**
23	**Telnet**
25	**SMTP**
53	**DNS**
69	**TFTP**
70	Gopher
79	Finger
80	**HTTP (also 8080)**
88	Kerberos
110	**POP3**
119	**NNTP**
123	**NTP**
135	RPC
137	NetBIOS Naming Service
139	NetBIOS Session Service
143	**IMAP: Internet Message Access Protocol**
161	SNMP: Simple Network Management Protocol
443	**HTTPS (SSL)**
1701	L2TP: Layer 2 Tunneling Protocol
1723	PPTP: Point to Point Tunneling Protocol
3389	RDP: Remote Desktop Protocol

*The most important ports are in bold.

Keyboard Shortcuts

For a complete list of Microsoft Word keyboard shortcuts, open the Tools menu, choose Macro, and select Macros. Then, in the Macro Name dialog box click ListCommands, and click Run. In the List Commands dialog box, click Current Menu and Keyboard Settings.

Table C.1 Shortcut Keys for Any Application	
Shortcut Key	**Function**
F1	Display help
Alt+F4	Quit a program
Shift+F10	View the object menu for the selected item
Ctrl+Esc	Display the Start menu
Alt+Tab	Switch to the window you last used
Ctrl+X	Cut
Ctrl+C	Copy
Ctrl+V	Paste
Del	Delete the selection
Ctrl+Z	Undo the last action
Alt+Enter	View properties
Ctrl+O	Open a document, spreadsheet, or what have you
Ctrl+N	Open a new template in an application
Ctrl+F4	Close a document, spreadsheet, or what have you
Ctrl+S	Save a document
Ctrl+P	Print a document
F11	Full screen

Table C.2	Shortcut Keys for Windows Explorer, a Folder Window, or on the Desktop
Shortcut Key	**Function**
F2	Rename an item
F3	Find a folder or file
Shift+Del	Delete an item, bypassing the Recycle Bin

Table C.3	Shortcut Keys for Windows Explorer or a Folder Window
Shortcut Key	**Function**
F5	Refresh a window
Ctrl+A	Select all
Backspace	Move one level up

Table C.4	Shortcut Keys for Windows Explorer
Shortcut Key	**Function**
Ctrl+G	Go to a file or folder
F6	Switch panes
Asterisk	On keypad, expand all subfolders
Plus	On keypad, expand a folder
Minus	On keypad, collapse a folder
Right arrow	Expand a folder
Left arrow	Collapse a folder

Table C.5	Shortcut Keys in Dialog Boxes (Usually in Tab-Delimited Format)
Shortcut Key	**Function**
Tab	Move to the next field
Shift+Tab	Move to the previous field
Ctrl+Tab	Move to the next tab
Ctrl+Shift+Tab	Move to the previous tab

Table C.6	Shortcut Keys in Open, Save, and Browse Dialog Boxes
Shortcut Key	**Function**
F4	Open the Save In or Look In list
F5	Refresh
Backspace	Move to the parent folder if you are in the list window

Table C.7 Shortcut Keys in Microsoft Exchange, Outlook and Outlook Express

Shortcut Key	Function
Ctrl+Shift+I	View the Inbox folder
Ctrl+Shift+O	View the Outbox folder
Ctrl+Shift+B	View the Address Book
Ctrl+N	Compose a new message
Ctrl+R	Reply to sender
Ctrl+F	Forward a message

Table C.8 Shortcut Keys in Internet Explorer

Shortcut Key	Function
Alt+left arrow	Back one screen
Alt+right arrow	Forward one screen

 The shortcuts for applications apply in Internet Explorer as well.

Table C.9 Accessibility Options

Shortcut Key	Function
Shift 5 times	Toggle StickyKeys on and off
Right Shift for 8 seconds	Toggle FilterKeys on and off
Num Lock for 5 Seconds	Toggle ToggleKeys on and off

D

Sub-netting Tables

Table D.1 Class A Subnetting

# of Bits						
NetID	SubnetID	HostId	Mask	# of Subnets	# of Hosts per	Increment #
8	0	24	255.0.0.0	/8	N/A	16,777,14	N/A
8	1	23	255.128.0.0	/9	N/A	N/A	N/A
8	2	22	255.192.0.0	/10	2	4,194,302	64
8	3	21	255.224.0.0	/11	6	2,097,150	32
8	4	20	255.240.0.0	/12	14	1,048,574	16
8	5	19	255.248.0.0	/13	30	524,286	8
8	6	18	255.252.0.0	/14	62	262,142	4
8	7	17	255.254.0.0	/15	126	131,070	2
8	8	16	255.255.0.0	/16	254	65,534	1
8	9	15	255.255.128.0	/17	510	32,766	128
8	10	14	255.255.192.0	/18	1,022	16,382	64
8	11	13	255.255.224.0	/19	2,046	8,190	32
8	12	12	255.255.240.0	/20	4,094	4,094	16
8	13	11	255.255.248.0	/21	8,190	2,046	8
8	14	10	255.255.252.0	/22	16,382	1,022	4
8	15	9	255.255.254.0	/23	32,766	510	2
8	16	8	255.255.255.0	/24	65,534	254	1
8	17	7	255.255.255.128	/25	131,070	126	128

# of Bits					# of Subnets	# of Hosts per	Increment #
NetID	SubnetID	HostId	Mask				
8	18	6	255.255.255.192	/26	262,142	62	64
8	19	5	255.255.255.224	/27	524,286	30	32
8	20	4	255.255.255.240	/28	1,048,574	14	16
8	21	3	255.255.255.248	/29	2,097,150	6	8
8	22	2	255.255.255.252	/30	4,194,302	2	4
8	23	1	255.255.255.254	/31	N/A	N/A	N/A
8	24	0	255.255.255.255	/32	N/A	N/A	N/A

Table D.2 Class B Subnetting

# of Bits						
NetID	SubnetID	HostId	Mask		# of Subnets	# of Hosts per	Increment #

NetID	SubnetID	HostId	Mask		# of Subnets	# of Hosts per	Increment #
16	0	16	255.255.0.0	/16	N/A	65,534	N/A
16	1	15	255.255.128.0	/17	N/A	N/A	N/A
16	2	14	255.255.192.0	/18	2	16,382	64
16	3	13	255.255.224.0	/19	6	8,190	32
16	4	12	255.255.240.0	/20	14	4,094	16
16	5	11	255.255.248.0	/21	30	2,046	8
16	6	10	255.255.252.0	/22	62	1,022	4
16	7	9	255.255.254.0	/23	126	510	2
16	8	8	255.255.255.0	/24	254	254	1
16	9	7	255.255.255.128	/25	510	126	128
16	10	6	255.255.255.192	/26	1,022	62	64
16	11	5	255.255.255.224	/27	2,046	30	32
16	12	4	255.255.255.240	/28	4,094	14	16
16	13	3	255.255.255.248	/29	8,190	6	8
16	14	2	255.255.255.252	/30	16,382	2	4
16	15	1	255.255.255.254	/31	N/A	N/A	N/A
16	16	0	255.255.255.255	/32	N/A	N/A	N/A